# The Broken Heart

# The Broken Heart

The Medical Consequences
of Loneliness

## JAMES J. LYNCH

Basic Books, Inc., Publishers     New York

Library of Congress Cataloging in Publication Data

Lynch, James J      1938–
    The broken heart.

    Includes bibliographical references and index.
    1.  Heart—Diseases—Psychosomatic aspects.  2.  Lone-
liness.  3.  Interpersonal relations.  4.  United States
—Social conditions—1960–      I.  Title.
RC682.L85        616.1′071        77–2173
ISBN: 0–465–00772–4

To Joe, Jim, and Kathleen

in the hope that in their adult years

they will find lovers

as exquisite as their mother.

# ACKNOWLEDGMENTS

The author gratefully acknowledges permission to reprint excerpts from the following sources:

"The Sound of Silence," by Paul Simon. Copyright © 1964 by Paul Simon.

Figures 2, 5, 6, 7, and 8 reprinted from: J. J. Lynch, L. Flaherty, C. Emrich, and M. Mills, "Effects of Human Contact on the Heart Activity of Curarized Patients in a Shock-Trauma Unit." *American Heart Journal* 88 (1974): 160–169.

Figures 3 and 4 reprinted from J. J. Lynch, S. A. Thomas, M. E. Mills, K. Malinow, and A. H. Katcher, "The Effects of Human Contact on Cardiac Arrhythima in Coronary Care Patients," *Journal of Nervous and Mental Disorders* 158 (1974): 88. Copyright © 1974 by The Williams & Wilkins Co., Baltimore.

Figure 9 reprinted from: James J. Lynch and J. F. McCarthy, "The Effect of Petting on a Classically Conditioned Emotional Response," *Behavioral Research and Therapy* 5 (1967): 55.

Tables B1, B2, and B5 reprinted from: Hugh Carter and Paul C. Glick, *Marriage and Divorce,* American Public Health Association, Vital and Health Statistics Monograph (Cambridge: Harvard University Press, 1970). Copyright © 1970 by Harvard University Press.

Table B3 reprinted from: Abraham M. Lillienfeld, Morton L. Levin, and Irving I. Kessler, *Cancer in the United States* (Cambridge: Harvard University Press, 1972). Copyright © 1972 by Harvard University Press.

Table B4 from: Statistics supplied by Satoshi Dohno, Hideko Ito, and Keiko Kawashima.

Tables B6 through B10 reprinted from: Iwao Moriyama, Dean E. Krueger, and Jeremiah Stamler, *Cardiovascular Diseases in the United*

*States,* (Cambridge: Harvard University Press, 1971). Copyright ©
1971 by Harvard University Press.

Victor R. Fuchs, *Who Shall Live? Health Economics and Social
Choice* (New York: Basic Books, 1974). Copyright © 1974 by Basic
Books, Inc.

Harold J. Morowitz, "Hiding in the Hammond Report," *Hospital
Practice,* August 1975, pp. 35–39.

George Engel, "Sudden and Rapid Death During Psychological Stress:
Folklore or Wisdom? " *Annals of Internal Medicine* 4 (1971): 771.

William N. Chambers and Morton F. Reiser, "Emotional Stress in the
Precipitation of Congestive Heart Failure," *Psychosomatic Medicine*
15 (1953): 38. Copyright © 1953 Elsevier North-Holland, Inc.

Julius Bauer, "Sudden, Unexpected Death," *Postgraduate Medicine* 22
(1957): A34.

# CONTENTS

## CHAPTER 9

## APPENDIX A

## APPENDIX B

# PREFACE

This book is about life and death—love, companionship, and health—and loneliness that can break the human heart. This book touches on complex themes that are in some ways as old as mankind itself, but its purpose is simple: to document the fact that reflected in our hearts there is a biological basis for our need to form loving human relationships. If we fail to fulfill that need, our health is in peril.

Many hospitalized patients, some of whom are now dead, shared with us their fears and hopes, their loves and loneliness, their very heart beats, so that we could better understand the power of human love. To them and to the nursing and medical staff at the University of Maryland Hospital who cared so deeply for them, I owe a special debt of gratitude. They helped write this book.

I asked Sue Thomas, a nurse who showed me the electrocardiogram of the first patient whose response to human touch we ever studied, how I should thank the many friends who helped me finish this book. She quickly responded that "friends need no thanks for friendship is its own reward." Therefore, I will not thank my friends, but only acknowledge some of them who helped me with this book: Eugene B. Brody, M.D., Alan Fertziger, Ph.D., Fred Fregin, D.V.M., W. Horsley Gantt, M.D., Kenneth Gimbel, M.D., Thomas Hackett, M.D., Aaron Katcher, M.D., Martin Kessler, James Mackie, Ph.D., Carole Marshall, Russell R. Monroe, M.D., Leonard Scherlis, M.D., Sue A. Thomas, R.N., Lourdes Weir, and Stewart Wolf, M.D.

This book was completed during 1976—the bicentennial anniversary of the United States of America. I mention that fact for two reasons. First, this book presents many facts and figures about social life and health in the United States of 1976 that are not particularly flattering. While the implications of all the health data are universal—companionship and loneliness are after all not idiosyncratic problems in the United States—the data and trends were taken from U.S. population statistics. These unflattering statistics are nevertheless presented with a deep love of this country, its people, and its ideals. Second, 1976 was an important year for another reason that is far more personal—in March of that year my father died. My parents were peasant immigrants from the Inishowen Peninsula of County Donegal in Ireland, and, clearly, the social ethic that pervades the latter part of this book owes much to them. Their values were simple: love of God, love of family, and love of neighbors. For their values and their love, I thank them.

# The Broken Heart

# INTRODUCTION

# Life and the Heart

"Man you must be kidding about love! I think our young college kids have really latched onto something. Why get married when you can simply screw some young chick and nobody gets hurt. In the end you owe her nothing and she owes you nothing."
—Comment made to the author by a 35-year-old steelworker, Baltimore, Maryland (1973)

"And in the naked light I saw / ten thousand people, maybe more. / People talking without speaking, / people hearing without listening, / people writing songs that voices never shared, / no one dared / disturb the sounds of silence."
—Paul Simon, *Sound of Silence*

There is a widespread belief in our modern culture that *love* is a word which has no meaning. A whole generation of detached, independent, self-sufficient, noncommitted individuals agree with the steelworker quoted above that no one really needs to get hurt in modern human relationships. You can be intimate with someone and then leave, and nothing bad will happen.

This book was written to document the opposite point of view: human relationships *do* matter. They are desperately important to both our mental and our physical well-being. The fact is that social isolation, the lack of human companionship, death or absence of parents in early childhood, sudden loss of love, and chronic human loneliness are significant contributors to premature death. Although, as we shall see, almost every cause of death is significantly influenced by human companionship, this book will concentrate chiefly on the leading cause of death—heart disease. My hope is that in this way the powerful impact of human companionship on our general physical and mental well-being will come into clearer focus. Quite literally, we must either learn to live together or face the possibility of prematurely dying alone.

Let me stress that this is not a book about heart disease or what to do about heart disease; a host of excellent books are already available on this topic.* Rather, we shall concentrate on premature death due to heart disease simply because it is the leading cause of death, and as such can be used to help illustrate the fact that health and human companionship do go together. In this regard, coronary heart disease is no different from any other cause of death. Cancer, tuberculosis, suicide, accidents, mental disease—all are significantly influenced by human companionship. Nature uses many weapons to shorten the lives of lonely people. On a statistical basis it simply chooses heart disease most frequently.

## A GAMBLER'S SHORTCUT TO PARADISE

Everyone is familiar with road maps which list the major geographical features of a region, often down to the dirt roads of local jurisdictions. Such maps help us find our way in unfamiliar territory. There are other maps, however, that very few people are familiar with. These depict disease rates and death rates in various parts of the country. They allow us to see, at a glance, in what part of the country diseases such as measles, mumps, polio, cancer, and cardiovascular disorders occur most frequently. These maps show that certain diseases occur only in one section of the country, while other diseases occur more frequently in urban areas than in rural areas, and so forth. Such maps not only give medical scientists

---

* Those who are unfamiliar with the function and malfunction of the heart may wish to consult Appendix A. Although every effort will be made to keep unfamiliar medical terms to a minimum in this book, a review of the appended description of the heart might prove helpful.

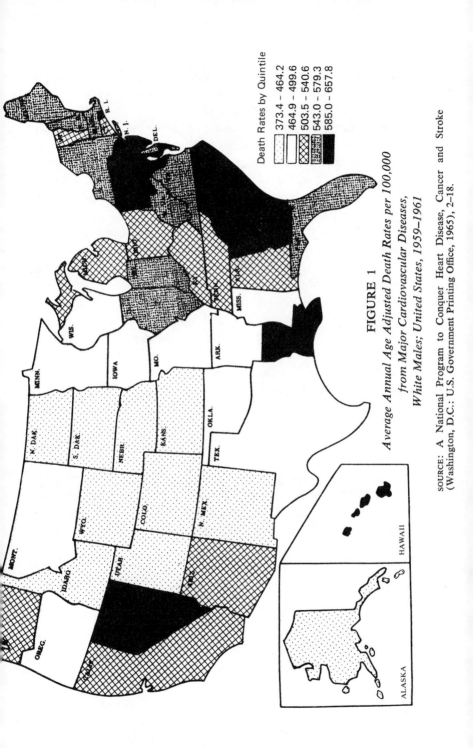

Death Rates by Quintile

| | |
|---|---|
| | 373.4 – 464.2 |
| | 464.9 – 499.6 |
| | 503.5 – 540.6 |
| | 543.0 – 579.3 |
| | 585.0 – 657.8 |

FIGURE 1

*Average Annual Age Adjusted Death Rates per 100,000
from Major Cardiovascular Diseases;
White Males; United States, 1959–1961*

SOURCE: A National Program to Conquer Heart Disease, Cancer and Stroke
(Washington, D.C.: U.S. Government Printing Office, 1965), 2–18.

clues to the causes of certain diseases, but they may also suggest means for controlling them. More germane to this book, however, is the fact that certain patterns of disease in one area can be used to predict the future course of disease and death in the entire country.

Take, for example, one of the maps drawn in 1965 for the President's Commission on Heart Disease as part of a detailed report called *A National Program to Conquer Heart Disease, Cancer and Stroke*.[1] This particular map (Figure 1) shows the annual death rates (per 100,000 people) from major cardiovascular diseases for the period 1959–1961 for white males in the United States. While this map has many intriguing features, one aspect stands out immediately—Nevada is a unique state, and its uniqueness is not enviable. Nevada is number one in the way it shortens white people's lives in the United States, and not only from heart disease but from almost every other cause of death. In 1960, in the age range 25–64 (and indeed at all age ranges), Nevada had the second-highest death rate in the United States, exceeded only by South Carolina. For *white males and females* between the ages of 25 and 64, Nevada had by far the highest death rates in the country. For females, no other state even ran a close second. Yet during that same period, Nevada had the second-highest level of education in the United States (for the age range 25–64), the second-highest median level of income, and a very small black population (a large black population might have accounted for the high death rates, since blacks live an average of seven years fewer than whites). Nevada also ranked about average in the number of physicians and hospitals per 100,000 population and had one of the lowest population densities in the United States.[2, 3]

Now consider neighboring Utah, which has one of the lowest death rates in the country. In 1960 Utah and Nevada had identical education rates for white adults (average 12.2 years), among the highest in the country. The average per capita annual income in Nevada was approximately $1,000 more than in Utah (about 16–20 percent higher). The number of people living in urban areas in the two states was practically identical.

How can the residents of these two neighboring states, comparably wealthy and well educated, differ so strikingly in longevity? Is the air different in Nevada? Or the water? Are people malnourished in one of the richest states in the Union? Do they jog less? Or play tennis less? Are they fatter? There seems little reason to think so.

In his recent book *Who Shall Live*, Victor Fuchs has pointed out some intriguing differences between these two states. Utah is an extremely religious state, with the Mormon religion being the dominant influence. Mormons neither drink nor smoke. They generally maintain very stable lives: marriages are generally secure, family ties remain strong, and most of the state's inhabitants stay in Utah. Nevada is quite the opposite. In the 1960s it was one of the divorce capitals of the United States. As Fuchs [4] points out, "More than 20 percent of Nevada's males ages 35–64 are single, widowed, divorced or not living with their spouses. Of those who are married with spouse present, more than one-third had been previously widowed or divorced. In Utah, comparable figures are half as large (p. 53)." Fuchs also notes that 9 out of every 10 middle-aged Nevadans were born someplace else, whereas 63 percent of the residents of Utah over the age of 20 were born in that state. Nevada, it appears, was a gambler's paradise—except for the odds on your life.

Nevada in the early 1960s was a foretaste of things to come. Divorce, mobility, living alone, uprootedness, these have now become acceptable middle-class norms throughout the United States. Consequently, the health of our infants, young people, and aged will, I predict, look more and more like Nevada's and less and less like Utah's for decades to come. The mortality data for 1960 offered sufficiently clear warnings about our future, but for reasons this book will examine, we have chosen to ignore the signs.

An entire generation has been raised to believe that dieting, exercise, inoculations, and other forms of preventive care are *the* means to avoid disease and premature death. The idea that another crucial element influencing well-being is the ability to live together —to maintain human relationships—seems strangely "unscientific" to our age. Yet that is the thesis this book will try to document: loneliness and isolation can literally "break your heart."

## HUMAN COMPANIONSHIP AS THE TWENTIETH CENTURY EBBS

Even the most cursory appraisal of our modern culture indicates that something has gone wrong with many human relationships. Almost every segment of our society seems to be deeply afflicted by one of the major diseases of our age—human loneliness. Yet we do not seem to be waging any kind of effective battle against its lethal domination.

Examples of the disturbance and disruption of human relationships can be seen almost everywhere. The divorce rate in the United States has accelerated at a truly astounding pace in the last two decades. In 1975 more than 1 million marriages ended in divorce, an all-time record. Allowing for the growth in population, the absolute divorce rate doubled in the decade from 1964 to 1974.*

The rapid rise in the divorce rate, however, is only the tip of an enormous social iceberg. The number of children under 18 years of age who now must endure the loss of a parent through divorce is growing even more rapidly than the divorce rate itself. Before 1955 almost 50 percent of all divorces occurred either among childless couples or among couples whose children had grown up and moved away. During the last two decades the number of children caught in the middle of parental divorce has more than tripled in the United States—from 330,000 children in 1953 to more than 1 million children in 1973, the last year for which there are reliable statistics. When one considers the decline in birthrate over the same period,

---

* I am deeply grateful to Dr. Alexander Plateris and the U.S. Office for Vital Statistics for providing many of the data cited in this section.

the increasing number of divorces involving children becomes even more striking. The reality is that children no longer serve as a restraint to keep couples married.

Demographic data suggest that traditional family life in the United States is also changing significantly in other respects. It is now generally known that the birthrate has fallen dramatically in the last decade; what is not so well known is that the illegitimacy rate has actually risen slightly during the same period. This has led to an increase in the *proportion* of the total live births in the United States that are illegitimate—children who have no legal fathers. In 1963 approximately 259,000 illegitimate children were born in the United States; by 1974 that figure had risen to 418,100. Contrary to popular belief, the widespread availability of birth control and abortion services has not reduced the illegitimate birthrate, although it has obviously acted to decrease the total birthrate in the United States.

The rapidly accelerating divorce rate has also produced a dramatic rise in the total number of one-parent households. Based on census estimates, the number of single-parent households in the United States increased from 2,715,000 in 1966 to 4,888,000 in 1975. In most instances the one parent (usually the woman) is forced out to work for economic survival, and therefore must leave the children in the care of others. (An ever-growing number of two-parent families must also leave their children in the care of others in order to survive economically.) An analysis of the figures shows that the number of single-parent households remained relatively stable between 1955 and 1965 (increasing from 2,100,000 to 2,727,000), and then began to accelerate rapidly to almost 5 million in 1975, reflecting the fact that the remarriage rate for divorced individuals is no longer keeping pace with the divorce rate.

All these trends—rapidly rising divorce rate, the growing number of single-parent households, the slower reentry of divorced individuals back into marriage, and proportional increases in the illegitimate birthrate—suggest the possibility that in the future the two-parent family may be the exception rather than the rule. (In 1973 husband-wife households constituted 67.8% of all households in the U.S.) As will be documented in this book, all available medical data indicate that these statistical trends portend serious physical and mental health hazards for many Americans in the decades ahead.

Nevertheless, popular magazines and books regularly discuss the possibility that the very notion of marriage and family will soon be outmoded. Marriage by contract, renewable every three to five years only upon the mutual consent of both partners, is seriously predicted by many.[5] Even more remarkable is the way in which books on health used daily in our high schools and colleges remain blind to the fact that divorce, infidelity, and marital swinging may have detrimental effects on health. For example, one textbook [6] on physical health used in American colleges asserts:

Far from being a wasting illness, *divorce is a healthful adaptation,* enabling monogamy to survive in a time when patriarchal powers, privileges and marital systems have become unworkable; far from being a radical change in the institution of marriage, divorce is a relatively minor modification of it, and thoroughly supportive of most of its conventions. . . . *Marital infidelity* is also *a frequently useful modification of the marriage contract* rather than a repudiation of it. . . . This lack of emotional involvement is the very essence of marital swinging, or as it is sometimes called, co-marital sex. Whether it consists of a quiet mate exchange between two couples, a small sociable group-sex party, or a large orgiastic rumpus, the premise is the same: As long as the extramarital sex is open, shared and purely recreational it is not considered divisive of marriage (pp. 199–204; italics added).

These are perplexing statements—a required college course on health implies a reality about marriage that is contrary to all available psychiatric data, and, as shall be described in the latter part of this book, contrary to the emotional nature of human relationships.

Symptoms of social disruption in the United States are not confined to the marital scene. It is estimated that the average young person of 20 entering the job market today will change jobs at least seven times during his working years. Only 57.4% of families in the U.S. lived at the same address in 1970 and 1974, indicating that many had to break ties with old friends and transfer children away from schools and playmates. Such mobility adds greatly to the burden of "life changes" that must be endured.

In his book *The Pursuit of Loneliness,* Philip Slater [7] suggests that the growth of social fragmentation is so severe in the United States that it is pushing our culture to the breaking point. This book was written to document the fact that loneliness is not only pushing our culture to the breaking point, but is also pushing our physical health to the breaking point, and indeed has in many cases already pushed the human heart beyond the breaking point.

## LOVE AND THE HEART

Almost as soon as man discovered the existence and function of the heart, he recognized that it was influenced by human companionship and love. Most of us have, at one time or another, felt our hearts beating rapidly when we are close to those we love or, occasionally, when we have been offended by others. Many of us have felt our hearts sink, as if pressed by some crushing weight, after the loss of loved ones. In an endless variety of verbal and nonverbal dialogues with others, we have learned that human beings have varied, and at times profound, effects on the cardiac systems of other human beings.

Long before scientists began, with the aid of sophisticated electronic monitoring devices, to catalogue the various ways that human companionship could alter the heart, physicians were already well aware of its influence. Indeed, the very antiquity and ubiquity of this knowledge has, unfortunately, led many of us to take it for granted. It has also served to obscure the fact that while we recognize the power of human contact, we do not understand it. The precise magnitude, generality, and (most importantly) the mechanisms of the effects of human contact on the heart have not yet been carefully examined. Still, it is now well known that a vast array of human interactions normally alter the heart in ways that range from barely detectable, transient reactions to changes that are profound—even deadly. There are, however, few conditions in life that do not involve some type of human contact, and so in one sense it would be remarkable if human contact did not influence our hearts. Like the air we breathe, it envelops every aspect of our lives. A simple visit to your doctor, arguments, reassurance and praise, sexual activity, social gatherings, competitive sports, the loss of a friend or loved one, jealousies, humiliations, human triumphs, the cuddling of a child in your lap, the silent hand-holding between two lovers, the quiet comforting of a dying patient—all these affect the heart.

It is this very pervasiveness of human contact that makes it so hard to sort out the unique influence of human companionship from all other factors that are known to influence the heart: genetics, dietary habits, smoking, exercise, and so forth. The array of human interactions just described often involves these factors, as well as human companionship, the lack of love, the threatened loss of love, the fear of rejection, or indeed the real loss of love. How important is human companionship when compared, for example, with physical exercise and diet? Until very recently most studies that examined the effects of exercise, diet, smoking, and similar practices on the heart usually did not consider whether the lack of companionship or human love or the general social milieu of the individual might have influenced their results. Incredibly complicated and expensive research projects have been carried out, involving the entire population of certain cities, in which investigators seeking the "causes" of heart disease never even bothered to record whether their subjects were married or not! Many examples of this peculiar state of affairs can be cited, but perhaps the most dramatic example of this type of scientific "benign neglect" is the failure to consider the effects of human love on the heart. For while the relationship between love and the heart has been universally recognized, the one factor that was long neglected by scientists studying the heart is love. To my knowledge, the word *love* is not indexed in any mainstream physiology textbook that deals with the heart, nor in any physician's manual on the heart. *Stress, pain, anxiety, fear,* and *rage* sometimes appear in indexes of textbooks on the heart, but never *love*. Take, for example, the *Index Medicus*, a scientific journal that annually prints the title and a summary of most medical research articles published in the world. In one four-year period (1970-1973) over 500,000 research articles were cited in this journal. Only 15 of those articles dealt with the topic of love (all from a psychiatric point of view), and not a single one of those articles discussed any effects of love or lack of love on the heart.

Apparently a peculiar type of intellectual schizophrenia exists between common sense and scientific attitudes when the human heart is considered. Does common sense recognize something that scientists and physicians cannot see? Why do we continue to use phrases such as *broken heart, heartbroken, heartsick, heartless, sweetheart*? Why do people persist in the notion that their fellow men die of broken hearts when no such diagnoses ever appear on twentieth-century death certificates?

Even though the effects of human love on the heart are still largely ignored by most scientists, times are changing. The larger question of the effects of human emotions on the development of cardiac disease is now being seriously considered by many scientists.[8, 9] Growing numbers of physicians now recognize that the health of the human heart depends not only on such factors as genetics, diet, and exercise, but also to a large extent on the social and emotional health of the individual.

The initial impetus to write this book came from observations made by me and many of my colleagues that human contact had important effects on the hearts of patients in coronary care and other hospital intensive-care units. These observations confirmed a large number of studies demonstrating that human contact can have marked effects on the hearts of various animal species.

Ultimately, however, the stimulus for writing this book was my deep concern about our apparent drift toward increased human isolation, fragmented human relationships, and loneliness. We live in a culture dominated by the power of science and scientific technology. One wonders, however, whether our increased understanding of the world "out there" has been accompanied by a similar growth in our understanding of our own private worlds. An appreciation of the importance of human love and companionship seems to be absent not only from our medical textbooks but also from the newspapers and magazines that mirror our lives, as well as from the very cities that are our technical masterpieces. The price we are paying for our failure to understand our biological needs for love and human companionship may be ultimately exacted in our own hearts and blood vessels. This book, therefore, will be divided into two sections. The first will describe the effects of human companionship and the loss of human contact on our cardiovascular systems, while the second will analyze some of the forces that seem to be contributing to increased human isolation, fragmented human relationships, and loneliness in modern society.

If the scope of this book is complex, its purpose is simple: to demonstrate that human companionship does affect our hearts, and that there is reflected in our hearts a biological basis for our need for loving human relationships, which we fail to fulfill at our peril. Since human dialogue is the elixir of life, the ultimate decision we must make is simple: we must either learn to live together or increase our chances of prematurely dying alone.

# CHAPTER 1

# Life and Death
# in Main Street America

> "The heart has reasons that reason knows not of . . .
> do you love by reason?"
>
> —Blaise Pascal,
> *Pensées* (1670)

Pause for awhile at the small cemetery plots of rural America, particularly in those parts of our country that were settled a few hundred years ago, and you cannot help but be struck by the harshness of the existence our ancestors had to endure. There is one such small plot in a rural part of Maine, no different really from thousands of similar graveyards throughout the countryside, that remains a mute testimonial to the suffering these people endured. No more than a hundred headstones marked the spot, but even in the warmth of that late summer's afternoon when I stopped by, you could still sense the pain and anguish of that era.

> *Here rests Sarah Ann, age 6, 1820, may she rest in peace*
> *John, age 6 months, 1810*
> *Mary Virginia, age 18, 1817*
> *My beloved wife, Martha Reynolds, age 24, 1826*
> *Our son, Mark, age 14, 1841, God's will be done*
> *My beloved husband, John, age 39, 1850*

More than half the tombs in this graveyard held the remains of people who died before they were 35 years old. Clearly these settlers knew firsthand the uncertainty and terror of disease and death. Their children could be healthy one moment, playing in the snow, then catch a cold and be dead in a week. Wives routinely died in childbirth or from mysterious fevers a few weeks later. A husband's cough would awaken the dread of pneumonia or tuberculosis in his wife's mind. They knew about disease and they knew about death. They were fully aware of their feelings of helplessness and hopelessness . . . they could not stop the ravages of diseases like pneumonia, which could disrupt their lives without warning. Death truly came like a thief in the night.

As I lingered awhile in this graveyard, I could not help but recall how just three weeks earlier I had contracted pneumonia and with a few simple injections had quickly recovered. Pneumonia to me was a kind of curiosity, but certainly nothing to fear. The legacy of terror was behind us now.

With few exceptions, science has eliminated almost all of the forces that had once caused premature death. Yet the medical triumphs of this century have not dispelled—and have perhaps encouraged—two persistent illusions. The rapidity with which disease has been conquered has, first of all, contributed to the widespread illusion that we are now living longer and longer lives. For the most part, this is simply not true. We are not living longer; rather, more people are surviving past infancy and childhood. Four-fifths of the entire statistical gain in our average lifespan has been due to the sharp reduction in infant mortality. The President's Commission on Heart Disease [1] noted in 1965 that the average American lived 69.9 years, which I believe is remarkably close to the Psalmist's estimate that "the days of our years are three score and ten—four score if we are strong," in other words, 70 years on the average, 80 if one was in particularly good shape. That was the average 4,000 years ago, and that seems to be the average today. The Psalmist in the Bible was not, however, averaging infant death rates in with adult statistics. He was estimating what the average life span was likely to be if you lived beyond the first years of childhood.

A second tenacious illusion, held even by some people within the medical profession, is the idea that disease is caused by factors outside of us, that we are helpless victims of malevolent forces in nature. This belief, which haunts us like a ghost from our tormented past, in turn obscures the fact that many people who die prematurely today are not the victims of mysterious and malevolent forces, but are instead the victims of their own behavior.

The obituary columns of American newspapers amply testify to the fact that many people still die long before age 70. They still die prematurely, although the causes of death today are very different from what they were 100 years ago. With the rise of effective antibiotics, the growth of immunization programs, and especially the rapid decline in infant mortality, the entire spectrum of forces that threaten our lives has changed. Cardiovascular disease (including stroke) now accounts for approximately 55 percent of all deaths in the United States, while cancer terminates the lives of another 25 percent. Since we all must die, and something must be listed as the "cause" of death, cancer and heart disease have emerged as the leading terminators of life in old age. But this is not a book about aging, or the natural forces that will eventually terminate our lives. Rather, this book will focus on one of the central factors that seems to cause us to die prematurely—our inability to live together.

When you examine the statistics on premature death (deaths not due to natural aging), you quickly begin to suspect that the way we live has a great deal to do with our long-term survival. Since 1950 the leading causes of premature death among U.S. adults between the ages of 24 and 65 have been, in the order of frequency: [2]

1. Heart disease;
2. Malignant neoplasms (among males the most prevalent neoplasm at these ages is lung cancer);
3. Cirrhosis of the liver;
4. Accidents (other than motor vehicle accidents);
5. Influenza and pneumonia;
6. Motor vehicle accidents;
7. Suicide;
8. Homicide.

Most people would agree that, with the exception of heart disease, influenza, and pneumonia, the leading causes of death are at least

partly, if not totally, avoidable—that is, they are due to the way
people behave. Three out of every four deaths among American
males between the ages of 15 and 25 are caused by either accidents,
suicide, or homicide.

The fact that heart disease is by far the leading cause of premature death, and the number-one crippling agent among people
below age 65, prompted the U.S. government after World War II
to undertake massive studies to find the causes of this problem.
Long after other major diseases had been conquered, heart disease
still appeared to come like a thief in the night. It seemed to victim-
ize people, to snuff out their lives prematurely and without warning. The mandate to medical science was simple: find the cause of
heart disease, especially premature heart disease, and seek out
means to eradicate it as a national problem.

In many ways the postwar period was a turning point in modern
medical science. The U.S. government, for the first time, began to
move into the health field, especially the research aspects of health,
in a really big way. Given our conquest of other diseases, it seemed
only a matter of time before scientists would snuff out the last
pockets of resistance barring our way to unbridled good health.
Cardiac disease, it was clear, had to go. It was in this spirit of scientific optimism that a small army of medical scientists and techni-
cians descended on the town of Framingham, Massachusetts, in
1948 to begin to seek out the causes of heart attacks.

## THE FRAMINGHAM STUDIES

To this day I still remember the town of Framingham in 1948.
At that time it was a small, rather beautiful and peaceful town of
28,000 people, some 20 miles or so from downtown Boston. In
many ways it was an ideal town for research. In its ethnic, social,

and economic mixes it appeared to be mainstream America—a model city, so to speak, for medical research.

The U.S. government joined forces with medical science to try something that had never been tried before—a kind of Manhattan Project for health.[3] Framingham was to be the testing ground, picked because it seemed such an average American community: hardworking, mostly white, mostly middle-class, and, in 1948, very stable. People didn't move around very much in Framingham, and the scientists hoped it would be rather easy to keep track of them. The mission was clear: find out what causes heart disease. By 1948 physicians were already well aware of how the healthy human heart functions. They were also very familiar with the events that immediately precede and follow a heart attack. They knew that the coronary arteries were vitally important to the healthy functioning of the heart, and that a process called atherosclerosis—especially coronary atherosclerosis—put a person at high risk for having a heart attack. Atherosclerosis is caused by a gradual narrowing of the inner walls of the arteries, which are thickened by soft, fatty deposits called atheromas or atheromatous plaques. This process increases the likelihood that the blood supply to various portions of the heart muscle will be temporarily or permanently cut off, leading to a heart attack. Before 1948, autopsies performed on heart attack victims had convincingly shown that their coronary arteries had lost their normal elasticity, becoming quite rigid and clogged. What was unclear was what led to atherosclerosis: how did it first develop, what caused it to lead to fatal heart attacks, why did it develop at such different rates in different people, and what could be done to ameliorate this condition?

To help answer these questions, the medical scientists picked 2,282 healthy men and 2,845 healthy women between the ages of 30 and 62 years, 5,127 volunteers in all, and asked them to participate in a study that might very well last the rest of their lives. Each participant was given a physical examination, including blood tests, electrocardiograms (to determine heart function), X rays, and blood pressure readings. A history of all participants' previous

medical problems was also documented. The initial phase of this
study involved mammoth amounts of work, but after that it was
just a matter of wait and see . . . who would remain healthy and
who would develop heart disease or other physical problems? Who
would be the first to die? Year after year this study has continued,
10 years, 20 years; soon it will be 30 years. At regular two-year
intervals all the participants have been called back for reexamina-
tion. Between intervals, their health has been followed by their
family doctors, who were requested to report major physical problems to the research team. When any of the volunteers died, a postmortem examination was conducted, if possible, in order to determine the cause of death.

Over the almost 30 years of the study, the computers have
churned out mountains of medical data about Framingham. Gradually it became clear that certain factors were statistically connected with the eventual development of coronary heart disease.
Five factors seemed especially important:

1.  Elevated blood pressure;
2.  Elevated serum cholesterol;
3.  Cigarette smoking;
4.  Electrocardiographic evidence of left ventricular hypertrophy;
5.  Glucose intolerance.

These were called *risk factors*. In a sense they were like weather
flags, signaling the impending approach of a storm, except that
these warning signs were hoisted long before the storm arrived—
even years in advance. These risk factors all seemed to be connected with the eventual development of heart disease, and if you
had all five of them your chances of developing heart disease and
dying prematurely increased significantly.

These studies had an explosive impact on the average citizen.
Americans may not have known exactly what cholesterol was, but
they did know it was in their diets and that it was linked to the
development of atherosclerosis. Foods were (and still are) adver-
tised on television specifically because they were low in saturated
fats, low in cholesterol. Americans also got the message from other

research studies that they had better start exercising to keep in shape, or else they would develop heart disease.

## A CLOSER LOOK

Over the years there were to be many other studies similar to the Framingham investigations, but Framingham was the prototype, and it remains the most famous. Because it has had such an explosive impact on the medical community (virtually every physician in the United States has heard about or read the Framingham reports), it is important to look more closely at many of the fundamental premises and findings of this pioneering work.

Perhaps the most important question is whether Framingham was really a representative town in which to study coronary heart disease. One wonders whether the research team would have discovered different relationships if instead of Framingham they had chosen the boomtown of Reno, Nevada, in 1948? Certainly it would have been a tougher research assignment, maybe even impossible, because people didn't seem to stick around Reno for very long. Besides, it would have been a messy research environment—what with all those people coming and getting divorced, they would hardly have been the type to come back to Reno every two years for a checkup. Many Reno citizens would have been mighty hard to find after two years. Framingham, by contrast, was perhaps one of the most settled communities in the United States in 1948—religious, churchgoing, nondivorcing type people. They were an ideal research population because their community was, on the whole, so dependable and so well integrated socially. This fact was not ignored by the original investigators,[3] for they wrote of Framingham: "As is true of New England towns, it included not only built-up business and residential areas, but also the outlying rural areas within the town limit. Framingham has the town-meeting form of government and the people were accustomed to and well versed in the group approach to their problems" (pp. 2, 3). After almost 30 years of study, the scientists have been able to keep track of almost 80 percent of the original population of those still alive—an astounding record of reliability.

If the entire United States were like Framingham, then the health data discovered there might be applicable to the whole country. The social realities of 1977, however, seem to make the Framingham of 1948 very different from mainstream America today. I suspect that very few of the people who lived in Framingham in 1948 had come from broken homes. I believe very few had experienced childhood deprivation or were from single-parent households. I suspect, I feel, I think, I believe these things but I do not know them, because the fact is that while blood pressure, weight, diet, and a host of other physical factors were painstakingly determined, social data were not analyzed by the original researchers. In 1948 social stability was more or less taken for granted.

Not only did the Framingham studies initially neglect social and psychological risk factors that might contribute to heart disease, but they also tended more and more to deemphasize the importance of emotional stress in heart disease. The Framingham investigators began to assert that emotional stress (and specifically divorce) was not related to coronary heart disease. In 1966, for example, one circular entitled *The Framingham Heart Study: Habits and Coronary Disease* emphatically stated that marital status was not related to coronary heart disease.[4] This circular was distributed to thousands of physicians across the United States and was seen by a large number of ordinary citizens. The brochure states:

*Marital status* was unrelated to risk of coronary heart disease, even though changes in marital status through separation, divorce, or death would be regarded by many as evidence of long-standing emotional upheaval.

Adjacent to a graphic display supposedly showing this lack of relationship between marital status and heart disease was another graph. This one, relating family size and heart disease, sought to make a similar point:

Family size appeared unrelated to risk of developing coronary heart disease. Some married couples with *no children* or with very *large families* might be construed as living under stressful conditions.

The message was clear: stress and heart disease were apparently unrelated.

The graph on coronary heart disease and marital status showed what was labeled as a "morbidity ratio." This ratio was based on the idea that the relative numbers of single, widowed, divorced (or separated), and married people in the Framingham population who died should be equivalent to the respective numbers of such people in their total sample. The researchers derived the ratio from the following data:

|  | *Expected* to have died in Framingham by 1966 | *Observed* to have died in Framingham by 1966 | *Difference* |
|---|---|---|---|
| Married | 328 | 322 | −6 |
| Single | 26 | 31 | +5 |
| Widowed | 19 | 23 | +4 |
| Divorced and separated | 8 | 6 | −2 |

What is most interesting about the researchers' claim that marital status had no bearing on coronary heart disease is that it was based on 6 observed cases of coronary heart disease in divorced or separated people where 8 cases had been expected! Two other situations, being single or widowed, actually had relatively higher incidences of coronary heart disease, while the married individuals had slightly less coronary heart disease than would have been expected. In other words, the three largest groups did show variations from the norm—all showing marital status to be related to heart disease—yet the one chosen to support the assertion of *no* relationship between marital status and coronary heart disease had a total of only 6 cases! No Las Vegas gambler in his right mind would have ever given you any odds on the reliability of that statement. What should have been clear even in 1966 was that these investigators did not have sufficient evidence to make *any* statement about the relationship between marital status and heart disease. Perhaps even more remarkable was the obvious fact that very few people in the Framingham study were getting divorced.

Assertions like the ones that first emerged from the Framingham studies reflected a widespread belief that emotional stress was not related to heart disease. While these assertions were made, we were told nothing about the rate of divorce in Framingham, how many of the divorcees remained alone, how many remarried, how isolated were the people living alone from their community, and so forth. In the early phases of these studies, emotional stress was not considered a serious risk factor in heart disease. Beyond that, the investigators were probably quite right in minimizing the impact of emotional stress on heart disease in Framingham. As noted, Framingham in 1948 may have been one of the more peaceful, socially stable towns in the United States. Emotional stress, especially that brought on by social disintegration and family disruptions, was obviously a minimal influence there.

Another aspect of the Framingham studies is generally overlooked. Many people who were relatively low on the scales for every risk factor still developed cardiovascular disease. If you analyze the most risk-prone 30 percent—that is, those people who ranked the worst on all five of the risk factors identified at Framingham (i.e., their blood pressure was highest, their serum cholesterol was highest, and they smoked the most)—they still accounted for only 50 percent of those who eventually developed coronary heart disease. Another 50 percent of those who got sick and died from cardiovascular disease ranked much lower on these risk scales. I do not mean to imply that the risk factors discovered at Framingham are not important contributors to the development of heart disease, but rather to emphasize that some risk factors were overlooked.

Over the years it has become apparent what some of the missing information might be—no psychological or social data were initially collected in Framingham. The focus of the medical scientists was instead on physical risk factors. At the risk of oversimplification, we might say that part of the legacy haunting the graveyards of regions like rural Maine helped create attitudes about disease and death that still pervaded postwar medical science. Disease was out there—somewhere—something mysterious—and it got inside us and killed us. Disease was not our fault, we were helpless victims, or so most of us believed in 1948. Framingham ever so slowly has helped us to dispel that illusion.

The Framingham findings generated controversies that now have been raging in the medical community for a decade. Serum cholesterol has been shown to be linked not only to diet but also to emotional stress: people who are more stressed psychologically can have higher levels.[5] Elevated blood pressure also has been linked to emotional stress,[6] as have smoking and obesity.[7] Strange questions began to emerge. Could the same dietary intake of cholesterol be absorbed differently, depending on your level of anxiety? Does food that is digested in a socially stable community like Framingham have the same effects as food that is digested in Reno?

In the 1960s, Dr. Stewart Wolf, a cardiologist, began to study the town of Roseto, Pennsylvania, a town in the foothills of the Pocono Mountains about 60 miles from New York City. Roseto's population was 1,630, largely Italians. They seemed to eat many things that would cause cardiologists to worry. Their daily caloric intake was above the national average. Strangely, while they had only one-third as many heart attacks as surrounding communities, their blood cholesterol levels were about the same as those of people in neighboring towns. Why? Dr. Wolf gave his opinion: "The most striking feature of Roseto was its social structure. . . . study revealed that unlike most American towns Roseto is cohesive and mutually supportive, with strong family and community ties. Because of the concern of the inhabitants for their neighbors, there is in Roseto no poverty and little crime. The family was found to be the focus of life in Roseto. . . . Few men over the age of 25 were unmarried." [8] (pp. IV–79)

As will be noted in later chapters, observations similar to those made in Roseto have been subsequently corroborated by other studies, and the suspicion is growing among medical scientists that social and psychological factors may not only significantly influence the course of heart disease—they may be the most important of all risk factors!

## HEALTH AND SOCIAL STABILITY

For nearly 30 years now, Framingham has been linked in the minds of the scientific-medical community with heart disease. For years, one study after another has been published linking various physical factors with this dreaded disease. But the greatest irony may yet turn out to be that the town was really another Roseto all along, disguised under miles of computerized medical data. This social reality about Framingham may prove much more important than all of the risk factors that have been linked thus far to heart disease. For the focus in Framingham has been so strongly oriented toward heart disease that a far more obvious fact has escaped general attention—the town was a very healthy place to live. Evidence supporting this assertion has been there almost since the beginning, but it was simply taken for granted.

From the very beginning of the Framingham studies, the incidence of coronary heart disease has been far below what the experts had originally estimated it would be. They based their original estimates on the national incidence of coronary heart disease in similar populations. At the very beginning of their studies, they pondered the question of what the likely incidence of cardiovascular disorders would be in 5,000 randomly chosen people who were initially free of this disease. They wrote:

Of these 5,000 [people free of cardiovascular disease at the initial examination] it was estimated that approximately 400 would be found to have cardiovascular disease at the end of the 5th year after the initial examination, 900 at the end of the 10th year, 1,500 at the end of the 15th year, and 2,150 at the end of the 20th year (see Gorden and Kannel[3]).

For the 13 years between 1953 and 1966, the number of deaths that were expected to occur in the Framingham population was 1,017 (based on national death rates for these age ranges). The number of deaths that actually occurred was 883—about 15 percent fewer deaths than predicted. Far more intriguing is the fact that nowhere near the expected number of people developed cardiovascular disorders. Twenty years after the study began, the figures simply didn't add up. In 1968 some 3,785 of the original 5,127 volunteers were still completely free of heart disease. Even throwing in the extra 127 people (the difference between 5,000 and the actual number of 5,127), only 1,342 people had developed any form of cardiovascular disease. That was 808 fewer people than the 2,150 the experts had originally estimated would have some form of heart disease after 20 years. Framingham had at least one-third fewer heart problems than they had originally predicted would occur in the town.

Of all the statistics emerging out of Framingham, the most revealing is that after 28 years of study, 73.2 percent of the original sample was still alive. The youngest members of this sample were approaching their 60s in 1976, while the oldest members were reaching 90.

In February 1976, 3,754 of the original group of volunteers were still alive. Comparing that against the national survival rates for a similar race-sex-age range, the number of people expected to live for 28 years was 3,116. Thus, at least 638 people are still alive in Framingham who might be dead in other parts of the United States. Using far more conservative figures, the life expectancy of people in Framingham can be compared to the life expectancy of whites covered by life insurance from the 15 largest insurers in the country.* These people are the "good risks", that is, they are screened

* I am indebted to Mr. L. Timothy Giles of the Fidelity and Guaranty Life Insurance Company, Baltimore, Maryland, for providing me with the comparative figures.

carefully for health; otherwise the companies that gamble on their health would lose money. Again, using the mortality figures of insured whites in the United States for the age and sex range at Framingham, one would have expected 3,438 people to have survived 28 years. By this criterion, at least 316 people are still alive in Framingham who should be dead even according to the very conservative figures of the life insurance companies. More people in Framingham are actually living longer than the estimates of insurance companies for their very best risks. Why so many people are still alive and so healthy in Framingham is, I believe, far more interesting than why 26.8 percent have died.

Is this simply a statistical fluke? Or did the fact that they were coming back for continuous medical checkups make the people of Framingham so health conscious that they have taken unusually good care of their bodies? Or was the social milieu of Framingham in 1948 similar to that of Roseto in the 1960's? Did the investigators inadvertently stumble upon a population that experienced such a low degree of emotional or social stress that the only risk factors likely to emerge from the medical data would have been physical in nature?

By 1970 the population of Framingham had reached almost 65,000, or more than double the 1948 total. The train station that once connected the town to Boston had been overshadowed by the Massachusetts Turnpike that passed nearby. The illegitimate birthrate in 1970 was 3 percent; there were no deaths by homicide, and only four suicides were recorded that year. In Massachusetts, divorce records are not kept by individual towns like Framingham, but are instead maintained by counties. In Middlesex County, of which Framingham is a part, the 1970 population was 1,400,000. In 1970 the county had 1,400 divorces, far below the national average.

Between 1970 and 1975, however, social patterns in the area began to shift rapidly; cultural tides from regions like Nevada began to affect these New England communities. "Framingham is changing very fast now," a town clerk (a lifelong resident) told me. "It wasn't too long ago that when you walked down the street you knew everyone. Now there seem to be so many strangers." She thought the illegitimate birthrate was "shockingly high," and she refused to believe that it was still ten times lower than the average of many American cities.*

Between 1970 and 1974 the number of divorces granted in Middlesex County tripled. All the signs pointed to the fact that Framingham is well on its way to "catching up" with the life-style of mainstream America. It would clearly be very difficult to begin a new Framingham study in 1978, yet one cannot help but wonder if its citizens will be as healthy three decades from now as they once were when our government moved in to snuff out the last pocket of resistance that barred their way to unbridled good health in 1948.

---

* In 1976 Washington, D.C. became the first American city where the illegitimate birth rate exceeded the legitimate birth rate.

# CHAPTER 2

---

# The Lonely Heart,
# the Broken Heart,
# and Sudden Death

"Just stay by my bed."
—Request of a coronary care patient who knew he was dying to his wife just before his death (March 1976)

While the Framingham studies have involved a huge amount of work, they are only one small part of a vast research enterprise aimed at controlling heart disease. Billions of dollars have been spent in the past decade attempting to eradicate this disease. Coupled with the research effort has been a clinical program that is nothing short of heroic. In terms of capital expenditures for the development of treatment facilities to care for those suffering from heart disease, the United States ranks first among all the nations of the world. The concern for providing the best treatment available is clear-cut, if not downright awesome in magnitude. In 1976 alone, the National Heart Institute and American Heart Association spent over $400 million on research into the cause of heart disease. That same year, the National Institutes of Health spent over $2 billion on all aspects of health research. The National Heart Institute estimated that in 1976 the total economic cost of heart disease—including hospital care, insurance losses, manpower losses, and other items—totaled over $58 billion in the United States alone.

This overwhelming cost and concern prompts an obvious question: Why does the United States still rank 24th among industrialized countries in life expectancy for its male citizens? Why is the mortality rate for males under age 55 double that of Denmark, Sweden, and Norway and six times higher than that of Japan? The coronary death rate for Japanese men between the ages of 35 and 64, for example, is 64 deaths per 100,000 population, while in the United States the coronary death rate at those ages is 400 per 100,000 population.[1] What is it about life in the United States that leads to these high mortality rates?

Despite the vast expenditure of our national treasury, we still find ourselves asking the very same questions raised in Framingham in 1948. What is it that causes heart disease, and how can our nation evolve effective methods for preventing this disease from striking down so many people in their prime of life? Is living in the United States a hazard to one's health?

## THE HEART'S WARRANTY

Diet, smoking, lack of exercise, and faulty living habits have all been identified by the experts as risk factors that affect the incidence of coronary heart disease in various countries. The central assumption of this book is that, in addition to these risk factors, a person's life may be shortened by the lack of human companionship. This idea is of special importance to the study of heart disease because the National Heart Institute has noted the likelihood that in the United States most men and many women over 50 years of age have moderately advanced coronary atherosclerosis. If most men already have moderately advanced coronary atherosclerosis after 50, then just what determines survival beyond this point?

As just stated, I believe one important factor is human companionship. By this I do not mean that, since human love and companionship affect the heart, all types of heart disease therefore stem from the lack of loving relationships. That would be absurd. The heart is a pump, and like other types of pumps it can malfunction through simple mechanical breakdowns. What I do imply is that the heart is a complex pump that is influenced by the most subtle human feelings and social situations. The presence of human companionship does not work in any simple fashion to prevent heart disease, any more than the mere existence of loneliness directly causes heart disease. If the relationship was that straightforward, it would have been recognized long ago. Since we all must die, it is clear that neither human companionship nor love can sustain life indefinitely. The question, then, is not whether human companionship or love can prevent cardiac disease. Rather, the question is whether the lack of human companionship and love, the sudden loss of human love, or the persistence of loneliness will lead to *premature* cardiac disease or excessive rates of disease and death. Does human companionship help sustain life? Does the lack of companionship hasten death?

In order to understand the relationship between human companionship and health, it is important to have at least a general comprehension of the magnitude of heart disease in the United States. Cardiovascular disease kills approximately 1 million individuals in the United States each year, and accounts for more than half of all the deaths reported in this country. Cardiovascular disease also disables a larger proportion of the U.S. population than any other disease. And while the toll is heaviest among individuals over 65 years of age, 25 percent of all heart disease deaths occur in people under age 65, and about one half of all disabling cardiovascular conditions occur in people under 65. Included among the major cardiovascular diseases are atherosclerotic heart disease, hypertension and hypertensive heart disease (elevated blood pressure), cerebrovascular disease (vascular problems in the brain), and rheumatic fever. Of these cardiac diseases, atherosclerotic heart disease is by far the most important, accounting for about 65 percent of all cardiac deaths.[2]

In the twentieth century there has been a sharp increase in the percentage of individuals dying from heart disease. In 1900 about

20 percent of the deaths in the United States were caused by heart disease. That percentage increased steadily until 1950, when heart disease accounted for 55 percent of all deaths. Since then the overall percentage has remained relatively constant. As noted earlier, part of the sharp increase in the cardiac death rate is explained by the sharp decreases in infant and young adult deaths from infectious disease, a fact which has resulted in the progressive aging of the population. In their exhaustive statistical survey *Cardiovascular Disease in the United States*, published in 1971, Drs. Moriyama, Krueger, and Stamler pointed out that "life expectancy at birth in the United States is 69.9 years, based on mortality experience during 1959–61. If cardiovascular-renal diseases were eliminated as causes of death, the gain in life expectancy would be 10.9 years —more than four times the gain that would be achieved by the elimination of any other cause of death." Nevertheless, aging seems to account for only part of the rise in heart disease. In 1969 the World Health Organization warned that "coronary heart disease has reached enormous proportions, striking *more and more at younger subjects*. It will result in the greatest epidemic mankind has ever faced unless we are able to reverse the trend by concentrated research into its cause and prevention" [3] (italics added).

One of the intriguing aspects of the differences in coronary mortality among various countries is the way in which these differences have been used to support divergent theories about the physical causes of heart disease. The explanations are reminiscent of the philosophy that guided the original Framingham studies. For example, the very low premature coronary death rate in Japanese men has been generally explained away with the argument that their diets contain far less cholesterol than typical American diets. To my knowledge, little reference is made to the fact that the divorce rate in Japan is also very low (almost nonexistent) and that social stability is a hallmark of Japanese culture.

Similarly, a well-known series of studies compared the coronary death rates of Irishmen who emigrated to America to those living in Ireland.[4] These studies were undertaken because the male coro-

nary death rate in America was observed to be four times higher
than that in Ireland. A large number of Irishmen living in Boston
who still had at least one brother in Ireland were identified and
examined. After exhaustive analysis it was found that the brothers
who stayed in Ireland had anywhere from two to six times fewer
signs of coronary heart disease (depending on which physiological
variable was used to detect this disease) than those who had come
to America. What made these findings even more interesting was
the fact that the brothers who remained in Ireland not only consumed at least 400–500 more calories per day than their Bostonian
siblings, but also seemed to pick menus far richer in saturated fats.
In short, the Irish diets were not the type of fare recommended by
either cardiologists or gourmets.

Why, then, the startlingly lower coronary death rate in Ireland?
The investigators decided it must have been due to differences in
exercise—the Irish who stayed in Ireland were apparently less
sedentary than their American brothers. Once again, this explanation was presented with minimal descriptions of the relative differences in social environments. Little recognition was given to the
social stability of Ireland versus Boston, and scant attention was
paid to the stresses involved in leaving one's family and homeland
to come to a new country. No data at all were given on the marital
status of the relative populations. So we are left to conclude that
it's the diet in Japan but exercise in Ireland that prevents heart
problems.

I do not mean to belittle the importance of diet and exercise for
the healthy functioning of the heart; since these factors have been
repeatedly linked to heart disease, they should be considered seriously by every reader of this book. Nevertheless, it is important to
recognize the type of premises that dominated such studies. Physical factors were examined exhaustively, while psychological and
social factors were, for the most part, ignored. Ironically, the inability of these studies to isolate *the* cause of heart disease gradually
led to the realization that this disease most likely was also influenced by factors not yet measured. A growing number of recent

studies have postulated that differences in national coronary mortality patterns might stem from important psychological and sociocultural divergences. Indeed, as shall be discussed subsequently, similar psychosocial factors may help account for the large racial differences in coronary mortality within the United States.

Recent research has pointed to the fact that many psychological, social, and interpersonal factors affect heart disease. In 1971, Dr. C. David Jenkins reviewed some of the psychological and social precursors of coronary heart disease in the *New England Journal of Medicine*.[5] Part of the introduction to Dr. Jenkins' review is especially relevant to this book:

The best combinations of the standard "risk factors" fail to identify most new cases of [coronary] disease. . . . And, whereas simultaneous presence of two or more risk factors is associated with extremely high risk of coronary disease, such situations only predict a small minority of cases. . . . A broad array of recent research studies . . . point with ever increasing certainty to the position that certain psychological, social and behavior conditions do put persons at higher risk of clinically manifest coronary disease (p. 244).

While the words *psychological* and *sociological* have at times a frustratingly large number of meanings, one sociopsychological factor that emerges from cardiac death statistics is, for our purposes, especially worth considering. The mortality statistics for heart disease among those adult Americans who are not married are striking—a death rate from heart disease that is as much as two to five times higher for nonmarried individuals, including those who are divorced, widowed, or single, than for married Americans. These statistics, which will soon be examined more closely, are most troubling when viewed in the context of our modern society, in which new patterns of living (marked by an accelerating divorce rate) have become well established.

If living patterns and human companionship do influence the incidence of cardiovascular disease, then it would appear that medicine has been misdirecting its preventive skills. A few heart transplants receiving worldwide attention have led to widespread euphoria—in just a few more years, perhaps, everyone will be able to receive new hearts, just as we replace worn-out tires on automobiles. It should be pointed out, however, that no one has yet suggested opening a "spare parts" department store for worn-out or defective human emotions. The repair of a "broken heart" from the loss of a loved one may present far more of a therapeutic challenge than the technical skills needed for a heart transplant operation.

## A TIME TO LIVE AND A TIME TO DIE

The growing body of evidence supporting the idea that psychological and social factors affect heart disease has led to the realization that many widely shared attitudes about disease and death must be reexamined.

The search for the causes of heart disease, and especially premature cardiac death, has inevitably stimulated one question that previous generations had more or less taken for granted. Every generation before this century was so busy trying to survive that it did not question the fundamental belief that "there is a time to sow and a time to reap, a time to work and a time to play, a time to live and a time to die." Before the triumphs of mid-twentieth-century medical science, the vast majority of people accepted premature death as an unpleasant but unavoidable part of life. It appeared as if the time to die was predetermined by forces far beyond individual control, and people generally resigned themselves to their fate without question. By the time the Framingham studies began, however, many of the major diseases that once terminated life prematurely had been controlled, freeing people to begin asking questions about life, death, and disease that had long been taken for granted. When is disease really disease, and when is it part of the natural aging process? Is there really such a thing as a "time to die"? Twenty-five years after the Framingham studies were initiated these questions erupted, sometimes with bitter intensity, in public debate and in the courts of the United States.

Is there a chronological time to die? Is the machinery of the body naturally programmed to last for a fixed period of time and then to stop functioning? The concept of *premature death* which permeates modern medicine ultimately has meaning only when there are some guidelines established as to just what is meant by the proper chronological time to die. It is similar to the idea of *premature birth*, a phenomenon that is intelligible only because we know the gestation period normally lasts nine months.

But the forces that lead to death are not nearly so precisely understood as those that bring about life. Earlier it was pointed out that the life span of the average American is approximately 70 years, a span that seems remarkably close to the estimates given 4,000 years ago by the Psalmist. But this average is the result of a kind of statistical lottery—jumbling together a large number of factors, totalling them all up, and looking at the bottom line figure. The average may be 70 in the United States, but there are very important variations within that total that should not go unnoticed. On the average, women live longer than men, the educated live longer than the uneducated, the rich live longer than the poor, and the married live far longer than the nonmarried. Race also seems to make a big difference. In the United States, for example, U.S.-born Japanese men have a life expectancy of 74.4 years at birth, 6.8 years longer than white men and 13.1 years longer than black men. Japanese women in the United States live on the average 80.4 years, which is 5.7 years more than white women and 13.2 years more than black women. The average Japanese woman born in the United States lives over 19 years longer than the average black American male.[6]

While there may be a time to live and a time to die, there certainly seems to be a huge variation in the amount of time allotted to various people within the United States. Moreover, when we examine average life spans in other parts of the world, we find regions of the Soviet Union, Ecuador, and Pakistan where surprising numbers of people live over 100 years. Unlike people in the United States, these people believe the average life span is around 100 years; they also believe there is a time to live and a time to

die, but they don't agree with our clocks. In all of these regions of
unusual longevity, factors like social integration, community cohe-
sion, and healthy long-term marriages seem to figure prominently.
Citing the parallels between the Italian community in Roseto,
Pennsylvania, and the longevity of the Abkhazians of Soviet Geor-
gia, Dr. Stewart Wolf quotes the work of Dr. Sula Benet, a professor of anthropology at Hunter College.* Dr. Benet described the
culture of the Abkhazians as having "the high degree of integration
in their lives, the sense of group identity that gives each individual
an unshaken feeling of personal security." Dr. Benet called them "a
life-loving optimistic people unlike so many very old 'dependent'
people in the U.S. . . . The elders preside at important ceremonial
occasions, they mediate disputes and their knowledge of farming is
sought. They feel needed because . . . they are." [7]

## LIVING TOGETHER AND DYING ALONE

The differences in longevity among various racial groups in the
United States, and the unusually long life spans of some groups, are
also reflected in the various mortality tables that measure the way
people live together.

It is a striking fact that U.S. mortality rates for all causes of
death, and not just heart disease, are consistently higher for divorced, single, and widowed individuals of both sexes and all races.
Some of the increased death rates in unmarried individuals are astounding, rising as high as ten times the rates for married individuals of comparable ages.

Corporations such as insurance companies that gamble their
money on their ability to evaluate health risks have long recognized
that a person's marital status is one of the best predictors of health,

---

* It should be noted that Alexander Leaf, who also studied these communities,
observed that those who lived the longest were almost all still married. He, too,
commented on the social stability and strong family ties of these communities.

disease, and death. Over two decades ago, in 1956, Drs. Kraus and Lillienfeld at The Johns Hopkins Medical School also recognized this relationship.[8] They summarized the medical data available at that time on the relationship between marital status and mortality rates as follows:

Married people experienced a lower mortality rate from all causes than did single persons, the widowed, and the divorced for every specific age group in each sex and color. For both sexes and colors combined, the ratios of the age-adjusted death rates in these three not-married groups to the age-adjusted rate in the married group were 1.47, 1.46 and 1.84, respectively. . . . The relative excess mortality in the not-married categories compared to the married group was greater at the younger ages. . . . The relative excess mortality in the not-married categories was consistently greater in males than in females (p. 207).

All three aspects of the Kraus and Lillienfeld review deserve special emphasis. First, all causes of death were higher in the nonmarried groups. Second, the differences were greatest at the younger ages. Third, the differences were more apparent in males.

Before we proceed to examine these conclusions in greater detail, however, several statistical concepts referred to by Drs. Kraus and Lillienfeld need to be clarified. The first of these is the concept of *age-specific death rates*. Within any given age group, a certain percentage of people die. At younger ages, obviously, fewer people die than at older ages. Excessive age-specific death rates, therefore, refer to any increase for a specific age group above the average death rate for that age. Quite often this is expressed in terms of a ratio. Thus, the 1.84 overall age-adjusted death rate for divorced people in the United States means that when the death rate at all ages is averaged together and adjusted for the average death rate at each age, divorced people die 1.84 times more frequently than married people. This is, of course, calculated from the relative numbers of divorced to married people at each age. A second concept that must be emphasized is that of *excessive mortality*. If for example, 1 out of every 100 males dies at the age of 30, while 2 out of every 100 30-year-old divorced males dies, then the excessive mortality of divorced males is said to be double that of their married counterparts for that specific age. *Premature death* as a statistical concept refers to deaths occurring before the ages of 65-70, while age-specific death rates are the death-rate patterns at any and all ages.

The Kraus-Lillienfeld finding of sharply increased death rates for nonmarried individuals has been confirmed repeatedly over the last two decades by other investigators, and these findings stimulate many questions. Why should nonmarried individuals have so much higher death rates than married individuals? What diseases contribute most to this marked increase in death rates? Why should the younger nonmarried groups suffer proportionally so much more than older individuals? Why should younger widows and widowers, for example, die at higher rates than older widows and widowers, who themselves die at higher rates than married individuals?

While the overall death rate for divorced individuals in the United States is almost double that of married individuals, a closer inspection of mortality figures reveals that the death rates of non-married individuals are far greater than might be initially deduced from Kraus and Lillienfeld's summary statements.

In 1970, in *Marriage and Divorce: A Social and Economic Study* Hugh Carter and Paul Glick reported *overall* increased death rates very similar to those observed by Kraus and Lillienfeld 14 years earlier.[9] Their text, however, provides additional valuable insights into the large number of diseases that contribute to increased death rates in nonmarried individuals. Using data obtained from the National Center for Health Statistics on all deaths that occurred in the United States from 1959 to 1961, Carter and Glick demonstrated that the *premature death rates* (deaths between the ages of 15 and 64) in men and women who were single, divorced, or widowed were significantly higher than those for married individuals. As is shown in detail in Appendix B, they classified death rates per 100,000 population according to marital status, sex, race, and cause of death. For every listed cause of death the single, widowed, and divorced had significantly higher death rates than did married people, both white and nonwhite and both sexes.

Representative comparisons, extracted from the detailed table in Appendix B, help show not only the magnitude but also the consistency of this phenomenon. The following table shows that for every major cause of death, the rates for divorced males ranged anywhere from two to six times higher than those of their married counterparts. Single and widowed males showed similarly high death rates when compared to those who were married.

*Death Rates of Divorced and Married Men per 100,000 Population,*
*Ages 15–64 in the United States, 1959–1961*

| Cause of Death | White Males | | Nonwhite Males | |
|---|---|---|---|---|
| | Married | Divorced | Married | Divorced |
| Heart disease | 176 | 362 | 142 | 298 |
| Motor vehicle accidents | 35 | 128 | 43 | 81 |
| Cancer of respiratory system | 28 | 65 | 29 | 75 |
| Cancer of digestive system | 27 | 48 | 42 | 88 |
| Stroke | 24 | 58 | 73 | 132 |
| Suicide | 17 | 73 | 10 | 21 |
| Cirrhosis of liver | 11 | 79 | 12 | 53 |
| Hypertension | 8 | 20 | 49 | 90 |
| Pneumonia | 6 | 44 | 22 | 69 |
| Homicide | 4 | 30 | 51 | 129 |
| Tuberculosis | 3 | 30 | 15 | 54 |

As can be seen in the table, for U.S. males heart disease is by far the leading cause of death. While in every case there were significantly higher death rates for the divorced males, there were also important differences in death rate patterns according to race. Death caused by strokes and hypertension was significantly higher in the nonwhite population, although again significantly altered by marital status. Unfortunately, however, until very recently U.S. census data grouped all nonwhite races together, including Orientals, blacks, and Indians, so that it is impossible to sort out the relative manner in which these different groups contributed to the nonwhite death rates. It is well known that hypertension and stroke afflict blacks significantly more than whites. Since blacks in 1960 comprised roughly 85 percent of the total U.S. nonwhite population, it would be reasonable to assume that they contributed to the bulk of the deaths given for nonwhite males. This point is especially critical in light of the fact that it has been assumed by many that the greatly elevated rates of hypertensive heart disease and stroke among blacks reflect some type of genetic predisposition to these diseases. And yet, as is clear from the figures, the incidence of hypertension is also significantly affected by marital status, strongly suggesting the possibility that environmental and psychological factors influence the course of this disease.

Similar changes in death rate patterns by marital status can be seen in women. In order to show the generality of the influence of marital status, the death rate patterns of widowed women can be compared to those of married women.

*Death Rates of Widowed and Married Females per 100,000 Population, Ages 15–64 in the United States, 1959–1961*

| Cause of Death | White Females | | Nonwhite Females | |
|---|---|---|---|---|
| | Married | Widowed | Married | Widowed |
| Heart disease | 44 | 67 | 83 | 165 |
| Cancer of breast | 21 | 21 | 19 | 28 |
| Cancer of digestive system | 20 | 24 | 25 | 41 |
| Stroke | 19 | 31 | 72 | 147 |
| Motor vehicle accidents | 11 | 47 | 10 | 25 |
| Hypertensive heart disease | 7 | 10 | 50 | 97 |
| Cancer of cervix | 7 | 13 | 17 | 34 |
| Cirrhosis of liver | 7 | 15 | 9 | 23 |
| Suicide | 6 | 12 | 3 | 6 |
| Accidental fires or explosions | 1 | 6 | 4 | 11 |

Several features can be quickly seen. First of all, the overall death rate before age 65 for women was significantly lower than for men. As was true with men, marital status significantly influenced the death rates, with married women always having lower rates. Again, there were important racial differences. Stroke and hypertensive heart disease were much higher among nonwhite females; as usual, the rate was double for widows.

In summary then, for both men and women, white and nonwhite, cardiovascular disease (including stroke and hypertension) was listed as the major cause of premature death. For divorced, widowed, and single men, both white and nonwhite, the overall death rates for cardiovascular disease were two to three times higher than for married men. Similar trends were also true for women. For almost every other major cause of premature death there were also marked increases for the nonmarried over the married, with differences in death rates as high as tenfold. Death rates for heart disease, motor vehicle accidents, cancer of the respiratory system, cancer of the digestive organs, stroke, suicide, cirrhosis of the liver, rheumatic fever, hypertension, pneumonia, diabetes, homicide, tuberculosis—all these were higher among single, widowed, and divorced individuals. The consistently higher death rates for so many different causes of death is itself remarkable.

Of all these causes of death other than heart disease, cancer is perhaps the most interesting, not only because it is the second leading cause of death but also because it is commonly thought of as a disease that is unambiguously physical in nature (that is, cancer is not usually thought of as being influenced by psychological or social factors). And yet, as is shown in the following table and in greater detail in Appendix B, almost every type of cancer is significantly influenced by marital status, with the widowed, divorced, and single individuals almost always having significantly higher death rates.[5]

The 4.10 ratio for white males for buccal cavity and pharyngeal cancer means that divorced white males died from this type of cancer *4.10 times more frequently than did married men.* What is remarkable about these figures, taken directly from Lillienfeld, Levin, and Kessler's text, *Cancer in the United States,* published in 1972, is that every type of terminal cancer strikes divorced individuals of either sexes, both white and nonwhite, more frequently than it does people who are married.[10]

*Ratios of Cancer Death Rates for Divorced to Married Persons ***
*for Persons of Age 15 and over, by selected sites or groups of sites,*
*color, and sex, 1959–1961*

| Primary Site | Divorced Male | | Divorced Female | |
|---|---|---|---|---|
| | White | Nonwhite | White | Nonwhite |
| Buccal cavity and pharynx | 4.10 | 3.14 | 1.67 | 1.44 |
| Digestive organs and peritoneum | 1.53 | 1.78 | 1.15 | 1.42 |
| Respiratory system | 2.11 | 2.46 | 1.49 | 1.89 |
| Breast | 2.50 | 2.00 | 1.13 | 1.42 |
| Cervix uteri | — | — | 2.38 | 1.60 |
| Female genital organs except cervix | — | — | 1.24 | 1.45 |
| Prostate | 1.30 | 1.45 | — | — |
| Male genital organs except prostate | 1.79 | 2.69 | — | — |
| All urinary organs | 1.52 | 1.83 | 1.40 | 1.70 |
| Other and unspecified sites | 1.70 | 1.95 | 1.22 | 1.37 |
| Lymphatic and hemotapoietic tissues | 1.21 | 1.65 | 1.05 | 1.71 |

* It is important to note that the ratio for married individuals would be 1.00 in *all* cases.

While these differences have been recognized for some time, they have not been investigated thoroughly. For example, in a recent publication by the National Institute of Health these differences are noted and then commented on as follows:

The apparent lower mortality of married persons may be, in part, the results of errors in reporting marital status to census enumerators and on death certificates. Another factor may be self-selection in marriage, since persons in poor health are less likely to marry or remarry (Levene, p. 55 [10]).

This explanation is perplexing. A fourfold rise in buccal and pharyngeal cancer and a twofold rise in lung cancer in white male divorcees, a doubling of the rate of genital cancer in white female divorcees, a near-tripling of the rate of nonwhite male genital cancer—a significant rise in all cancers for divorced individuals—are unlikely to have been caused by "census errors" or marital selection factors. One could even ask why the census enumerators did not err in the other direction and possibly mask even greater differences? The fact is that these differences will not be understood without further study. Commenting on these differences Lillienfeld,

Levin, and Kessler recommended "We would suggest that a group of recently widowed and divorced persons be followed and their mortality experience compared with that of a suitable married group . . . similar comparisons being made between those who remain single and those who marry" (pp. 148–149).

Data on many leading causes of death suggest that marital status also significantly influences the general life-style of the individual. The sevenfold increase in premature death rates from cirrhosis of the liver among divorced white males and the general increase in death rates from this disease among all nonmarried groups (except single white females) suggest that unmarried individuals in general consume more alcohol. There are marked increases in death rates due to motor vehicle accidents and "accidental fires," with widowed men and women having four- to sevenfold increases in death rates from these causes. Suicide increases fivefold in the widowed white male and fourfold in the widowed nonwhite male and white female, while death by homicide also increased dramatically. This doubling of cancer of the respiratory system and the tenfold rise in tuberculosis among divorced white males led Carter and Glick to suggest that perhaps differential patterns of cigarette smoking had influenced these results.

Yet even something as obvious as the relationship between cigarette smoking and health is not so clear-cut as one might think. Dr. Harold Morowitz, a professor of biophysics at Yale University, recently called attention to intriguing data he found buried among the masses of health statistics in the Hammond Report.[11] The Hammond Report, first published in 1963, was the study that followed the smoking habits of about a half million men; it led, ultimately, to the warning printed on every package of cigarettes that "smoking is dangerous to your health." Without quarreling with the overwhelming mass of data which support that conclusion, Dr. Morowitz points out that the relationship is not a simple one. For example, he extracted the following table from the Hammond Report on the relationship between marital status, smoking, and premature death:

*Age-Standardized Death Rates*
*per 100,000 Men, Ages 40–69*

|           | Nonsmokers | Smoke 20+ cigarettes a day |
|-----------|------------|----------------------------|
| Married   | 796        | 1,560                      |
| Single    | 1,074      | 2,567                      |
| Widowed   | 1,396      | 2,570                      |
| Divorced  | 1,420      | 2,675                      |

The overall influence of marital status on premature mortality closely resembles the ratios cited earlier. Moreover, it is fascinating to note, as Dr. Morowitz points out, that "being divorced and a non-smoker is slightly less dangerous than smoking a pack or more a day and staying married." He adds with tongue in cheek that "if a man's marriage is driving him to heavy smoking he has a delicate statistical decision to make" (p. 39).

By no means should these data be construed to minimize the very real dangers of cigarette smoking. What these data also reveal, however, is that the ultimate medical consequences of behavioral variables like smoking must be examined in the larger context of a person's total social existence. Of even greater significance, these data suggest that it is possible to sort out statistically the relative influence of both smoking and marital status. As can be seen, the relative impact on mortality remains proportionately the same between marrieds and nonmarrieds, although the overall death rate rises when smoking is added to the equation.

In 1973, Kitagawa and Hauser attempted to correct for statistical factors that might have influenced the higher death rates that have been routinely reported for the nonmarried. In their book *Differential Mortality in the United States,* based on death rates in the United States during 1959–1961, they estimated that divorced white males between the ages of 35 and 64 had a death rate more than double that of their married counterparts (130 percent higher), while white male widows had a death rate of 78 percent higher and single males 75 percent higher. Among white females, divorcees had an overall death rate 37 percent higher than that of married women, whereas the widowed were 30 percent higher and the single 34 percent higher. Among nonwhite males, the widowed had the greatest increase, being 89 percent above the married levels, while divorced nonwhite males had a death rate 87 percent above that of married nonwhite males. Among nonwhite females of the same age range, the death rate for widows was 65 percent, for divorcees 57 percent, and for singles 42 percent above the rate for nonwhite married females. In summary, they pointed out that the greatest increases in death rates occurred for divorced white males and widowed nonwhite males, with cardiovascular disease in all cases being the leading cause of death.

Such mortality statistics cannot be completely understood without a keen awareness of the general cultural climate in which these deaths occur. Compare, for example, the death rates in the United States for 1940 and 1963. For married men and women of all races, health status and longevity significantly improved during this period. By contrast, while the health status of married individuals steadily improved during those 23 years, the health status of the nonmarried did not change significantly. Thus, the differences in death rates between the married and the nonmarried were greater in 1960 than they were in 1940. Carter and Glick [9] described this phenomenon as follows:

During the approximate generation between 1941 and 1963, several consistent changes occurred in death rates by marital status and age. For both men and women the death rate of the married declined more than that of the unmarried in each age group from 25 to 64 years of age. Moreover, the proportional reductions in death rates for married persons were progressively larger towards the younger ages (p. 342).

There are few satisfactory explanations of why this has occurred, but it does not seem unreasonable to propose that social isolation, alienation, and loneliness are no easier to cope with now than they were two decades ago, and those who live alone still find it difficult to adjust in a fashion that aids survival.

The increased death rates for the nonmarried are by no means peculiar to the United States. Every industrialized country in the world exhibits similar patterns, although there are some important cultural differences. In Japan, where overall coronary death rates are low, the increase in death rates in the nonmarried is similar to that observed in the United States. As is shown in Appendix B, at every age for both males and females the death rates from all causes of death for the nonmarried range anywhere from 2 to 25 times greater than those exhibited by married individuals. The consistency of these increases at all ages, for both sexes, and for different cultures only serves to emphasize the universality of the phenomena in question. In England, unmarried males between the ages of 45 and 54 have a death rate that is 53 percent above the rate for married males, while in the United States unmarried men at the same age have a death rate 123 percent higher than those who are married. Why these types of cross-cultural differences exist is difficult to determine, but it seems clear that life for unmarried men in the United States is just as hard as, if not harder than, it is in any other industrialized country.

The influence of the nonmarried state on health can also be gauged by other indices. Mortality is by no means the only statistic that reveals the strong relationship between marital status and health. Another barometer of health is the amount of time spent in all types of residential institutions, both of a voluntary and involuntary nature. (Detailed tables are given in Appendix B.) Almost every type of institution has extraordinarily high proportions of the nonmarried in their populations. For example, Carter and Glick pointed out that among middle-aged persons in institutions providing long-term hospital care, "widows had three times and widowers had eight times the institutional rate of comparable married persons. Bachelors had a rate twenty-one times that of married men, and fully 9 percent of bachelors and 5 percent of spinsters 45 to 64 years old were confined to an institution" (p. 410).

Differential rates of mental hospital residence among the married and nonmarried reflect the same pattern. Carter and Glick reported that "where rates of mental hospital residence for married men of middle age in 1960 were set at 100, bachelors of the same age had a comparable rate of 2,350 (23.5 times greater), separated and divorced men around 1,000 and widowers about 500. Likewise, where mental hospital residence rates for married women of middle age were set at 100, comparable rates were nearly 1,000 for spinsters, around 500 for the separated and divorced, and 200 for widows" (ibid.). At ages 45–64, divorced males had a detention rate in prisons 20 times higher than married men, the separated 18 times higher, and the widowed 7 times higher.

Another way to assess the impact of marital status on health and health costs is to examine the differential manner in which chronic health conditions affect those who live alone. Health conditions are considered chronic if they last more than three months; included in this category are both mental and physical disorders. Of interest in this regard is the manner in which chronic health conditions affect the activity of individuals—for example, whether they can continue to work. Married individuals have significantly fewer chronic conditions (50 percent fewer) which limit their activities, even though they suffer slightly more chronic diseases overall. This suggests that they can cope with diseases better than people who live alone.[9]

On the other hand, the differential patterns of confinement in mental hospitals, prisons, and other institutional settings help to emphasize the fact that any attempt to consider the effects of marital status apart from all the changes in personal and cultural lifestyles that go with it would seriously distort reality. This issue reduces to one that health statisticians call an *analysis of variance*. If, for example, ten different factors hypothetically contribute to heart disease, statisticians would try to determine the relative importance of each factor—that is, how much of the "variance" in heart disease each factor accounts for. In the case of one of these factors, marital status, the issue becomes even more complex. Marriage not only apparently influences the heart itself but also affects other behaviors, such as eating, drinking, smoking, and general life-style, all of which also influence the heart. Thus, in many instances, marital status appears to *co-vary* with other fac-

tors that also influence the heart. And as we have already seen
with cigarette smoking, the impact of such behaviors is in turn
influenced by marriage.

Even beyond the manner in which marriage may act to change
an individual's behavior, the very process of selection in marriage
no doubt also tends to leave those who are sick unmarried. In general, those who are healthy are likely to marry, while those who are
seriously ill are less likely to find a partner. This selection factor is
also likely to influence death statistics, especially in early adult life
leading to a higher statistical death rate among nonmarried individuals. What percentage of the increased death rates among the nonmarried is due to this type of selection factor has not been thoroughly examined. However, this selection factor cannot be the only
factor accounting for the wide variety of causes of death that are
influenced by marital status, or the differential manner in which
people of different ages are afflicted by the same disease. It is hard
to apply the same "selection factor" to differences in death rates
from phenomena as diverse as tuberculosis, automobile accidents,
fires, cancer, suicide, and coronary heart disease.

All these complicating factors make it imperative for us to focus
more carefully on just one cause of death, heart disease. The multitude of factors that mix with marriage to influence health can be
sorted out more clearly by concentrating on the heart.


## LIVING TOGETHER AND THE HEART

An examination of cardiovascular death rates helps to sharpen
our understanding of the influence of marital status on the development of this disease. The increases in death rates due to cardiovascular disease have been examined in detail by Drs. Moriyama,
Krueger, and Stamler in their 1971 text *Cardiovascular Disease in
the United States*.[2] The following table shows the *ratios* of death
they reported for single, widowed, and divorced persons, as compared to married persons, for the principal type of heart disease,

*coronary heart diseases,* for all individuals in the United States between 1959 and 1961. Again, as in previous tables, the numbers are expressed as death ratios of the *nonmarried to the married,* so that the 2.83 listed for divorced white males between the ages of 25 and 34 means that their death rate at that age from coronary heart disease is 2.83 times greater than that of married men of the same age.*

What is clear from this table is that the death rates for single, divorced, and widowed individuals are significantly greater than the rates for married individuals; this is true for both sexes and for

*Ratio of Death Rates of Single, Widowed, and Divorced to Married Persons,†
for Coronary Heart Disease, United States, 1959–1961*

| Age | Male | | | Female | | |
|---|---|---|---|---|---|---|
| | Single | Widowed | Divorced | Single | Widowed | Divorced |
| *White* | | | | | | |
| 15 and over, | | | | | | |
| age adjusted | 1.34 | 1.51 | 1.79 | 1.22 | 1.45 | 1.32 |
| 25–34 | 1.52 | 1.98 | 2.83 | 3.17 | 5.17 | 2.28 |
| 35–44 | 1.47 | 1.84 | 2.47 | 2.08 | 2.34 | 2.14 |
| 45–54 | 1.39 | 1.66 | 2.16 | 1.33 | 1.69 | 1.60 |
| 55–64 | 1.28 | 1.55 | 1.92 | 1.03 | 1.48 | 1.30 |
| 65–74 | 1.37 | 1.45 | 1.67 | 1.05 | 1.35 | 1.20 |
| 75–84 | 1.35 | 1.39 | 1.56 | 1.26 | 1.35 | 1.32 |
| 85 and above | 1.27 | 1.35 | 1.37 | 1.63 | 1.56 | 1.40 |
| *Nonwhite* | | | | | | |
| 15 and over, | | | | | | |
| age-adjusted | 1.53 | 2.07 | 1.88 | 1.39 | 1.94 | 1.37 |
| 25–34 | 2.24 | 4.24 | 2.64 | 1.61 | 2.37 | 1.26 |
| 35–44 | 2.04 | 2.61 | 2.42 | 1.83 | 2.42 | 1.35 |
| 45–54 | 1.77 | 2.65 | 2.32 | 1.39 | 2.15 | 1.40 |
| 55–64 | 1.33 | 2.24 | 1.91 | 1.15 | 2.08 | 1.39 |
| 65–74 | 1.46 | 1.83 | 1.79 | 1.40 | 1.87 | 1.39 |
| 75–84 | 1.55 | 1.59 | 1.49 | 1.39 | 1.56 | 1.33 |
| 85 and above | 1.42 | 1.58 | 1.73 | 1.91 | 1.91 | 1.29 |

† The ratios for married individuals would be 1.00 in all cases.

* To reemphasize a point made earlier, this does not mean that more non-married people are dying from coronary heart disease, but only that, based on the relative numbers of each group in the population, the rate of disease is much higher in the nonmarried.

both whites and nonwhites. The magnitudes of some of the increases in death rates in the nonmarried groups are most impressive, sometimes exceeding the married death rates by as much as five times. The differences *are greatest at younger ages* (a fact that confirms Drs. Kraus and Lillienfeld's observations about all other causes of death) and tend to diminish somewhat with age. But *never* do the death rates of the unmarried groups *ever* fall below those for married individuals. Young white female divorcees and widows show marked statistical increases in coronary death rates, although divorced and widowed white and nonwhite males generally have far greater increases in death rates than do females and significantly higher death rates from coronary heart disease overall.

An interesting feature of the relatively high death rates of white single females is that this difference almost disappears by age 55. There is, to my knowledge, no satisfactory explanation for this finding, although it has been suggested that perhaps this reflects the possibility that physically healthy women tend to marry, leaving the physically unhealthy females unmarried and therefore dying at higher rates. While such a possibility cannot be discounted, it must be considered in light of the consistently higher coronary death rates for the widowed and divorced females. One cannot use the same explanation for higher death rates in both widows and single females—especially in light of the fact that the most marked increase in the death rates of widows (as shall be examined momentarily) occurs during the first six months of bereavement.

As documented in Appendix B, *all other types of cardiovascular disease* show the same significant rise in death rates for the non-married groups. That is, in addition to coronary heart disease, deaths attributed to hypertensive disease, cerebrovascular disease, rheumatic fever, chronic rheumatic heart disease, and cardiovascular renal disease all show the same pattern. *At all ages, for both sexes, and for all races in the United States, the nonmarried always have higher death rates, sometimes as much as five times higher than those of married individuals.* The tables showing the effects of marital status on hypertensive heart disease are especially interesting because of the well-known fact that blacks are much more prone to this disease in young adulthood and middle age than are whites. As discussed earlier, for years investigators have thought this racial difference in hypertension to be evidence supporting the theory of genetic predisposition to this disease. And yet, as can be seen in Appendix B, in the critical ages between 25 and 50, non-white* men and women who are divorced or widowed die from hypertensive heart disease at a rate more than double that of married individuals of comparable ages, a fact that would seem to suggest a strong environmental influence.

Other correlational evidence linking cardiovascular death to marital status can be seen by comparing the death rates of white males between 1940 and 1960 with the divorce rates during that period. All age groups showed a slowly increasing death rate due to coronary disease during these two decades. Of special interest, however, is the abrupt rise in 1945–1946 (a doubling of the coronary death rate) and equally abrupt subsequent fall of coronary heart disease for the two youngest age groups (25–44). While there is, to my knowledge, no satisfactory explanation for this abrupt increase in these specific age groups, it is interesting to note that the highest rate of divorce for this group was also reached in the United States in 1945–1946; their divorce rate then fell abruptly, not to be exceeded until the late 1960s. That is, the pattern of divorce for this age group precisely mirrored the coronary death pattern for this age group—an abrupt rise in divorce immediately after the war and then a rapid fall in subsequent years. The divorce rate per 1,000 married couples was 10 in 1942, rising to 18 in 1946, and back down to 10 in 1949.

The link between marital status and early death due to heart disease has also been established in a different and very intriguing fashion by Drs. Bainton and Peterson in Seattle, Washington.[12] In

* Again, it is important to note that while these figures include other racial groups in addition to blacks (a fact that complicates these data), nevertheless the black population is by far the largest component (approximately 85 percent). Orientals generally have a very low incidence of hypertension at early ages; thus, the trend among blacks may be more marked than it appears in these tables.

an article published in the *New England Journal of Medicine* in 1963, these investigators examined all deaths from coronary heart disease in persons 50 years of age or younger in the Seattle region during 1960–1961. They observed that 133 persons younger than 50 years of age (11 women and 122 men) had died from coronary heart disease during this period. Interestingly, 13 of those individuals were listed as separated, divorced, or widowed, about twice as many as would be expected based on the relative percentage of those groups in the total population. Moreover, 98 of the deaths were in individuals reported to have been married, which was 8 less than the 106 deaths one would have expected according to the percentage of marrieds in the total population. Eleven deaths were observed among single individuals, only one more than expected. Their finding of a doubling of the death rate in separated, divorced, and widowed people younger than age 50 parallels the statistical data documented by Drs. Moriyama, Krueger, and Stamler.

In light of the consistent relationship between marital status and cardiovascular death that emerges from every national health survey, it is frustrating to discover that most biomedical research studies dealing with coronary heart disease have ignored this influence. Electrocardiograms have been taken on thousands of individuals, elaborate blood chemistry studies have been conducted and followed up for decades, plasma cholesterol has been measured again and again, smoking habits have been carefully checked, dietary habits have been painstakingly monitored—obesity, catacholamines, lipids, proteins, almost anything that could be "objectively" quantified has been scrutinized. Scientific data on all these factors have been collected again and again on business executives and dockworkers, farmers and fishermen, Indians and immigrants, country dwellers and city dwellers, Irish and Italians, Jews and Japanese, Lithuanians and Liberians. And yet most of these elaborate studies neglected to evaluate whether marital status was correlated with any of these measures, what type of families these individuals had come from, whether they had experienced early parental loss, whether their subjects were lonely or anxious when their cardiovascular status was measured. If one does not bother to collect certain data, then of course those unmeasured factors will never be seen as influencing heart disease.

Nor have the implications of such studies been lost on the citizens of the United States. People jog, play tennis, and ride bicycles; margarine advertisements on television broadcast the fact that "they have low saturated fat content." Meanwhile our divorce rate skyrockets. The joggers and tennis players who exercise to "keep their hearts in shape" apparently see little connection between the "shape" of their marriage, the "shape" of their general social milieu, and the "shape" of their hearts! Unfortunately, the medical effects of the rapid increase in divorce rates that began to occur in the late 1960s cannot be accurately assessed for another decade.

## THE BROKEN HEART AND SUDDEN DEATH

In the case of single and divorced individuals it is often difficult to sort out the specific link between the lack of human companionship and cardiac disease. Many divorced and single people who contribute to the marked increase in cardiovascular death rates not only lack human companionship but also alter their life-styles in a number of ways that contribute to cardiac disease. In other cases, divorced individuals quickly remarry and are therefore listed on statistical tables as married. Many other single and divorced individuals live with other human beings and therefore need not lack either human companionship or love. Furthermore, many individuals listed as married on statistical tables are married in name only. Through excessive dedication to their jobs or life-styles, many individuals live in a state of complete "psychological divorce" from their mates. Their lives are essentially devoid of love.* From a "scientific" point of view, therefore, the widow or widower who

---

* Evidence suggests that dissatisfaction with one's marriage is correlated with increased cardiac disease and death; see below.

suddenly loses a loved one presents a far less ambiguous picture than single, divorced, or even certain married individuals. The sudden loss of a loved one abruptly removes human companionship and a source of love from one's life. Loneliness and grief often overwhelm bereaved individuals, and the toll taken on the heart can be clearly seen. As the mortality statistics indicate, this is no myth or romantic fairy tale—all available evidence suggests that people do indeed die of broken hearts.

In his book *Bereavement*, Colin Parkes points out that the real cost of a deep personal love for another human being can only be seen in the shattering loss that is felt when that love is suddenly and permanently taken away.[13] This idea is not new. A few hundred years ago "grief" was openly recognized as a cause of death. Today, however, a broken heart would never be listed as a cause of death in any U.S. hospital. We have grown far too "medically wise" to tolerate such an ill-defined diagnosis. Patients now die of atherosclerosis, ventricular fibrillation, or congestive heart failure brought on by age, damaged hearts and arteries, or poor eating habits.

Despite modern medical science's reluctance to recognize the killing potential of human grief, most physicians are intuitively aware of its lethal power. While most physicians would never list "grief" or "loneliness" or a "broken heart" as a cause of death, that does not mean they do not recognize the importance of these emotional factors in heart disease. When you raise this topic with physicians at social gatherings they will often recall their own clinical experiences. In these stories the physicians implicitly recognize the importance of human companionship and the devastating effects of loneliness. For example, a physician-friend once asked me with a great deal of anguish upon the death of his mother-in-law, "How much time do you think my father-in-law has now?" Most people seem to recognize the medical reality of a broken heart. Many of us have watched couples who have lived together die "coincidentally" within a few months. Many of us have had uncles, aunts, cousins, or grandparents who showed the same pattern.

Adding empirical evidence to this intuitive perception, Drs.

Kraus and Lillienfeld in 1959 were among the first to call attention to the abrupt rise in mortality among widows and widowers, especially in the young widowed group.[8] Carefully examining data published by the National Office of Vital Statistics, they observed that "the excess risk in the widowed under age 35, compared to the married, was greater than tenfold for at least one of the specific age-sex groups, involving several leading causes of death, including *arteriosclerotic heart disease* [author's emphasis] and vascular lesions of the nervous system" (p. 217 ). Arteriosclerosis is generally thought of as a degenerative disease that can begin in childhood and then usually progresses slowly through life. In light of the observations of Drs. Kraus and Lillienfeld, one would have to wonder what it is about bereavement that seems to hasten a process that usually develops at an imperceptibly slow pace over a period of decades.

Parkes has pointed out that the increased mortality among the bereaved is especially high during the first six months after the loss of a loved one. This finding is especially important because it clearly implies that the increase in mortality in widows and widowers is not due to the fact that these individuals are simply too sick to remarry. Most of the increase in sudden deaths occurs before there would have been sufficient time to remarry in any event. In 75 percent of the cases Parkes studied, the cause of death in bereaved individuals was coronary thrombosis or arteriosclerosis. Parkes also cites the work of Michael Young and his colleagues in England,[14] who studied 4,486 bereaved males over the age of 54. They found that death rates increased over 40 percent during the first six months of bereavement, and then began to decline back to the death rates for married men of the same age. Parkes also cites the work of Rees and Lutkins, who studied a rural community in Wales. These investigators studied 903 close relatives of 371 residents who died between 1960 and 1965. Of these relatives, almost 5 percent died within one year of being bereaved, compared to a death rate of 0.7 percent for nonbereaved individuals of the same age living in the same community.[15]

It should be noted that the abrupt rise in death rates during the first year of bereavement is seen in many other causes of death. For example, Drs. Brian MacMahon and Thomas Pugh examined the incidence of suicide among the widowed in Massachusetts during the years 1948–1952. Consistent with many other studies, they found the incidence of suicide to be higher in widowed compared to married individuals. As was also true with coronary deaths, they found the greatest incidence during the first year of bereavement (2.5 times greater), with a 1.5 times geater incidence of suicide in the second through fourth years of bereavement. This death rate pattern bears a striking relationship to that established for coronary heart disease.[16]

A series of intriguing clinical cases of sudden death, scattered through the medical literature, reinforce this statistical evidence on bereavement. With astounding regularity, most of these clinical cases appear to involve some type of interpersonal loss. One of the more unusual cases I have come across in the scientific literature is a report on the simultaneous deaths of two 32-year-old schizophrenic sisters by Ian Wilson and Dr. John Reece.[17] The circumstances surrounding their deaths in a mental hospital in North Carolina are truly remarkable. Neither twin was ever married, nor were they ever separated from each other for any prolonged period. At about age 21 both began to deteriorate psychologically, with a progressive flattening of their emotional expressions, loss of social interest, and disturbances of sleep and appetite. This was accompanied by growing suspiciousness and delusions, until they were simultaneously institutionalized in 1961, at the age of 31. They were discharged twice from this mental hospital under pressure from their parents, but in neither case could they function adequately outside the institution. On their final readmission on April 1, 1962, they refused to eat, withdrew from all social contact, and gave only minimal answers to questions. When their refusal to eat grew serious, it was decided to separate the twins into different wards, since the staff felt they were reinforcing each other with negativistic attitudes. The description of events following their first evening of separation was as follows:

Statements by the nursing and attendant staff showed that during the evening they had been under constant observation. . . . Both patients were ambulatory and went to bed as usual. At 10:20 p.m., 11:30 p.m. and 12:00 midnight both patients were observed in routine checks. Both were sleeping and examination of their respiratory movements showed nothing unusual. At 12:45 a.m. on April 12, twin A was found dead. An immediate investigation was made as to the condition of her twin and she was also found to have died. It was considered from immediate examination of the bodies that death in both cases was recent. Twin A's death was unobserved, but another patient shared the room with twin B. Apparently a short time before their deaths were discovered, twin B had stood looking out of the window of her dormitory, looking up at the window where her sister was a patient. She then sank to the floor and her body was found in this position. The patient who shared her room was accustomed to peculiar behavior in other patients and felt that there was no cause for alarm in this unusual incident (pp. 378–379).

Walter Cannon, a professor of physiology at Harvard University some years ago, wrote about the phenomenon of "voodoo death," the sudden deaths that have frequently been reported among primitive peoples in Brazil, Africa, New Zealand, Australia, the Hawaiian Islands, Haiti, and the former British Guyana.[18] Examining numerous reports, Cannon concluded that these deaths were commonly preceded by alienation, intense loneliness, social isolation, and the total lack of any social support for the doomed victim. Death was the only escape from this oppressive social climate. Cannon concluded that "the social environment as a support to morale is probably much more important and impressive among primitive people because of their profound ignorance and insecurity in a haunted world than among educated people living in a civilized and well protected community." He concluded that without the social support of the tribe, fear ran wild, leading to massive physiological changes that could abruptly terminate life.

Recent data, however, persuasively argue against Cannon's assertion that modern man is less vulnerable to sudden voodoo-like deaths. Dr. George Engel at the Rochester University Medical School in New York reported in 1971 a large number of sudden deaths that are reminiscent of the voodoo deaths described by

Cannon.[19] During a six-year period he collected 170 newspaper
reports, many from the Rochester press, of sudden deaths, in which
he could rule out suicide as a cause of death and in which the circumstances surrounding the sudden death could be reconstructed.
In 59 percent of these cases, Dr. Engel was able to document that
the specific life events that preceded the sudden death involved
some type of interpersonal loss. In both men and women these
sudden deaths occurred:

| | |
|---|---:|
| (1) After the collapse or death of a close person | 36 people |
| (2) During a period of acute grief (within 16 days) | 35 people |
| (3) Threat of the loss of a close person | 16 people |
| (4) After loss of status or self-esteem | 9 people |
| (5) During mourning or the anniversary of some event | 5 people |

Many of the cases documented by Dr. Engel are truly remarkable. He cites the cases of two teenagers who died abruptly after
being told of the death of someone close to them. In another case,
a 14-year-old girl died after being told that her 17-year-old brother
had suddenly died; in a third case, an 18-year-old girl died upon
being told of the death of a grandfather who had helped to raise
her. In a case similar to that of the schizophrenic twins, Dr. Engel
noted that a pair of 39-year-old twins who had been closely
attached to each other died within a week of each other, with no
cause of death being mentioned. Among other cases cited by Dr.
Engel:

(1)   *"A 52-year-old man had been in close contact with his physician
      during his wife's terminal illness with lung cancer. Examination,
      including electrocardiogram, 6 months before her death showed
      no evidence of coronary disease. He died suddenly of a massive
      myocardial infarction the day after his wife's funeral"* (p. 774).
(2)   *"A 40-year-old father slumped dead as he cushioned the head
      of his son lying injured in the street beside his motorcycle"*
      (p. 775).
(3)   *"A 17-year-old boy collapsed and died at 6 a.m., June 4, 1970;
      his older brother had died at 5:12 a.m., June 4, 1969, of
      multiple injuries incurred in an auto accident several hours*

*earlier. The cause of the younger boy's death was massive sub-arachnoid hemorrhage caused by a ruptured anterior communicating artery aneurysm" (p. 775).*

*(4)   "A 55-year-old man died when he met his 88-year-old father after a 20-year separation; the father then dropped dead" (p. 775).*

*(5)   "A 70-year-old man died 6 hours after his wife came home from the hospital, presumably recovered from a heart attack. She herself then had another attack and died 13 hours later" (p. 777).*

The "coincidence" of grief and human loss that seemed to surround so many of the sudden deaths noted by Dr. Engel in these newspaper accounts prompted Dr. William Greene and his colleagues to carefully reexamine the psychosocial circumstances that surrounded sudden coronary deaths.[20] They interviewed the surviving next of kin (usually wives) of 26 male patients who died suddenly while employed by the Eastman Kodak Company in Rochester, which has an industrial population of 44,000 employees. They found that in most instances the sudden death was preceded by a combination of circumstances that included both feelings of depression and increased work. Common to at least 50 percent of the sudden deaths "was the departure of the last or only child in the family for college or marriage, in response to which the patient had been depressed." They also observed that a large number of patients who had a heart attack but survived to reach the hospital also mentioned that a child had recently left home. Dr. Greene concluded that "there is some wisdom in the lore which Engel has read into the reports in the newspapers."

Other investigators have also noted the link between interpersonal difficulties, depression, and sudden death from a coronary heart attack. At the University of Oklahoma Medical School, Dr. Stewart Wolf examined 65 patients who had documented myocardial infarctions and 65 matched control subjects who were physically healthy.[21] All 130 of these individuals were interviewed monthly and given a battery of psychological tests to determine their levels of depression and social frustration. Predictions were then made after a series of interviews as to which 10 subjects would most likely have a recurrent heart attack and die—the prediction being based solely on the level of depression and social frustration, without any knowledge of who, in fact, had even had a heart attack. All 10 patients selected by purely psychological criteria were among the first 23 who died within the four-year period after these predictions were made. Dr. Wolf adds that all 10 had failed to find meaningful satisfaction in their social and leisure activities.

The pattern of human loss or separation from a loved one, followed by depression and disease, has long been recognized. Dr. Arthur Schmale studied 42 consecutive patients admitted to the Rochester Memorial Hospital with medical problems that ranged from cardiovascular disorders to respiratory, digestive, and skin problems.[22] Twenty-nine of these patients or their families reported the loss of a loved one (spouse, child, even fantasized losses), coupled with feelings of helplessness and hopelessness, immediately preceding the illness that led to hospitalization. Furthermore, "31 patients developed the onset of their disease within one week after what was considered the final or only change in relationship to which the patient experienced a feeling of helplessness or hopelessness" (p. 271). The experience of these losses also recalled to the patients their own early loss of parents or their traumatic reactions to past separations.

About ten years ago a series of studies began to suggest that sudden changes in an individual's life were often followed by the sudden onset of a wide variety of illnesses. Conversely, these same studies began noting that if relatively few changes were occurring in an individual's life, little or no illness would occur. Drs. L. T. Holmes and Richard Rahe at the Naval Neuropsychiatric Unit in San Diego, California, who explored this phenomenon intensively, developed a scale they called the "Life Change Index Scale."[23] They began with a questionnaire, called the "Schedule of Recent Experiences," which had been developed at the University of Washington in Seattle in order to document systematically a variety of life events that had preceded the onset of illness in patients. Holmes and Rahe noted that while this original questionnaire had revealed interesting connections between changes in a person's life and the development of disease, it had one serious flaw—all changes were simply catalogued and given equal importance or weight. The death of a spouse was given equal weight with a recent change of address. The researchers therefore decided to ask a large group of individuals to rate a whole variety of life changes according to their importance. As their standard of reference, Holmes and Rahe arbitrarily assigned marriage a score of 500 and asked their subjects to rate other life changes as more or less important. The scale that emerged reflected a high degree of agreement among people in many nations. Of the major life events, the loss of companionship, which included the death of a spouse, divorce, marital separation, and the death of a close family member, were consistently ranked as the most stressful and important. Divorce was seen as far more stressful, for example, then going to jail or losing one's job.[24]

Equipped with this new scale, Holmes and Rahe began exploring a large number of different populations to measure life change events that occurred before the onset of disease. They arbitrarily divided these events into time intervals before the illness, and then computed the degree of life change two years, one year, six months, three months, and one week before the onset of disease. In study after study they observed the same pattern: usually six months to three months before the onset of illness there was a sudden increase in the weighted value of life change events occurring in the individual's life. Among U.S. Navy and Marine Corps personnel, on naval vessels (in essence, these were self-contained, quarantined environments, since the ships were at sea), in underwater demolition teams, in the Royal Norwegian Navy—those who fell ill were those who had been experiencing significant and recent life changes.

In a series of studies in Sweden and Finland, Dr. Rahe and his colleagues Drs. Tores Theorell and Matti Romo began to examine the specific relationship between cardiac disease, sudden death, and life changes. [25, 26] They demonstrated that the development of a myocardial infarction was frequently preceded by an abrupt increase in life change events six months to three months earlier. The greater the changes in life events, the shorter the time interval. Moreover, by interviewing the spouse or close friends of the heart attack victims, Theorell and Rahe observed that the greater the life changes before the heart attack, the more likely it was that sudden death would occur.

Drs. Rahe and Romo found similar connections between severe life changes and the risk of sudden coronary death. They compared 272 consecutive patients under the age of 65 in a Helsinki clinic who survived a heart attack with 286 patients under the age of 65 who died abruptly after a heart attack. In the six months preceding the heart attack, both groups had a significant rise in life change event scores, but the rise for those who died was significantly greater than for those who survived. For those patients who died, the researchers noted: "Generally the spouses, but on occasion a close relative, of these subjects were contacted for interview. . . . *Twenty-five of the two hundred eighty-six subjects proved to have no spouse and no close relative from whom life change information could be obtained.*" This last statement has been italicized to emphasize the high percentage of patients who died suddenly who had to be dropped from the study because they had no one close to them! This suggests, if anything, that Drs. Rahe and Romo may have underestimated the importance of the lack or loss of human companionship for sudden death from a heart attack.

Drs. Liljefors and Rahe have pursued the relationship between interpersonal problems and heart disease even further. In 1970 these investigators reported their findings on 32 pairs of Swedish identical twins, all males, between the ages of 42 and 67, where coronary heart disease had appeared in only one of the twins. Effectively controlling for genetic influences on coronary heart disease, they found that smoking habits, obesity, and cholesterol levels were not significantly different in the twin who had suffered a myocardial infarction and the twin who was still healthy. Factors which did distinguish these twins were their behavior patterns regarding work, how they spent their leisure activity, and especially home problems and general dissatisfaction with life. While divorce and separation were rare in these twins, Drs. Liljefors and Rahe observed that "Swedish subjects with relatively severe cardiovascular heart disease frequently expressed poor childhood and adult interpersonal relationships, felt they had too low a level of income, and regretted their past and/or current working conditions." [27]

Evidence that the lack of human companionship or disrupted social relationships may lead to the development of arteriosclerosis and sudden death can also be found in the work of Drs. Meyer Friedman and Ray Rosenman.[28] For over 30 years these San Francisco investigators have explored the relationship between personality and the development of coronary heart disease. Eventually they identified a number of personality traits linked to the development of coronary heart disease; these they labeled Type A behavior. They characterized the Type A person as someone who is "aggressively involved in a chronic incessant struggle to achieve more and more in less and less time, against the opposing efforts of other things and other persons." The Type A person suffers from a combination of what Friedman and Rosenman called "hurry sickness" and hostility. They found that people suffering from this personality syndrome tend to develop arteriosclerosis prematurely and are far more subject to sudden death than individuals who do not have these personality traits. Even when the Type A person exercises moderately and maintains a well-balanced diet, he is much more likely to suffer from the development of premature cardiac disease and death than the non-Type A person. Friedman and Rosenman examined thousands of individuals from all walks of life, long before these individuals developed any measurable symptoms of coronary heart disease. If the individual had a Type A personality profile, the researchers were able to predict with a high degree of certainty that premature cardiac disease would eventually manifest itself. While the great majority of the individuals they examined were married, Friedman and Rosenman observed that the Type A personality engaged in a life-style that guaranteed a high degree of social isolation, not only from acquaintances but also from the immediate family. Often the Type A males were work addicts, to the point where they grossly neglected their wives and children.

Drs. Friedman and Rosenman state that the only real preventive cure for the coronary heart disease that emerges in Type A personalities is to alter the behavior patterns that are relentlessly driving these people toward their premature demise. In their advice to patients, the two doctors clearly recognize that the best hope of changing the Type A behavior pattern rests in revitalizing human companionship and the pleasures derived from social intercourse:

A reviving personality must be nourished with another kind of new communication—communication with people. Besides opening yourself to the riches of art and knowledge, you must also open yourself to new friendships, particularly to those which can reinforce your newly expanded interests. How long has it been since you noticed yourself warming to someone new, how long since you made even the mildest effort to bring a new person into your life and affections?

Do not underestimate the difficulty of this process: the Italian novelist Ignazio Silone was probably only too accurate in remarking that "the true revolution of our times is the disappearance of friendship." Most of us are so far out of the habit of searching for friends and retaining them that we feel it awkward and painful to begin. But there is nothing so satisfying as success in this regard, and nothing so basic to the problem of subduing the Type A's free-floating hostility (p. 195).

As Drs. Friedman and Rosenman imply, the rise of human loneliness may be one of the most serious sources of cardiovascular disease in the twentieth century. And yet, while it is easy enough to advise patients to seek out new friends and acquaintances, this simple advice is often difficult to obey. The reasons for this will be examined later.

What is particularly fascinating about the Friedman-Rosenman analysis is that it underscores the fact that acute social isolation and loneliness can, and indeed frequently do, exist even when an individual is married. Such marital breakdowns can be linked to the Type A personality and to the ultimate development of cardiovascular disease. But this raises the intriguing question of whether the large statistical differences in cardiac mortality between married and nonmarried individuals cited earlier in this chapter might not be even greater if one could statistically sort out those individuals classified as married but who were in fact living in total psychological isolation. In order to completely understand the link between human loneliness, lack of love, and cardiac disease, it will ultimately be necessary to differentiate the happily married from those who are unhappily married. While scientific data on this question are just now beginning to be gathered, the preliminary evidence is most suggestive. In describing their own research on psychosocial characteristics of Swedish cardiac patients, Drs. Theorell and Rahe cite the work of Dr. J. H. Medalie, who screened 10,000 Israeli adult males before any symptoms of coronary heart disease had appeared.[29] During five years of observation, Dr. Medalie noted that those men who later had a myocardial infarction reported far more frequent dissatisfaction with their marital life. For example, men who reported that they felt a lack of emotional support from their wives were far more likely to become heart attack victims. In a retrospective study, Dr. Stewart Wolf and his colleagues also found that patients with coronary heart disease reported a greater number of marital problems then did a control sample.[30] In addition to these studies, a series of recent reports have commented on the fact that the occurrence of marital problems and a sense of interpersonal rejection antedate a surprising number of acute myocardial infarctions. Dr. J. J. Groen at the University of Leiden has also linked marital status and the lack of love to the development of coronary heart disease.[31] He observed: "It appears that the individuals who are supported by love and secure family and community bonds can cope much better with stressful psychological situations than individuals who are deprived of such support." Drs. Bonami and Risne have reported similar findings. They observed that men who placed an inordinate emphasis on their work and therefore neglected their wives and families were more likely to develop subsequent cardiac problems.

A great deal of additional research is needed before all of the relationships between marital dissatisfaction and subsequent myocardial infarctions can be completely understood. There is, however, sufficient evidence now available for us to anticipate a connection between marital discord and the development of coronary heart disease and premature death. This does not mean that marital discord or loneliness causes every myocardial infarction, for clearly such a position would be absurd. And yet, in a surprising number of cases of *premature* coronary heart disease and *premature* death, interpersonal unhappiness, the lack of love, and human loneliness seem to appear as root causes of the physical problems.

# CHAPTER 3

# Children: Innocent Victims of Isolation

The evidence presented in the last chapter indicated that there was something about divorce, bereavement, or being single that made these states hazardous to one's health. The inference was made that the "something" common to these states was either the lack of human companionship or the disturbance and disruption of human relationships. And yet, despite the large number of statistics put forward to support this inference, the health mosaic being pieced together is still far from complete. Many hidden factors enter into the production of these mortality statistics which tend, I believe, to obscure their full medical impact.

The one overriding concern of this chapter is that the adults reflected in these mortality statistics were once children, raised in complex worlds, the impact of which remains largely hidden from our view. The fact is that the loss of human contact is not an experience restricted to adulthood; it is something felt by many children, often in a physically crushing manner. When adults experience divorce or bereavement, quite often a child is caught in the middle—and if adults suffer measurable medical consequences from such experiences, there is no reason to expect that children will remain totally immune. One consequence is readily measured. Children who experience the early disruption of parental contact —whether through divorce, separation, or death—are among the very ones who, upon maturation, will contribute in increased numbers to the ranks of those who encounter interpersonal difficulties. This does not mean that every child who loses one or both of his parents in childhood will end up divorced, but only that such children are more likely to experience interpersonal difficulties and unstable marriages than will children from intact families.

The relationship between early childhood experiences and the excessive death rates that appear so consistently among nonmarrieds is a question of great concern. This concern is especially central to coronary heart disease, for it raises the intriguing question of whether this major killer can begin in the lonely and broken hearts of childhood.

## THE SOURCE OF DISEASE: A NEW PERSPECTIVE

In a very real sense, attempting to understand a disease like coronary atherosclerosis, which can develop ever so gradually over the years, is like trying to understand a great river like the Mississippi. The flood of water that flows into the Gulf of Mexico is the end result of contributions from thousands of small streams from all over the midsection of the United States. While the headwaters can be traced back to Lake Itasca in Minnesota, the Missouri and Ohio rivers bring water from as far away as the Rockies and Appalachians.

If atherosclerosis is like a river, its headwaters—how, when, and where it begins—remain shrouded in mystery. Nor is the manner in which various life events contribute to the buildup of this disease known precisely. The search for the sources of heart disease has been further complicated by the long span of time that intervenes between the initial stages of this disorder and the appearance of visibly detectable symptoms.

The aim of this chapter is to point out that certain experiences in infancy and childhood—especially those involving the loss of parental contact—can make important contributions to the eventual premature development of atherosclerosis in adulthood, and may also contribute to many other causes of premature death. However, in order to better understand the evidence supporting this idea, we must first examine our society's current perspective on childhood diseases.

There are few attitudes more widely shared than a universal revulsion toward diseases that strike down children. Everyone knows about the existence of such diseases, and every industrialized nation wages an unrelenting war to control them. Poliomyelitis, spinal meningitis, pneumonia, diphtheria, and typhoid fever once were dread diseases that terminated the lives of many children; the efforts expended to control them have been truly impressive. While certain diseases, such as leukemia, still await cures, most life-threatening pediatric illnesses have now been controlled in industrialized countries through drug therapies and immunization programs.

There is little reason to doubt the universal commitment to this goal. The role of Drs. Salk and Sabin in helping to control polio elevated these two men to the status of international heroes. Their accomplishments removed a terrible scourge from the earth. Other examples quickly spring to mind. On a single Labor Day weekend in 1976, the entertainer Jerry Lewis, in one telethon, was able to raise more than $20 million for medical research aimed at curing muscular dystrophy. While this was a remarkable feat and a testimonial to one individual's humanitarian efforts, it is also vivid proof of a shared universal concern about diseases, especially those that cripple and kill children.

There is, however, one important but frequently overlooked aspect of these diseases that *compels* everyone to be concerned . . . the effects of these diseases are highly visible. Everyone realizes what polio does; the crippled child lying helpless in bed makes it painfully obvious what this disease is and what it does. Visibility is a powerful psychological force that influences attitudes about disease and death, especially in children. If the effects of certain diseases are visibly horrible, then people are understandably horrified and they struggle to take every possible action to alleviate the situation.* But in many cases the visible impact of a disease, or at least its relationship to certain life events, is either dampened or completely obscured by its gradual onset and development. This fact, compounded by serious logistical research problems, has led most people to overlook some potentially serious childhood situations that may lead to physical disease decades later.

In a broad philosophical sense, every human being begins to die the very moment his or her life begins. Although everyone is inexorably marching toward his or her demise, the trek can be significantly hastened or slowed by factors which appear extraneous to that inevitable biological process. While certain forms of adult death occur abruptly and without precursors, most fatalities typically involve a long period between the onset of the illness, the appearance of symptoms, and eventual death. Certain forms of death, however, appear in a manner which tends to obscure this latter reality. For example, heart attacks often strike an individual suddenly, with few apparent warning signs, leading to the widespread illusion that the precursors of such attacks also developed rapidly. And yet, the opposite situation more closely approximates clinical reality. Typically, years before a heart attack occurs, the process of coronary atherosclerosis is already slowly placing the individual at greater and greater risk.

While certain physical and behavioral factors have been singled out as contributors to the process of coronary atherosclerosis, by no means have the exact mechanisms been identified. Nor is it at all clear exactly when this disease begins, although it has been established that by age 50 most American males already have what the National Heart Institute has labeled moderately advanced coronary atherosclerosis. It now seems possible that atherosclerosis, once viewed as a degenerative disease restricted to older people, may even begin during childhood. By late adolescence some people

---

* The psychological influence of the visible impact of disease is by no means a phenomenon restricted to childhood diseases. The same reactions occur toward diseases that strike at adult populations. Two such highly visible diseases are cancer and heart disease. In 1976 the U.S. Government spent the overwhelming proportion of its money in health research trying to control just these two diseases.

already have reached an advanced stage of this disease. Autopsies performed on U.S. servicemen killed on the battlefield during World War II revealed that a startling number of these young men, mostly in their early twenties, already had developed significant coronary atherosclerosis; their coronary arteries resembled those usually seen in men over 60 years of age.[1] Even now, the reasons for their premature development of this disease have not been clarified, in part because the necessary research studies have not been conducted.

While there are many ways to approach the study of physical diseases which develop slowly and have multiple causes, the methods employed are generally labeled as either *prospective* or *retrospective*. As the name implies, retrospective studies look backward. They are, in a sense, an *after-the-fact, best-guess* approach. Most of the data reviewed in the last chapter can be classified as retrospective. For example, *after the fact* of death, marital status was correlated with death rates and a *best-guess* hypothesis proposed that companionship is conducive to longevity. Despite its evident merits, this approach has certain inherent scientific limitations, for theories and hypothesis based on retrospective data simply cannot be tested directly. In order to test such hypotheses, medical scientists utilize another approach, which they label as a prospective, or *before-the-fact* investigation. This procedure is very much akin to the prospector who goes out to dig for gold, never absolutely certain that his hypothesis that gold is in "them thar hills" is really correct. The proof ultimately is in the gold strike.

By their very nature, prospective studies in medicine are enormous undertakings—time-consuming, costly, and often excruciatingly difficult. As already mentioned, the first and most famous prospective studies on heart disease were the Framingham studies, and it is well worth reiterating that these investigations were, and still remain, extraordinarily valuable. The problems with these studies stemmed from the hunches the investigators initially formulated about heart disease. Using the best retrospective data available in 1948, they formulated certain guesses about what caused heart disease and then proceeded to test whether these hunches were correct. The point here is that all prospective studies depend on some interpretation of retrospective data. Therefore, the very existence of the Framingham prospective studies allows us to examine the way scientists in 1948 formulated their hunches about the root causes of heart disease. Their hunches were reflected in what they chose to measure and how they collected their data. One hunch was clearly missing. Nowhere is the avoidance of questions about the relationship of childhood experiences to adult physical disease more obvious than in the Framingham studies.

In light of the enormous efforts expended in these prospective studies . . . to follow 5,127 healthy people for the remainder of their lives . . . and the importance of the question being asked . . . what causes heart disease? . . . one is struck by the fact that no children were included. For that matter, to my knowledge, infants still have not been included in any prospective study that has attempted to trace the natural course of any disease that develops slowly over a period of decades. The youngest healthy subjects studied at Framingham were already 30 years old when the project began. While one can sympathize with some of the reasons for this exclusion—especially in light of the fact that if children had been included, more than likely they would have outlived the original investigators—the exclusion of children from all long-term prospective studies of physical disease has unfortunately contributed to the implicit and widespread belief that childhood experiences are not linked to adult physical disease.

To repeat a point made earlier, if only physical factors such as blood pressure, diet, and exercise regimens are monitored, while early childhood experiences are ignored, then quite naturally only blood pressure, diet, and exercise can possibly be linked to the development of coronary heart disease. By not studying the relationship of childhood experiences to adult disease, most scientists have remained blind to its potential importance.

The lack of long-term prospective medical studies that follow children into adulthood also helps to clarify the peculiar split that has evolved in our understanding of human emotions and human disease. No concept is more central to psychiatric and psychological thinking than the belief that human personality and emotional development are significantly influenced by childhood experiences. And of all developmental experiences, the interpersonal relationships between the child and its parents appear to be the most crucial. Virtually no psychiatrist or psychologist would argue that early experience is not critically important to later development. Indeed, it would not be an exaggeration to call the importance of early developmental experiences the central dogma of all psychiatric theory. And yet, despite its central importance in psychiatric thinking, the link between early experience and adult disease seems almost a nonexistent problem in medical science.

## THE PSYCHOLOGICAL IMPACT OF EARLY LOSS

The psychological literature pointing out the important connection between early loss and subsequent emotional disturbance is very large, and only the most pertinent studies will be cited here. Lytt Gardner reported a series of studies showing that children raised in emotionally deprived environments can suffer serious physical and emotional damage, including the permanent stunting of their physical growth.[2] In a report entitled "Deprivation Dwarfism," Gardner retold the legendary story of Frederick II, ruler of Sicily in the thirteenth century. Frederick believed that all men were born with a common language, which he suspected must have been an ancient language, such as Hebrew. In order to test his theory, he took newborn infants away from their natural mothers at birth and gave them to foster mothers. He ordered these foster mothers to care for these babies physically but never to speak to them, so that he might learn what language they would naturally speak. The experiment was, however, a failure—all of the children died. "For they could not live without petting and the joyful faces and loving words of their foster mothers" (p. 101).

Sigmund Freud convincingly demonstrated at the beginning of the twentieth century that human personality does not emerge out of a social vacuum: childhood experiences are vitally important to the ultimate development of the adult personality. If, for example, the Type A personality described by Friedman and Rosenman is linked to the development of cardiovascular disease, it would seem reasonably safe to assume that such a personality profile emerges at least in part from childhood experiences. The psychiatric research clearly indicates that bereavement, divorce, sudden loss of love, lack of love, and chronic human loneliness are by no means felt only by adults. Children suffer from the loss of love and the lack of love perhaps even more than adults do.

Psychiatric researchers from Freud onward have recognized that early parental loss is directly related to a wide variety of childhood, adolescent, and adult psychological problems.[3] Many of the scientific data in this field stems from the now classic research of Dr. John Bowlby, who investigated the relationship between maternal care and mental health for the World Health Organization in 1950.[4] He documented in great detail the extensive physical, emotional, and intellectual damage that can result from a child's separation from its parents (especially from the mother) for extended periods of time, particularly if this separation occurs in the first few years of life. Dr. René Spitz, now at the University of Colorado Medical Center, first described more than 25 years ago the "marasmus," or physical wasting away, of infants who suddenly lost their mothers.[5] Spitz observed that some infants who suddenly lost their parents would refuse to eat and would eventually die even when force-fed. In one study with Katherine Wolf, for example, he carefully followed 91 infants raised in foundling homes in the United States and Canada.[2] All of these infants were physically very well cared for. In spite of this care, Spitz and Wolf reported that most of the infants appeared to be very depressed, and many of them also seemed quite anxious. They did not grow as rapidly as other infants; they did not gain weight, and some even lost weight. Of the 91 infants studied, "34 died in spite of good food and meticulous medical care." The last trimester of the infants' first year of life seemed to be of special significance, because most of the deaths occurred during this period. But even among those who survived, almost all showed varying degrees of physical and emotional retardation.

Observations such as these have fortunately led to important changes in the way orphanages and foundling homes care for children. Hospitals also have become more enlightened: mothers visiting their sick children are no longer seen as administrative nuisances but are instead encouraged to live-in with their infants during critical periods, so that serious physical illness need not be compounded by emotional disturbance.

Similarly, Dr. Nelson Ordway and his colleagues at the University of Oklahoma reviewed the cases of three infants who had been hospitalized for a variety of physical problems.[6] All three infants had been deprived of parental love, and all initially "failed to thrive" while in the hospital. These infants began wasting away until the physicians provided them with warm interpersonal support, given exclusively by one or two nurses (mother surrogates). All three infants significantly improved after this nurturing care was introduced. Ordway and his associates noted, as have many other investigators, that the infants deprived of parental love "failed to develop strong attachments to people. Their lack of interest extended also to objects. . . . They did not show anxiety in the presence of strangers or distress when a person or toy was removed."

Still, it is rather easy to dismiss much of the research showing the destructive effects of social deprivation as irrelevant to most human situations. After all, few children in the United States are raised in total isolation. The kinds of cases described by Spitz or Ordway are highly unusual, even extreme. Nevertheless, they hint at the potential effects of the kind of partial social deprivation that appears to be growing in our society.

While most infants and children are not raised in total social isolation, large numbers—and the number is growing at a rapid rate —are being raised in homes that could easily become environments of partial social deprivation. Not only are there now significantly fewer children in each home (and consequently less dialogue between siblings), but there is also an overall diminution of social interaction in many homes. One-sixth of all children in the United States under the age of 18 now live in one-parent households, and this number is growing. Coupled with this trend is the fact that a majority of mothers now hold jobs outside the home; certainly the vast majority of adults in single-parent households are forced to work for economic survival. Many of these parents do not want to leave their children. They simply have no other choice—economic necessity dictates their behavior. These situations create environments where something usually has to give, something has to be sacrificed. Most parents who work all day and then come home to cook a meal and clean a house will naturally be tired. It takes a concerted effort for that parent, after working all day long, to come home (and stay home) and pay attention to his or her child. Time and personal pressures will naturally tend to compress the quantity of dialogue. It is not a question of whether parents love their children; rather, it is a question of time. More and more, the vital function of interacting with infants and children is left by default to schools, day-care centers, nurseries, baby-sitters, and television, none of which may have even the slightest interest in serving as a surrogate parent.

A wide variety of adolescent and adult psychiatric disorders have now been unequivocally linked to lack of parental contact during infancy. Hundreds of studies have shown that the lack of parental contact or the early loss of parents can seriously undermine the emotional stability of children. Severe adult depression, dependency, psychosis, various neuroses, and suicide have all been frequently reported among individuals who suffer early parental loss. For example, C. N. Wahl studied 392 male schizophrenics who had once been in the U.S. Navy.[7] He found that 40 percent of his total group had lost a parent by death, divorce, or separation before 15 years of age, compared to only 11 percent in the general naval population. Dr. Roslyn Seligman and her colleagues at the University of Cincinnati College of Medicine examined 85 adolescents who had been referred for psychiatric evaluation from a general adolescent population in their hospital.[8] They found that 36.4 percent of these adolescents had experienced early parental loss (through either death or permanent separation), with the loss of a father being reported twice as frequently as the loss of a mother. The relative incidence of similar parental loss in the general adolescent school population was 11.6 percent. Dr. Glueck in the United States and Dr. Greer in Australia have shown that adult sociopathy occurs significantly more often in individuals who have experienced early parental loss.[9,10] An exhaustive study of almost 12,000 ninth-graders from all geographic and socioeconomic sectors of the state of Minnesota by Gregory in 1965 showed that adolescent delinquency rates and school dropout rates were much higher for children who had lost a parent through death or divorce.[11] Dr. J. H. Nolan at the University of Maryland, who has studied cross-cultural evidence of schizohrenia, noted that over 90 percent of the psychotic adults of the Loma tribe in Liberia had lost a parent when they were young.[12]

## THE PHYSICAL IMPACT OF EARLY LOSS

Perhaps the most direct theoretical link between such early psychological trauma as the loss of one's parents and subsequent physical illness can be drawn from the fact that adult psychopathology itself leads to serious problems in interpersonal relationships. And, as already noted, almost all psychiatrists believe such problems stem from early childhood. Those people who are unable to form close personal ties in adulthood would likely appear in the mortality tables described in the last chapter—that is, they would be over-represented in the single and divorced categories.

Evidence supporting this idea can be gleaned from several sources. The Rochester Medical School research group that has included Drs. George Engel, William Greene, and Arthur Schmale has been pointing out for the past two decades that a strong relationship exists between early parental loss and the subsequent development of various physical diseases. For example, when Schmale[13] examined the relationship between separation and depression and the development of physical disease (such as cardiovascular disease), he found that a significant number of adult patients in the hospital with physical disease had suffered the early loss of one or both parents. Confronted again as adults with some new loss or the threat of such a loss, these patients tended to become very depressed and developed various physical diseases, including cardiac disorders. Schmale noted that

the 16 patients listed under "rejection" had lost one or both parents through separation, not including that by death, or had one or more demanding parents or had many siblings so that the patient felt unaccepted, unwanted and at a distance from the parents. Nine patients were still grieving or again grieving over a significant loss which had occurred 3 to 32 years prior to the onset of the current symptoms. Thus 33 out of 42 patients were preoccupied, or because of the nature of the current changes in object relations, became preoccupied with past conflicts never completely resolved (pp. 268–269).

Very similar observations have been made by Dr. Claus Bahnson in Philadelphia, who has been studying for over a decade the connection between early child-parent relationships and the subsequent development of coronary heart disease and cancer.[14, 15] Examining the data from both the Middlesex County Heart Study and the Midtown Manhattan Mental Health Study, Bahnson observed that a significant number of fathers of coronary patients had died prematurely, usually when the son was between the ages of 5 and 17 years of age.

A similar pattern has also been observed in a series of prospective studies by Drs. Caroline Thomas and Karen Duszynski at The

Johns Hopkins School of Medicine.[16] They examined 1,185 Johns Hopkins medical students who had attended medical school between 1948 and 1964. All the students, while still in medical school, were given a questionnaire concerning their attitudes toward their family and the "closeness" they had felt to their own parents. At the time of this questionnaire, all students were physically healthy. Ten years later in 1974 the authors began to report on the relationship between family closeness and disease. They concluded that those physicians who eventually committed suicide, had to be hospitalized for mental illness, or developed malignant tumors had initially reported significantly greater amounts of interpersonal difficulties and had suffered more from loneliness from one to 23 years before the onset of the disease and/or death. To begin to explain how the development of malignant tumors might be related to the lack of meaningful relationships, Thomas and Duszynski proposed the following:

The possibility that there are early psychological antecedents of malignant neoplasm has gradually been introduced into medical thinking as the result of detailed retrospective studies. LeShan's hypothesis concerning the emotional life history pattern associated with neoplastic disease is that early in life, damage is done to the child's developing ability to relate to others, resulting in marked feelings of isolation, a sense that intense and meaningful relationships bring pain and rejection, and a sense of deep hopelessness and despair. Later, a meaningful relationship is formed in which the individual invests a great deal of energy. For a time, he enjoys a sense of acceptance by others and a meaningful life, although the feeling of loneliness never is completely dispelled. Finally, with the loss of the central relationship, whether the death of a spouse, forced job retirement, or children leaving home, comes a sense of utter despair and a conviction that life holds nothing more for him (p. 265).

In what remains one of the most comprehensive retrospective studies of early predictors of disease and premature death, Dr. Ralph Paffenbarger and his colleagues examined the records of up to 50,000 former students from Harvard and the University of Pennsylvania who were in college during the period from 1921 through 1950.[17] They carefully examined the college records of the first 590 male students who had died of coronary heart disease and contrasted them with 1,180 randomly chosen classmates of equivalent age who were known to be alive. Nine factors distinguished the coronary heart disease victims: heavy cigarette smoking, higher levels of blood pressure, increased body weight, shortness of body height, *early parental death, absence of siblings, nonparticipation in sports* (coupled with a general college style of *secretiveness* and *social isolation*), *a higher emotional index,* and scarlet fever in childhood.

One obvious and frequently proposed explanation for this relationship between early parental death and subsequent coronary heart disease is genetic predisposition. But in another report Paffenbarger and his colleagues also examined the incidence of suicide (which is not generally thought of as a genetically determined phenomenon) in a sample population of 40,000 students and found that 225 former students committed suicide in the years following graduation. Again comparing these suicide cases with a large number of randomly selected former students, they found that those former students who committed suicide were likely to have come from families whose parents were college trained, where the father had a professional status (frequently a physician), *parents were separated, or the father died early.* Other distinguishing characteristics were exactly the same as for death by coronary heart disease: heavy cigarette smoking, nonparticipation in extracurricular sports, secretiveness, and social isolation. Paffenbarger [18] goes on to speculate that

lack of participation in extra-curricular activities seems to acquire meaning in loneliness, fear, hostility or frustration. Wealth or success of the father may have an adverse influence on the son through paternal absence, deprivation of companionship and counsel, overbearing demand for emulation, possible lack of interest or lack of need for individual success or effort in the son (p. 1035).

In sum, the picture that emerges from these fascinating prospective studies of early death among Harvard and Pennsylvania university students reveals that very similar physical factors, personality traits, and life histories—including early loss of a parent, social isolation, and loneliness—were highly predictive of both suicide and premature death from coronary heart disease. In describing the cause of premature coronary death in these former students, Paffenbarger and his colleagues[17] summarized their findings as follows:

> Students who later died of coronary heart disease were more likely than their controls to be without siblings, and also were more likely to have lost one or both parents before entering college. It seems, however, that *only-child status and early death of a parent were independent precursors of coronary death.* . . . * Early parental death might signify some hereditary weakness or environmental trait transferable to the child in the form of a predisposition to heart disease. Any of these circumstances might have psychological significance, since feelings of lassitude and anxiety were reported more frequently by the future coronary decedents. The insecurities commonly noted on separation from home to enter college may have been enhanced by overly possessive or protective family ties often associated with loss of a parent or with the status of only child (p. 327).

There are, unfortunately, very few other studies that have analyzed the relationship between early childhood experiences and the subsequent development of terminal diseases. Is the divorce, separation, or death of parents related to the eventual development of heart disease? Are children more vulnerable at certain ages? It seems obvious that the relationship between early parental loss, the lack of love in infancy and early childhood, and the eventual adult development of disease and premature death must be more intensely examined. At a time when more and more couples are divorcing or separating and more and more families have only one child, Paffenbarger's studies pose a rather ominous warning for the future. As we have noted, increasing numbers of children are now raised by only one parent, who is, in most cases, forced to work and therefore must leave the child in the care of others. As Dr. Gilbert Kliman points out in his book *Psychological Emergencies of Childhood,* there is a great deal that can be done to ameliorate and prevent the future development of psychiatric and medical problems if the seriousness of this situation is generally recognized.[19]

Many cultural factors have served to compound the problems of

---

* Italics added.

children who experience the early loss of a parent. Perhaps the most serious is the disappearance of the extended family. In previous generations most individuals came from larger families which tended to remain in the same location. In the absence of a parent or if the parents were forced to work, the child usually was cared for and given ample love by grandparents or even aunts and uncles. In our current era of significantly smaller families and high social mobility, the extended family has shrunk and, in many cases, totally disappeared. Readily available sources of love and emotional support that were often provided by the extended family have largely disappeared. Many children are, of necessity, raised in impersonal settings whose medical effects may not be fully apparent for decades. This entire topic requires a text in itself, and I mention it here only to complete the outlines of the picture being sketched in this book—how every human being, young or old, can be seriously affected by the lack of love and human companionship.

If the social deprivation in infancy is acute, the physical effects will show up quickly. There are, however, external forces that tend to check such obvious neglect and abuse. Most children are able to evoke at least minimum amounts of love and attention necessary for their survival. They are not totally shut off from parental love. Still, many are cheated . . . many children are seriously shortchanged. Parents can reduce contact with their children in the short run, and nothing may be apparent; but over the long run, serious emotional and physical problems may appear, even to the point of significantly shortening the child's life span some 30 to 40 years later.

Nor is this all. Urie Bronfenbrenner, a social psychologist at Cornell University, recently pointed out that current trends in child rearing represent a national pattern of downward mobility.[20] "In terms of such characteristics as the proportion of working mothers, number of adults in the home, single-parent families, or children born out of wedlock, the middle-class family of today increasingly resembles the low-income family of the early 1960s."

What does this development mean? The fact is that low-income families of the early 1960s had a life expectancy significantly shorter (5–7 years) than middle-class families. While all low-income groups suffer disproportionately from health problems, one group, the black Americans, seems to be especially vulnerable. The suggestion of a strong relationship between familial disruption and shortened life span may help shed some light on the reason why black Americans have significantly shorter life spans than whites, a difference that averages more than seven years. Only 56 percent of all black children in the United States live in households where both parents are present.[21] Illegitimacy rates are higher than for whites, and death rates are significantly higher at all ages than they are for whites. There is no reason to suspect that the physical-emotional effects on black children of the loss of a parent through early death, divorce, or separation are any less severe than they are for white children. All available evidence suggests, if anything, that these effects may be worse when compounded by poverty. If this suggestion proves correct, then the greater percentage of familial disruptions now occurring among black families may mean continued ill health and shorter life spans (relative to whites) for at least another generation. Retrospective medical attempts to alleviate conditions such as elevated blood pressure, conditions which may very well be the end result of years of social deprivation and familial disruption, seem to be an inefficient and thus far not fully effective way of approaching the problem.

To date, the only medical data that bear directly on this question are Paffenbarger's, Bahnson's, and Thomas and Duszynski's. Their studies focused almost exclusively on whites, and in two cases the populations were generally from high-income families. For the rest, perhaps as many as 99 percent of all studies on the effects of early childhood experiences have focused on how these situations affect psychological and psychiatric development. It would appear that there is a desperate need to begin carefully examining the relationship between factors like early childhood, lack of love, parental divorce, and only-child status, and the eventual development of physical disorders such as heart disease. In light of the fact that over 1 million children in the United States lost one of their parents through divorce in 1974, it is clear that far more data on the medical and psychological consequences of such experiences are desperately needed.

As with the chronic overuse of pesticides, which Rachel Carson's *Silent Spring* warned us about in 1962,[22] the seriousness of this situation may only be recognized when the medical effects become devastating. Carson pointed out that many of the negative side effects of pesticides could not be seen until 20–30 years after the pesticides had been sprayed on the fields. The effects of these chemicals often were felt far from where they were sprayed. For example, DDT which might have been sprayed on a Kansas farm played a role years later in the destruction of bald eagles in the Rocky Mountains and the extinction of wildlife in the arctic. So, too, many of the effects of early loss of parents may not appear for decades after the loss occurs.

Again and again we have stressed the need for additional prospective and retrospective medical studies that begin in infancy and childhood. But we must also remember another aspect of the connection between health and companionship. Everyone's life is unique. No two people experience precisely the same social support, either in childhood or in adult life. Thus, while overall health trends can be assessed by examining mortality statistics in large populations, eventually that macroscopic view must be complemented by an examination of the unique social experiences of the individual. In order to bridge this gap and examine how human relationships affect the health status of individual people, another approach must be used—clinical rather than statistical—focusing on individual cases rather than large groups—an approach that follows the individual through his unique life experiences. The next chapter will examine this heart of human companionship, the unique social life of every human being.

## CHAPTER 4

# Beyond Statistics:
# Lessons from the Clinic

"How many persons we meet in houses, whom we
scarcely speak to, whom yet we know, and who
know us! How many we see in the street, or sit with
in church, whom though silently, we warmly rejoice to
be with! Read the language of these wandering eyebeams. The heart knoweth."
　　　　　　　　　　　—Ralph Waldo Emerson,
　　　　　　　　　　　*Essays on Friendship* (1841)

As can be seen from the population mortality statistics reviewed in
the last three chapters, the warning signs all seem to point in one
direction: the lack of human companionship or the loss of a loved
one can have serious effects on our physical and mental well-being.
In terms of cardiovascular disease, the evidence is remarkably consistent . . . human companionship appears to play a vital role in the
healthy functioning of the heart. And yet, despite the consistency of
the data, many readers will refuse to believe them. And for many
who do accept them, the statistics will, nevertheless, make very
little difference in the conduct of their lives.

The fact of the matter is that the form in which population mortality statistics must be presented tends to mute their impact.
Abstract statistics, based on large populations, simply do not seem
real—the world of the individual is not a statistical world at all, but
a highly personal, experiential world. A death rate from coronary
heart disease for 40-year-old divorced males that is 2.5 times
greater than for married males of the same age may not be very
disturbing for any particular individual. It is remarkably easy to
convince oneself that such data do not apply to oneself. We can all

point to many apparently healthy male contemporaries married to absolute witches who seem to get their main joy in life from making their husbands miserable. And we can all cite cases of 40-year-old married men who appeared to be happy who suddenly died from heart attacks.

There are many other examples of this response to statistics. Millions of Americans shrug off the data that show a strong correlation between lung cancer, cardiac disease, and smoking by immediately pointing toward some fat, jolly, chain-smoking neighbor who is 75 years old. This psychological maneuver, which permits so many people to deny the reality seen by pathologists every day at the morgue, helps explain why the per capita consumption of cigarettes in the United States is still quite high, in spite of the Surgeon General's Report, massive amounts of scientific evidence, and warnings printed on every pack of cigarettes.* The human condition is such that we generally resist hearing, or at least resist incorporating into our behavior, information we do not like.

The gap between statistical data and the conduct of our individual lives is also further widened by the pervasive, rugged-individualist, devil-be-damned attitude that dominates our culture. Evel Knievel is but one of many examples of how easy it is to become an American folk hero by simply shaking your fist at statistical reality. By defying the odds against survival, the stunt cyclist became a household word and the basis of a wide variety of children's games and toys. "What a way to go" a medical school student joyously exclaimed to the delighted applause of his classmates during a lecture on the relationship between bachelorhood and premature death. A sevenfold increase in death from cirrhosis of the liver, a fivefold increase in death in car accidents, an eightfold increase in death by explosions and fires, and a sevenfold increase in death by homicide—all are reminiscent of the Wild West "where men really were men." The same students are more solemn when reminded that over 1 million children were also in-

* This dissociation between objective reality and individual behavior often borders on the incredible. Even a medical school pathologist has been seen smoking during a lecture to medical students in which he was describing the relationship between lung cancer and cigarette smoking.

volved in parental divorce in 1975 but then again, they know—or at least they think they know—many children of divorced parents who seem to be happy.

This does not mean that all the resistance these grim data encounter is psychological; there are also very real problems in interpreting the meaning of these statistics. Correlations, after all, do not prove cause but only point out relationships. The more factors involved in any specific correlation, the more difficult it is to interpret the meaning of the relationship. While cigarette smoking, for example, has been linked to coronary heart disease, one could hypothesize that people who smoke have peculiar personalities or suffer from high anxiety, and one could therefore propose that it is these factors, and not the smoking itself, which lead to the high correlations between heart disease and smoking. One way scientists attempt to resolve this problem is to conduct research with animals where these extraneous factors can be controlled. This is precisely how the carcinogenic agents in cigarettes were discovered after the correlation between lung cancer and cigarette smoking was observed. Another way scientists can proceed is to control these extraneous influences by utilizing the natural differences among people. One could, for example, examine two groups of highly anxious people, one of which smokes while the other does not, and then determine whether the incidence of coronary heart disease differs in these two groups.

However, when it comes to correlating coronary heart disease with something like marital status, these issues become infinitely more complicated. First of all, there are no completely satisfactory animal models that can be used to evaluate the effects of human relationships. Marriage, for example, is a uniquely human condition.* Furthermore, unlike cigarette smoking, where certain facets of the behavior can be objectively quantified (for example, numbers of cigarettes consumed per day), human relationships are difficult to quantify. The state of marriage is by no means either a

---

* I should quickly point out, however, that there are important aspects of companionship, human contact, and cardiac functioning that can be evaluated with animals (see Chapter 6).

constant or a discrete phenomenon either among couples or even between the same couple over a period of years. Like the billions of snowflakes that fall in a single winter storm, no two marriages—no two human relationships—are precisely alike. Neither is divorce, widowhood, or being single a discrete, quantifiable human condition; these situations vary as much as marriages do. Furthermore, many married people live in a state of complete psychological divorce and social isolation from their mates, while the lives of some divorcees, widows, and single people are filled by satisfying, loving human relationships.

While the constant flux of human relationships creates enormous variance that is problematical and troublesome from a scientific point of view, it also provides us with the best hope of understanding what it is about human companionship that prevents premature death. There are literally thousands of exceptions to the general statistical rule that unmarried individuals die prematurely. One cannot be blind to the fact that there are many happy and healthy 80- and 90-year-old unmarried men and women, and many people who live active, productive, and happy lives for decades after they have lost a husband or wife. Their physical and psychological adjustment must be carefully studied, for their lives clearly point out that being unmarried need not be a physical and mental disaster. It is, in all likelihood, not the physical state itself that leads to disease and death but rather one's social adjustment to it. Before focusing on this point, however, it would be helpful to examine some of the factors that do influence the relationship between living together and the healthy functioning of the human heart.


## BEYOND STATISTICS

The statistical data reviewed thus far have primarily focused on the destructive impact of the lack of human companionship. As striking as the statistical facts might be, however, they generate far more questions than answers. What is it about human contact that makes it so important to our health? Why should marriage be statistically so beneficial to the health of the heart? Why is loneliness so physically destructive? Why do people die of broken hearts? Perhaps one helpful way to begin examining why the *absence* of human companionship can be so detrimental to the heart would be to explore the opposite side of the same question: how does the *presence* of human contact affect the heart?

For over a decade, a number of colleagues and I have explored the effects of human contact on the cardiac functioning of both humans and animals. In order to carry out certain parts of this research, we have spent several years observing both the staff and patients of hospital coronary care units, as well as patients in a hospital shock trauma unit (a unit where critically injured patients, often automobile accident victims, receive care). Our role in these studies has been akin to that of neutral observers on a battlefield, one in which the most intense war is constantly waged against death. While we have witnessed many victories, some of the patients we observed did not survive. As our studies have continued, we have been increasingly struck by the uniqueness of every patient, as well as by the responsiveness of the human heart to the most ordinary types of human contact.

Very recently, for example, we watched a 54-year-old man die. He succumbed after 14 days of the most intense medical care that could be imagined. When it was clear that this man was not going to survive, the medical personnel reluctantly shifted their concern to one of making his death as comfortable as possible. As will be described in more detail in the following chapter, we watched this man's heart change abruptly when a nurse held his hand. She quietly comforted him at a point when he was in a deep coma, shortly before his death. Not only was the patient in a coma, but every muscle in his body had been completely paralyzed by a drug known as d-tubocurarine, and he was able to breathe only with the help of machine-regulated artificial respiration. And yet, in spite of, or perhaps because of, his acute condition, the heart rate change in the comatose man when the nurse comforted him was striking (Figure 2).[1]

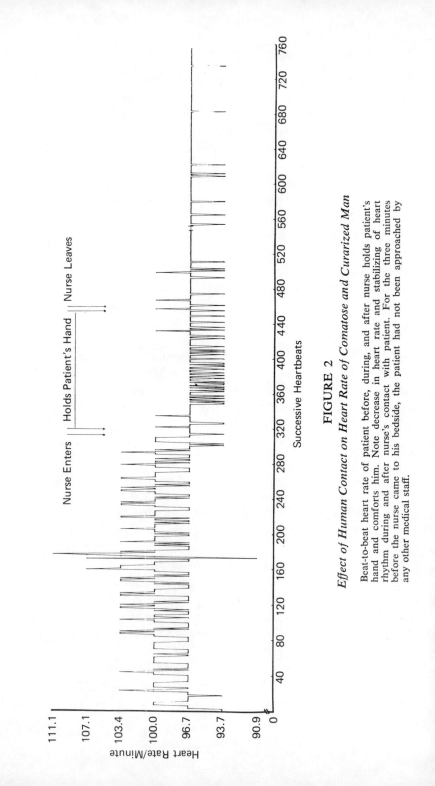

**FIGURE 2**

*Effect of Human Contact on Heart Rate of Comatose and Curarized Man*

Beat-to-beat heart rate of patient before, during, and after nurse holds patient's hand and comforts him. Note decrease in heart rate and stabilizing of heart rhythm during and after nurse's contact with patient. For the three minutes before the nurse came to his bedside, the patient had not been approached by any other medical staff.

When the struggle between life and death terminated for this man, the "cause" of his death was succinctly summarized in one sentence: "death caused by ventricular fibrillation secondary to a ruptured heart valve." There was, of course, page upon page of medical records that had meticulously charted his demise, and in the end, it seemed remarkably easy to diagnose and summarize the "cause" of his death, although there was a vast amount of information about this man that no one really knew. No doubt most of the medical personnel felt that the missing information had little to do with the immediate treatment of his life-threatening illness, but one had to wonder about that assumption. What really *was* the cause of his death? Did he die of ventricular fibrillation secondary to a ruptured heart valve? Technically, that was an accurate assessment of his pathology. His medical charts did mention a history of anxiety attacks and chronic alcoholism, suggesting that perhaps his life had not been a particularly happy one.

He also had no visitors during the 14 days that he struggled in the hospital and in a real sense this man was alone in a world surrounded by strangers and a strange technology. It was unsettling to think that we had watched this man for so long and yet we did not know who he really was, what he had experienced in his life, what gave him joy or caused him sadness, what gave his life meaning. The questions were now all unanswerable, and perhaps it was more comfortable simply to state that the cause of death was ventricular fibrillation. But were his joys and his sorrows related to his ruptured heart valve? Was his life filled with love, or was it one of loneliness? Did he, like so many other alcoholics, eventually end up all alone and totally isolated? And were his loneliness and anxiety related to his ruptured heart valve? Somehow all of these questions seemed inappropriate, strangely out of place on the battlefield of the intensive care unit. How could one ever hope to repair the damage created by a lifetime of loneliness and constant drinking?

And yet, as complicated as these questions might be, one fact could not be ignored . . . the heart of this comatose patient did respond to the simple quiet comforting of a nurse. One had to wonder what it was about human contact that made it such a potent stimulus for the heart of this dying patient.

## HUMAN COMPANIONSHIP IN CONTEXT

Long before scientists began to catalogue the various ways that human contact could alter the heart, physicians were already well aware of its influence. In his book *The Story of Heart Disease*, Terrence East described how the Greek physician Erasistratus, head of the medical school in Alexandria in 250 B.C., used patients' heart reactions to human contact to advance his own medical career.[2]

Antiochus I had fallen in love with his stepmother, Stratonice—and had really become ill. Erasistratus diagnosed the disorder by observing the patient's pulse change when the lady of his affections entered the room. Marriage cured him, and established the doctor's fame and fortune (p. 15).

Similarly, Aulus Cornelius Celsus, perhaps the most famous Roman medical scribe during the era when Christ was born, recognized the power of human contact on the heart. He gave the following advice to physicians on bedside manner in his text *De Medicina* [3]:

Bathing, exercise, fear and anger, and any other state of mind, may often be apt to excite the pulse, so that when the medical man first comes, the anxiety of the patient, who is in doubt as to what he may seem to him to have, may upset the pulse. For this reason it is not the part of an experienced doctor that he seize the arm with his hand at once; but first of all sit down with a cheerful expression, and inquire how he feels, and if there is any fear of him, to calm the patient with agreeable talk; and then at last, lay his hand on the patient's body. How easily a thousand things may disturb the pulse, which even the sight of a doctor may upset (p. 15)!

The heart reactions of a dying patient to human comforting, as well as the reactions described long ago by Erasistratus and Celsus, are all of one kind—immediate responses to brief and transient types of human interactions. In trying to understand the influence of human companionship on the heart, it is important to distinguish between these types of interactions and the social milieu or social life-style of an individual. It must be remembered that diseases such as atherosclerosis develop slowly over decades, and any single transient human interaction is likely to contribute only minimally to the course of the disease. Loneliness is a more pervasive, chronic human condition, and feelings of loneliness usually emerge out of a life-style generally devoid of human contact. On the other hand, brief human interactions can *precipitate* immediate heart reactions that vary all the way from harmless to deadly. The distinction between social conditions that predispose a person to develop an illness such as atherosclerosis and those that precipitate transient heart reactions must be kept in mind.

Beyond these global distinctions, transient human interactions themselves occur within several very important contexts. While many human interactions are fleeting, they nevertheless occur within a far larger cultural and interpersonal setting. A brief handshake with a friend we see weekly is very different from a brief handshake with a friend we have not seen in years. The acute loneliness resulting from the sudden loss of a loved one is very different from the chronic loneliness experienced by someone who has spent his childhood or adult years in social isolation, which differs, in turn, from the loneliness experienced by someone who is recently divorced. The impact of loneliness on the heart in these varied settings itself differs greatly. Thus, in order to understand the effects of any single episode of human contact on the heart, it is necessary to have at least some understanding of the entire life-style of the individual.

A second important distinction must be made between the effects of transient human interactions on individuals who have healthy hearts and on individuals who already suffer from cardiovascular disease. While the heart reactions might be the same in both, the consequences can be very different. In the first case the heart changes usually have no immediate clinical consequences, while in the second case the changes could very well be lethal.


## TRANSIENT HUMAN CONTACT IN INDIVIDUALS WITHOUT CARDIAC DISEASE

There are, perhaps, no bodily reactions more familiar to the readers of this book than the feelings of apprehension we experience when visiting the family physician. When he attempts to take our blood pressure, we may feel a bit anxious and even be aware that our heart is beating faster. Physicians routinely measure blood pressure several times in order to get a "true reading," since they are quite cognizant that the medical interaction itself usually influences blood pressure.

With the aid of modern electronic monitoring equipment, it is now known that transient human contact can precipitate some of the most extreme changes the heart can exhibit. For example in 1970, Drs. Arthur Moss and Bruce Wynar at the University of Rochester Medical School demonstrated that the average heart rate of 10 healthy young medical residents, with a mean age of 26 years, increased from 73 beats per minute up to 154 beats per minute while they were presenting various medical cases to their senior physician-teachers. While virtually no physical exertion was required to produce these results, Drs. Moss and Wynar noted that such an increase was approximately 80 percent of the *maximal heart rate change* that could be obtained under *any* condition in this age group. The magnitude of this reaction was greater than the fastest heart rate obtained in skiers of comparable age during vigorous cross-country competition. Clearly, the residents' senior medical colleagues, their teachers, had an amazing capacity to influence the hearts of these students.[4]

Heart rate responses to transient human interactions have also been examined in a different type of medical encounter, psycho-therapy. Dr. Milton Greenblatt and his colleagues at Harvard University Medical School have described a series of fascinating experiments in which they recorded the heart rates of both patients and psychiatrist-interviewers.[5] A typical scenario described by these investigators went as follows:

At times during the psychiatric interview, the patient, a 34-year-old married man and father of five children, became jittery; the pitch of his voice rose, and his facial expressions grew tense and rigid. At other times his speech became slower and softer, the pitch of his voice dropped, and his overall expression was one of sadness and hopelessness. During the therapeutic session his psychoanalyst, a staff physician at the clinic, also appeared to change moods and to alter his manner of speech and bodily movements. In an adjacent room a polygraph simultaneously recorded the changes in the heart rates of both the psychiatrist and patient. During some sessions the changes in the heart rates of both the psychiatrist and patient were similar. When the patient's heart rate would increase (usually when he described anxiety-provoking experiences), the psychiatrist's heart rate also increased, often more than the patient's. When the patient's heart rate slowed down, the psychiatrist's heart rate also slowed down.

Dr. Greenblatt and his colleagues repeated these observations for as many as 44 psychotherapy sessions with particular patients. In those sessions where the psychiatrist felt the least disturbed and believed that he and the patient had communicated very well, their cardiac relationship (the concomitant changes in their two heart rates) was closest. In those therapy sessions where the psychiatrist reported the most disturbance—because he was preoccupied either by something other than his patient's communication or by certain segments of what the patient had said—the relationship between their heart rate changes was poor. Neither the patient nor the psychiatrist knew what his heart rate was, and yet somehow when they felt they were communicating with each other, their heart rates changed in a similar fashion.

Heart rate changes also have been observed in patients in therapy by Drs. Stanek, Hahn, and Mayer at Heidelberg University in Germany.[6] During a series of psychoanalytic interviews they monitored patients who were specifically fearful of having a heart attack, even though they exhibited no detectable cardiac pathology. The most crucial moments in the psychoanalytic interviews (as judged by independent observers) were accompanied by the largest changes in the heart rates of both the therapist and the patient. In several patients the cardiac reactions were marked. During one interview the heart rate of one patient gradually rose until it reached a peak of 200 beats per minute. Another patient went into a prolonged period of abnormal heartbeats while discussing sexual problems, even though prior routine electrocardiograms had revealed no cardiac pathology.

Dr. Robert Malmo and his colleagues at the Allan Memorial Institute of Psychiatry, McGill University in Montreal, simultaneously recorded the heart rates of a psychiatrist and a psychologist as they interacted with 26 different "psychoneurotic" female patients.[7] In individual interviews with these patients, the psychologist-examiner presented each patient with a series of ambiguous-looking pictures and asked her to tell him stories about each picture. As the patient told the story, the psychologist was "blindly" instructed on sealed orders to either praise or criticize the story the patient told about each card, irrespective of what the patient said. Following a series of these card stories, the psychologist left the room and a psychiatrist then came in to interview and reassure the patient. The results of this study revealed very different cardiac reactions to praise and criticism, not only in the patients but also in the psychologist who had presented them with the ambiguous pictures. When the psychologist was critical, his tension level was much higher than when he praised the patient. The psychologist-examiner also kept a three-month diary during the course of this experiment, and each day he subjectively rated whether he had had a "good" or a "bad" day in general. It was found that the patient's heart rates rose significantly more on those days the examiner had called "bad" than on his "good" days.

It has even been suggested by Dr. Kaplan and his colleagues at Baylor University Medical School that the common waxing and waning of bodily changes, such as heart rate, might provide an objective index of the degree of rapport that occurs between a therapist and his patient. They found that cardiac interactions were much more likely to occur between two individuals who either liked or disliked each other than between individuals who had neutral attitudes or were uninvolved with each other.[8]

To repeat a point made earlier, the nature of every human interaction is both subtle and obvious, and it is this paradoxical combination that complicates analysis of even the briefest interpersonal contact. Thus, Dr. Morton Reiser and his colleagues at Yale University have shown how seemingly trivial aspects of interpersonal relationships can have significant effects on the way the heart responds.[9] They have emphasized that physiological changes occurring, for example, between an experimenter and a subject, can only be understood if the total situation is assessed:

Differences in the experimenter-subject relationships may alter the total meaning of the experimental situation so that different psychological and physiological mechanisms or responses are evoked by an otherwise identical test procedure. . . . The findings strongly support the concept that the circulatory measurements reflect responses to these interpersonal transactions as well as responses to more obvious and standard stimuli.

The effect of transient human interactions is not limited to changes in heart rate and blood pressure. A large body of scientific literature has shown that our blood chemistry is similarly changed by human companionship.[10] This topic is complex and can only be dealt with here in passing. But it should be noted that, both in the slow development of atherosclerosis and in the maintenance of general electrical stability in heart tissue, various bodily hormones and electrolytes play a vital role, and these aspects of blood chemistry respond immediately and often profoundly to interpersonal interactions.

Such changes in blood chemistry extend far beyond what one might at first imagine possible. Even the menstrual cycle appears to be influenced by human friendship. Dr. McClintock observed several years ago that the menstrual cycles of close friends and roommates in a college dormitory appeared to be related, while randomly selected girls on the same campus showed no such correspondence.[11] Dr. John Mason at the Walter Reed Army Institute has observed that the blood chemistries of three crewmen working closely together on a lengthy B-52 flight reached similar elevated levels of 17 hydroxycorticosteroids (involved in stress reactions) at the same time of the day.[12] Similar findings were also seen in two all-female groups of college-age volunteers placed on a research ward; the blood chemistries of these two groups of women began to change in similar fashion during the day. A mixed-sex ward of volunteers showed no such correlations, even after five weeks of measurements. The investigators pointed out that something other than common exposure to a similar environment seems to influence blood chemistry—and that something appears to be companionship.

## HUMAN COMPANIONSHIP IN TIMES OF STRESS

Literally hundreds of recent studies have shown that transient types of emotional stress can have significant effects on heart, blood vessels, and blood chemistry. All the major risk factors for heart disease identified in the Framingham studies have now also been linked to emotional stress.[13] Human companionship, in turn, can significantly change physical and psychological reactions to emotional stress, a phenomenon that was perhaps demonstrated most clearly in World War II.

In 1973, some 28 years after the end of World War II, the Office of the Surgeon General completed its thorough analysis of American casualties during the war.[14] In the volume on neuropsychiatric casualties, the staff of the Surgeon General's Office summarized the main lesson learned from World War II:

Perhaps the most significant contribution of World War II military psychiatry was recognition of the sustaining influence of the small combat group or particular members thereof, variously termed "group identification," "group cohesiveness," "the buddy system" and "leadership." This was also operative in noncombat situations. Repeated observations indicated that the absence or inadequacy of such sustaining influences or their disruption during combat was mainly responsible for psychiatric breakdown in battle. These group or relationship phenomena explained marked differences in the psychiatric casualty rates of various units who were exposed to a similar intensity of battle stress (p. 995).

In his book on *Air War and Emotional Stress,* Dr. Irving Janis reached similar conclusions. He showed that a soldier's willingness to endure the severe stresses of combat was primarily dependent on his identification with and the cohesiveness of his combat unit.[15] Other studies have demonstrated that wartime stresses and natural disasters greatly increase people's needs to be with one another—and that people can reduce their feelings of stress and anxiety by seeking out each other's company.

This fact has also been confirmed in laboratory investigations. For example, Dr. Stanley Schachter at Columbia University demonstrated in 1959 that individuals facing danger seek out human companionship.[16] He threatened a group of volunteer subjects with a series of either mild or painful electric shocks and then gave them the choice of waiting alone or in the presence of other subjects. Schachter observed that subjects who were threatened with "painful shock" showed a stronger preference for waiting with others than those who were threatened with a "mild" shock. He concluded that "people do serve a direct anxiety reducing function for one another, they comfort and support, they reassure one another and attempt to bolster courage. There can be little doubt that the state of anxiety lead to the arrival of affiliative tendencies" (p. 133).

The close relationship between emotional stress and human contact has a direct bearing on the health of the heart. Dr. Bogdonoff and his colleagues at the Duke University School of Medicine have described one such link.[17] They have shown a relationship in changes in heart rate and elevations in free fatty acids (which have been linked to the development of atherosclerosis) between two human beings, one of whom was simply listening while the other was forced to answer highly personal questions. After the experiment, individuals who had been told merely to listen passively reported that they felt very personally involved in the answers of their partners. And their bodily changes closely mirrored the types of changes exhibited by their partners who were directly under stress. The Duke University investigators also observed that free fatty acids were significantly higher in subjects recruited individually for an experiment than in pairs of recruits who had been prior acquaintances. Apparently the emotional support provided by the presence of a friend or companion changed the "objective stress" inherent in the situation, generally making the situation far less stressful for the heart. One cannot help but conclude that, in general, unpleasant life experiences or aversive situations are far more upsetting to humans who lack companionship. As we shall see in Chapter 6, a very similar phenomenon exists at the animal level.

Those individuals who lack the comfort of another human being may very well lack one of nature's most powerful antidotes to stress. Thus, individuals who live alone—widows and widowers, divorcees, and single people—may be particularly vulnerable to stress and anxiety. The presence of a friend or companion may not only help suppress fear and physical pain, but it may also reduce the "wear and tear" on the heart that occurs under stress and chronic anxiety. The increases in cardiac death rates for those who live alone may be due, in part, to the fact that these individuals continuously lack the tranquilizing influence of human companionship during life's stresses. Tranquilizing drugs may not be able to fill the void, and in the final analysis they may not be anywhere near as effective as the calming capacity of human friendship.

Later on I shall cite additional studies to support my claim that human contact can calm the cardiovascular system of a person in stressful situations. This influence, however, is of most immediate concern to those people who already have developed cardiac problems.

## TRANSIENT HUMAN CONTACT AND THE HEART
## PATIENT

Transient cardiac changes that occur in individuals who have had a heart attack or who are experiencing other types of cardiac difficulties, such as atherosclerosis, angina pectoris, and congestive heart failure, create very special problems that need not particularly worry the healthy individual. First of all, after a heart attack many transient cardiac changes can threaten a patient's life. The importance of human contact in this circumstance ought not to be minimized: human contact can serve as one of the primary healing agents for the injured heart, or it can be the source of lethal distress!

The power of transient human contact to influence the cardiovascular system of individuals suffering from heart disease has been recognized by physicians for hundreds of years. The noted eighteenth-century English physician John Hunter, who himself suffered from angina pectoris,* once remarked that his "life was in the hands of any rascal who chose to annoy and tease him." Ironically, he predicted the precise circumstance of his own death. One day at a medical board meeting, Hunter got into an argument with a colleague who had contradicted him. He became so enraged that he ceased speaking, stormed out of the room, and immediately dropped dead.[18]

Sir William Osler, one of the foremost pioneers of medicine at The Johns Hopkins Medical School and one of America's most eminent physicians, once remarked that "palpitation of the heart in a medical student may be the result of a lobster salad the night

---

* Angina pectoris, as described in greater detail in Appendix A, is a pain in the chest (heart) that is caused by lack of oxygen to the heart muscle, brought about by a diminished blood supply. The pain usually occurs intermittently, often in association with physical exercise, eating, or emotional stress. These activities all increase the needs of the heart muscle for increased oxygen-rich blood, which cannot be delivered. The pain occurs because the heart muscle continues to work with a diminished blood supply. It is very much like cutting off the blood supply to one of your fingers with a rubber band; if you try to move your finger, you notice that it becomes increasingly painful to do so.

before or the girl left behind." While this statement suggests a clinical lightheartedness about cardiac disturbances in a healthy young student, Osler realized that "the girl left behind" could cause cardiac arrhythmia even in a healthy medical student. He also recognized the power of human contact on patients who were suffering either from cardiac disorders or from a wide range of other serious medical problems.

Osler became the chief spokesman in the twentieth century for the medical importance of bedside manner and the crucial role of human companionship in physical well-being. Osler recognized the connection between angina pectoris, sudden death, and the socio-emotional life-style of his patients. In his famous Lumleian Lectures on Angina Pectoris, delivered at Oxford University in 1910, he noted: [19]

In a group of 20 men, everyone of whom I know personally, the outstanding feature was the incessant treadmill of practice; and yet if hard work—that "badge of all our tribe"—was alone responsible, would there not be a great many more cases? Everyone of these men had an additional factor—worry; in not a single case under 50 years of age was this feature absent. . . . Listen to some of the comments which I jotted down of the circumstances connected with the onset of attacks: "A man of great mental and bodily energy, working early and late in a practise, involved in speculations in land," *"domestic infelicites,"* "worries in the Faculty of Medicine," "troubles with the trustees of his institution," "lawsuits," *"domestic worries,"* and so through the list (p. 698; italics added).

A large scientific literature has since unequivocally confirmed the clinical impressions of physicians like Osler.[20] Patients who have recovered from a myocardial infarction are but one class of examples. Many interpersonal situations influence heart rate, blood pressure, and the frequency of cardiac arrhythmia in individuals who have recovered from a heart attack.

In 1949, Drs. Stevenson, Duncan, Wolf, Ripley, and Wolff published a paper that has since become a classic prototype for many subsequent investigations in this field.[21] Working at Cornell University Medical School, these physicians examined 12 unselected patients who had previously had cardiac difficulties and who had come to the hospital complaining of "chest palpitation." They took exhaustive life histories on all 12, and then interviewed them repeatedly while continuously recording their electrocardiograms. The authors found that anxiety was a prominent feature in 11 of the 12 patients examined. All had experienced the lack of parental love in childhood, had not married, had encountered serious marital problems, or were divorced. In every case, the onset of the patient's cardiac problems could be traced to a specific traumatic interpersonal event in the patient's life. Furthermore, while being interviewed by these physicians, 8 of the 12 patients exhibited marked heart rate increases; when interviewed on topics they were known to be sensitive about, these patients began to develop premature ventricular contractions and other types of cardiac arrhythmias that were not previously present. Here is a typical case:

A 45-year-old housewife came to the hospital with complaints of palpitations both at rest and upon exertion, which she had had for four years. . . . For almost 20 years prior to the onset of her symptoms the patient had wavered in her attachment to two men. One she had loved, but feeling unsure of him, she had married the other who appeared to be stronger but proved to be also unkind. As her husband increasingly maltreated her she finally resolved to divorce him. In the setting of this decision she became aware of marked tension and anxiety and noted the onset of her symptoms. These continued as her conflict was prolonged by her inability to detach herself from her husband [following the divorce] and marry the second man. Anxiety was joined by resentment when she blamed both men for her unhappiness [an exercise tolerance test at the height of her anxiety showed a marked inability of the heart to tolerate standard exercise tests in the laboratory]. . . . Following this the patient came to the clinic over a 7-month period during which she ventilated and discussed her conflicts and the origins of her emotional disturbance. During this period she gradually became more relaxed and all her symptoms greatly improved (p. 1540).

What makes this case particularly interesting is the manner in which it demonstrates how emotional problems can interact with physical factors to influence the overall efficiency of the heart. It suggests that even the ability to engage in physical exercise is not determined strictly by one's physical condition but is also affected by emotional tension.

In 1967, Dr. Louis Sigler, a New York cardiologist, showed that changes in heart rhythm and abnormal heartbeats could be induced in cardiac patients by having them recall earlier traumatic emotional experiences.[22] The following case is typical of those described by Dr. Sigler:

A highly emotional 58-year-old female, complained of . . . recurring anterior chest pain on any upset, and insomnia. She had been married 25 years and had had two miscarriages and one Caesarean birth where the infant died. Her husband died at 59 years of age from acute myocardial infarction and she felt "lost to the world". However, 4 years later she remarried, but her new husband was "very cruel" to her. Her blood pressure varied between 196/110 and 160/94, and the heart rate between 68 and 104 beats per minute, at various times and moods (p. 57).

An electrocardiogram obtained while she was resting showed major heart changes when she talked about emotionally disturbing events, including the loss of her first husband.

Dr. Sigler described another patient who showed marked changes in her electrocardiogram, along with manifest anxiety, when she began to discuss her sister, who was seriously ill. Still another case involved a 48-year-old man who was forced to witness the murder of seven members of his family in a Nazi concentration camp. Recollection of this horror produced severe cardiac irregularities in the patient's heart. A fourth patient was a 69-year-old female who showed marked heart changes while recalling "the agonizing events" connected with the death of three sisters some years before. Dr. Sigler suggested not only that these acute memories produced the heart changes he observed during his recordings, but also that the events recalled were probably significant factors in the production of the cardiovascular disease his patients were all suffering from.

The cases cited by Dr. Stevenson and his colleagues, as well as those cited by Dr. Sigler, have an uncanny similarity—they all involve interpersonal disasters, marital difficulties, or the loss of a loved one. These case reports also underscore a point made earlier: all conversations—indeed, all human interactions—can be completely understood only when they are viewed within the larger context of the entire interpersonal life experiences of the individual.

Dr. Stewart Wolf, a cardiologist at the University of Texas, showed that clinically serious abnormal heart reactions, including atrial fibrillation and ventricular tachycardia, occurred even in individuals with apparently normal hearts when they discussed topics that were emotionally stressful to them.[23]

Indeed, Drs. Weiner, Singer, and Reiser observed that the cardiovascular systems of young healthy subjects changed far more during an experiment in which they were asked to tell a story about a series of ambiguous pictures than did the cardiovascular systems of comparable subjects who were suffering from essential hypertension.[24] They noted, however, that individuals suffering from hypertension uniformly remained distant, uninvolved, and socially insulated from the experimenter, while healthy individuals readily and even eagerly interacted with the experimenter:

There is clinical evidence to suggest that hypertensive patients are sensitive (both in the direction of amelioration and worsening of the medical status) to the vicissitudes of emotional interchange with physicians with whom they have established long-standing close emotional relationships. The insulating device we describe here and elsewhere may be looked upon teleologically as protection erected by these patients against their vulnerability in such close relationships (p. 494).

The observations of Dr. Weiner and his colleagues suggest that a circular type of life-style exists for patients suffering from hypertension. Given their propensity to show exaggerated cardiovascular changes during various social interactions, such individuals try to protect themselves from cardiac reactions by socially insulating themselves. They try to remain detached and aloof in many social situations, a strategy which leads to exaggerated social "over-involvement," with elevated blood pressure responses, when they do begin to interact.

## THE STRAW THAT BREAKS THE CAMEL'S BACK

That emotional stress is a frequent precipitating factor in the development of congestive heart failure* has been shown by several different studies. Drs. Chambers and Reiser[25] found that in 24 of 25 consecutive cases of congestive heart failure they examined at the Cincinnati General Hospital, the onset of the crises had been precipitated by severe emotional upset. Of even greater interest, in light of the theme of this book, is the list of causes they found had precipitated the "emotional stress." Sudden death of a son, desertion by a wife, desertion by a husband, rejection by a husband—the emotional events all seemed to involve the loss of some type of human love or the loss of security gained from human contact. In almost every case, the emotional crises involved types of interpersonal disasters similar to those that have been observed by other investigators. Chambers and Reiser noted that the interpersonal life histories of these patients were most likely of major significance in predisposing them to develop cardiovascular disease.

The following are the factors that Chambers and Reiser were able to identify as precipitating the onset of congestive heart failure:

| Patient # | Factors Leading to Congestive Heart Failure |
|-----------|---------------------------------------------|
| 1. | Desertion by relative |
| 2. | Relatives' refusal to care for her |
| 3. | Sudden death of son |
| 4. | Desertion by one son and landlady; serious accident to other son |

---

* Congestive heart failure is a serious medical problem that occurs when the heart is unable to completely pump out all the blood that returns to it. This leads to a situation in which the venous blood returning to the heart begins to back up, since there is still blood in the chambers of the heart. Congestion, or an accumulation of fluids in various parts of the body (for example, in the lungs, legs, arms, or abdomen), results from the heart's inability to maintain adequate circulation.

| | |
|---|---|
| 5. | Illness of mother; argument with wife |
| 6. | Desertion by wife |
| 7. | Sudden death of husband |
| 8. | Husband's death; rejection by relatives |
| 9. | Rejection by husband and son |
| 10. | Marriage of daughter; wife's leg amputated |
| 11. | Desertion by husband |
| 12. | Rejection by children |
| 13. | Desertion by brother and sister-in-law |
| 14. | Rejection by employer |
| 15. | Rejection by husband |
| 16. | Rejection by employer |
| 17. | Eviction from home of 18 years |
| 18. | Eviction from home of 17 years |
| 19. | Loss of pseudomasculine defenses |

Drs. Chambers and Reiser suggested that lack of social support, coupled with a variety of interpersonal stresses, had led to total circulatory collapse. The lack of love or sudden loss of love, they pointed out, acted like "the straw that breaks the camel's back." Two of the typical cases cited by Drs. Chambers and Reiser are included here to underscore the similarity of these life histories to those described by other investigators.

*Patient #3,* a 66-year-old black man, was diagnosed as having, among other medical problems, chronic bronchial asthma, pulmonary emphysema, chronic alcoholism, and chronic progressive congestive heart failure of a year's duration.

BACKGROUND

The patient reported that he had been separated from his wife for 15 years and that he had been living alone for this period without maintaining much, if any, direct contact with any of his five children. His life story was characterized by mild pseudomasculine denial of dependency and chronic alcoholism. Life relationships had been tenuous; his work record was sporadic. He was extremely reluctant to discuss his children, stating that they were all failures and that they did not "figure" in his life situation. He was obviously depressed and talked repeatedly of his aloneness and the fact that there was no one to help him.

### PRECIPITATING FACTOR

The sudden death of a son (age 33) who had been living with the patient for many years. Although the patient had not mentioned the fact of his son's death or talked of his relationship with him, it was learned through social service contacts that there had been an extremely close relationship between them. They had been living together, and the patient had been quite dependent upon him. Following the son's death, mild congestive failure developed. On hospitalization, digitalis intoxication was found to be present (p. 55).

*Patient #9,* a 67-year-old white woman, was diagnosed as having arteriosclerotic heart disease [as well as many other medical problems]. . . .

### BACKGROUND

This patient, the oldest of 6 siblings, had developed a pattern of hard work and caring for others early in her life. Her first marriage had failed and had been followed 9 years later by a second unsatisfactory, but permanent marriage to an irresponsible alcoholic. Her total adjustment had remained fairly satisfactory as long as she had been able to work productively and carry the responsibility for rearing a number of small children. Although she had been unable to have children of her own, she had cared for a series of "adopted" and foster children. . . .

### PRECIPITATING FACTOR

Three weeks prior to the patient's admission, the unmarried mother of an infant that the patient had taken to raise changed her mind and decided that she wanted the baby back. The mother, knowing the patient's temperament, had sneaked into the apartment and "stolen" the child. When the loss was discovered, the patient flew into a rage and developed an exacerbation of her failure, which eventually required that she be hospitalized. This incident was superimposed upon the chronic strain of the gradual deterioration of her relationship with her husband and "son" and upon multiple organic predisposing and contributory influences, such as malnutrition, low grade infection, and advanced arteriosclerotic heart disease (p. 56).

One of the more dramatic cases of cardiac change that occurred during a medical interview was reported by Dr. Julius Bauer in 1952.[26] He cited the verbatim notes of an interview in which a 27-year-old woman suddenly died after recounting how one of her brothers attempted to rape her. She became very upset emotionally as she described what she had endured. She then said she "wanted to die," whereupon she collapsed and died. The interview was conducted by an intern at the Los Angeles County General Hospital, which the patient was visiting to be treated for occasional asthmatic attacks. A partial transcript of their interview was as follows (p. A44):

PATIENT: Well, where do you want me to start? From the beginning of my troubles?
DOCTOR: Yes, of course.
PATIENT: Well, when I was a child we lived in Arkansas. My mother was quite religious and brought us up in the Baptist faith. I have never known my father and nobody knew his whereabouts. To tell the truth, I think my parents never were married at all. When I went to school I made some money as a baby sitter. The baby's mother was always good to me, better than my own mother, and when I moved to California later on she still used to send me checks occasionally. I came to Los Angeles at the age of 17 and first my asthma improved quite a bit here.
DOCTOR: Did you move to California because of your health?
PATIENT: Well, this was not the only reason, but must I tell you all those things?
DOCTOR: Certainly. You should relieve your mind by speaking about everything that happened in those days.
PATIENT: Well, back in the little town in Arkansas a man fooled me

into an affair and I became pregnant. When the child was born my mother was very mad at me and became awfully nasty. I never heard any nice word from her and was feeling that she wanted to get rid of me and the child.

DOCTOR: What about the father of the child?

PATIENT: He was no good. He threatened to kill me if I ever told his name to anybody as the father of the child. He repeated that time and again and even told me that he would come to Los Angeles to kill me if ever I would mention him as the child's father. For that reason I never dared to ask for help from any state agency. The only one helping me with money was the lady from my home town once in a while, so I was able to register in junior college. I could stay then with my two brothers who had come to Los Angeles and found jobs.

DOCTOR: Did you finish junior college?

PATIENT: (very agitated and nervous): No, I did not. I had to quit because I could not stay with my brothers any longer.

DOCTOR: Why?

PATIENT: Do I have to tell you that too?

DOCTOR: Certainly, you should. You have no reason to be ashamed of anything.

PATIENT: Mind you, it was impossible for me to live with my brothers. One of them frequently made advances at me and even tried to rape me [very excited]. So I moved to a single apartment on county aid. As I had to make a living I had to quit junior college and took occasional domestic jobs.

DOCTOR: What about your asthma?

PATIENT: Oh, it became much worse at that time. You know, I had to go to the hospital every so often and also had to stay here a few days for treatment. Naturally I always lost my job and had no hope any more to recover. That's why I wanted to die and want to die all the time because I am no good, no good! [Crying, agitated, hyperventilating, reaches for ISUPREL nebulizer, gets a generalized tonic seizure and loses contact with environment.]

The patient never regained consciousness. In spite of intense emergency medical treatment, she died within a few minutes after stating that she wanted to die. Several other reports, including those by Dr. James Mathis at the Veterans' Hospital in Oklahoma City and Dr. Dennis Leigh at the Maudsley Hospital in London, have also noted the strange sudden deaths of asthmatics after they suffered some severe personal loss or when they were recalling this loss to a physician.[27]

Dr. John C. Coolidge of Cambridge, Massachusetts, reported a case in which a 45-year-old woman "collapsed suddenly and very unexpectedly about an hour after an incident which may well have been perceived as a profound rejection by her psychoanalyst and within several minutes after a rejection by her husband." The death of this lady by cardiac arrest had been preceded by a life history with an all-too-familiar ring to it: lack of love in childhood, final departure from home by her daughter, the death of both her parents in the past year, and serious marital problems. The events that precipitated her death seemed to emerge out of a life history that predisposed her to sudden death. The coincidence of the nearly simultaneous deaths of both her parents shortly before her own death, as described by Dr. Coolidge, should also be noted. First, "her father succumbed to Parkinsonism. Like a Greek tragedy, within two weeks her mother became jaundiced, and died of bilary cancer seven terrible months later." [28]

## HUMAN CONTACT AND THE RECOVERY PROCESS

The data described thus far have indicated that interpersonal situations can produce cardiac changes which are dangerous and even lethal, especially in individuals who have already suffered a heart attack or who are presumably predisposed by severe atherosclerosis. But the reverse is also true. If the lack of human love or the memory of earlier personal traumas can disturb the heart, then just as clearly the presence of human love may serve as a powerful therapeutic force, helping the heart to restore itself.

Nowhere is the power of human contact more readily apparent than in the period of emotional crisis that follows the sudden occurrence of a heart attack. Warm, interpersonal support is a critical element in the recovery process of such a patient. The therapeutic power of human contact, as Osler pointed out, begins immedi-

ately after a heart attack, in the form of the bedside manner of
those who first come in medical contact with the patient, and continues thereafter in the loving support given by the patient's family.

The personal impact of the medical team is compounded (for
better or worse) by friends and relatives of the patient. The coronary patient desperately needs not only the medical support of the
doctor and nurses, but also the support of family and friends long
after he or she leaves the hospital. Irrespective of what might have
caused the cardiovascular difficulties in the first place, the experience of an attack can be emotionally shattering. For many patients
the sudden onset of a heart attack involves far more than physical
weakness, dizziness, acute chest pain, or even total physical collapse; it forces many patients to reassess their lives. Heart attacks
can strike individuals in the prime of life who have never previously had any serious physical difficulty. One day an individual is
leading a full and active life, and the next day he suddenly finds
himself flat on his back in a hospital coronary care unit, confronting the very real possibility of his own death. Much that was previously taken for granted must now be questioned. Can I return to
work? How will I support my family? How will I relate to my
spouse and children? What about my favorite activities? What about
my sex life? A heart attack is both a physical and an emotional
trauma, and often the emotional scars are far more serious than
the physical scar left on the heart muscle.

Dr. Gunnar Bìörck examined 223 cardiac patients in the town
of Malmö, Sweden, and found that the most serious medical problems were encountered by these patients *after* they left the
hospital.[29] Having regained their physical and psychological
strength in the hospital, many patients feel deserted and very lonely
when they return to their homes. A special problem in convales-
cence and in cases of chronic disability "is the lack of contact with
friends and neighbors—sometimes also with children. The intervals
between visits become stretched and finally the contact ceases
entirely. . . . Time gets long, and feelings of loneliness and even of
desertedness may present themselves."

According to Dr. Lipowski's estimates, about 50 percent of all patients hospitalized for heart disease show moderate to severe depression, with the most severe depression usually accompanying the more serious disease.[30]* It has been estimated that up to one-third of all patients who have had a heart attack fail to return to work not because of physical problems but because of psychological problems. This failure to return to work will itself often lead to increased social isolation, loneliness, and depression—all of which are quite certain to affect the heart adversely. The problems caused by this new type of loneliness may ultimately be lethal.[31]

Perhaps no area can crystallize the multidimensional interpersonal concerns that follow the sudden occurrence of a heart attack so clearly as human sexuality. What happens to sexuality after a heart attack? Can the heart that has suffered a myocardial infarction tolerate the strain of sexual excitement? Can a man or woman simply stop sexual intercourse after many years, without a wide range of emotional problems flooding their lives? If human love and affection are major influences on the heart, can the heart patient tolerate a significant reduction of the human affection that is shared in sexual activity?

Several years ago I received a letter (from a woman I had never met) which summarized concisely the problems many couples must face after a heart attack and which shows the vital support one human being can give to another. (Indeed, one wonders whether her husband would even be alive today without her loving support.) When her husband was recovering from a heart attack, their internist instructed them to avoid all future orgasmic sexual activity. She wrote, in part:

We have been married for 34 very interesting and challenging years. We always had had a very affectionate life, and it was not until my husband's internist discharged him from the hospital following his heart attack in 1968 with the words, "eat and drink moderately, don't

---

* A growing body of scientific evidence has linked psychological depression to the development of coronary heart disease, and so in Dr. Lipowski's study it is not at all clear which is cause and which is effect.

smoke and no orgasms" that I had paid attention to the significance of our sex life.

At the time of the heart attack, we were experiencing not uncommon concerns for middle age people. One son, 26 years old, was in Vietnam, our daughter, 23, a good student, had just resigned from graduate school in disgust, and our second son, 21, was in the Sixth Fleet in the Mediterranean. My husband's job, a research scientist, was periodically being threatened by cutbacks in research funds, so that he was under considerable stress.

His health had up to that time been reasonably good, although he had always suffered from what we kiddingly called "bellyaches." . . . Following his discharge after the myocardial infarction, we were careful. He, being a very affectionate guy, needed physical contact, so we engaged in considerable play. Thankfully we both have a sense of humor; and late in August, he suggested "fitting jobs." We managed these very well for some months without orgasm. However, they began to result in orgasms. When I wondered aloud about the advisability his response was "What a way to go." So we began enjoying "side jobs" and later "top jobs" with orgasm.

After that, we proceeded to ignore the doctor's advice about orgasms but we often talked about the damage to marriage and to life in general such advice must be inflicting on numberless couples.

Eight years after ignoring their internist's advice, this couple is living an active and happy married life.

While, in some cases, severe atherosclerosis and cardiac difficulties will seriously impair sexual capacity and performance, it is far more common for sexual problems to emerge after a heart attack as a result of psychological rather than physical problems. The sex life of many couples is needlessly destroyed by the occurrence of a heart attack. Many men become impotent after a heart attack, while many wives of heart attack victims live in an unspoken fear that their husbands will die during intercourse. Drs. Weiss and English report that one-third of the cardiac patients they studied reported impotence as a frequent sexual difficulty.[32] Dr. Tuttle and his associates reported in the *American Journal of Cardiology* in 1964 that 10 percent of postcoronary males become permanently impotent; they also noted that in 26 male coronary patients under the age of 50, 13 reduced their sexual activity by 50 percent or more.[33] Similarly, Dr. Hellerstein and his colleagues found that about one-third of postcoronary patients reduced their sexual activity and 10 percent became total abstainers.[34]

Sometimes sexual difficulties are the direct result of poor or ambiguous medical advice, or even a complete lack of discussion. For example, in their investigation on this topic, Drs. Masters and Johnson discovered that two-thirds of their patients who had suffered heart attacks received no advice whatsoever on sexual activity after a myocardial infarction, while the instructions received by the other patients were so vague that they were of no use at all.[35] Physicians often advise patients to "use your own judgement" or "do what you think you can do." Such advice not only shifts responsibility from the doctor to the patient, but it also communicates a certain degree of ambivalence about the whole topic. Unfortunately, many cardiac patients are hypersensitive to even the slightest ambivalence on the part of their physicians, and their sexual capacity suffers because of this medical ambivalence.

Most often, however, sexual difficulties seem to be the result of the patient's fears and anxieties following a heart attack. Such fears and anxieties are felt not only by the person who has suffered the heart attack but also by the patient's mate. Many women, for example, either consciously or unconsciously blame themselves for their husbands' cardiac difficulties, and these complex feelings (coupled with the fear of additional cardiac difficulties) interfere with sexual performance. Unlike the couple in the letter just cited, many couples never discuss these matters and thus unwittingly create sexual problems that might otherwise not exist.

Medical ambivalence about this topic is not difficult to understand. Until recently there were few data available on normal cardiac function during sexual activity in the postcoronary patient. Given this widespread ignorance, it is not surprising that physicians have tended to avoid this topic, or to be somewhat ambivalent in discussing sex with their patients. Moreover, when the first scientific data on cardiac function during sexual activity were published by Dr. Bartlett [36] in 1956 and then subsequently by Masters and Johnson, the accounts did little to reassure cardiologists. For instance, Masters and Johnson found that sexual intercourse produced large changes in heart rate and blood pressure. In the males they studied in their laboratory, they found that the heart rate typically increased up to 100–175 beats per minute during the plateau stage of sexual excitement and increased further during orgasm to a rate of 110–180 beats per minute. Systolic blood pressure changes increased between 40 and 100 millimeters of mercury, while the diastolic pressure increased from 20 to 50 millimeters of mercury. Very similar cardiovascular changes were recorded in female subjects during climax and orgasm, with the highest heart rates being recorded during the periods of most sustained or repeated orgasmic experiences. These cardiac changes are very impressive and would cause most cardiologists to hesitate before advising their patients to engage in an activity that could so dramatically alter the heart. The Masters and Johnson data especially have been widely circulated and are well known to most physicians and the lay public. And yet, are the data obtained by Masters and Johnson representative of what occurs routinely during sexual intercourse? The typical heart patient is generally older, married for many years, and usually engaging in sexual intercourse in the privacy of his or her own home. In contrast, the Masters and Johnson data were collected from healthy subjects, generally younger in age, who were recently married, or from older subjects who were having sexual difficulties or were unmarried or divorced. Furthermore, the Masters and Johnson data were necessarily collected in a laboratory—an environment quite unnatural to most of the subjects —often with photographic and other monitoring devices being attached directly to the participants. These problems are not pointed out in any way to belittle their very important scientific contributions, but rather to question whether these data are relevant to the heart patient. Do such cardiac changes usually occur within the confines of one's own bedroom, and more importantly, do such changes occur in a cardiac patient who has experienced many years of sexual intercourse with a spouse?

Questions such as these prompted Drs. Hellerstein and Friedman of Case Western Reserve University Hospital to reexamine cardiac changes during sexual activity in patients after they have recovered from a heart attack.[34] They often use a Holter Monitor, a small cassette tape recorder that the patient carries around all day, continuously recording his or her heart rate while eating, traveling, working, and so forth. The patient only has to keep a log of what he or she does during the day, and the cardiologist can then assess the effects of a wide range of daily activities on the functioning of the patient's heart. Using this technique, Hellerstein and Friedman were able to assess cardiac changes in 91 male patients with an average age of 48. The mean maximal heart rate they observed during sexual intercourse was 117 beats per minute, with a range between 90 and 144 beats per minute, rates significantly lower than those observed by Masters and Johnson. Interestingly, Hellerstein and Friedman noted that patients' heart rates increased to that degree many times during the course of their routine working activities. For example, they calculated that sexual activity consumed an amount of oxygen equivalent to climbing one flight of stairs. These authors also found that sexual activity was influenced favorably by the enhancement of physical fitness. They concluded that in advising postmyocardial patients about returning to sexual activity, physicians should consider these factors: (1) the prior history of sexual activity and sex drive of the patient; (2) the age of the patient; (3) the attitudes of the wife, her health, etc.; and (4) the patient's psychological reactions to his illness.

Statistics regarding coronary death during sexual intercourse are quite scarce and difficult to come by. In the past, physicians were likely to record such deaths as "sleep deaths," and it is not difficult to imagine that an individual's mate might hide the true occasion of death. However, what few data do exist on this question appears almost "moralistic" in implication. Thus, the Japanese pathologist M. Ueno reported in 1963 his findings on 5,559 cases of sudden death. Thirty-four of these cases involved sexual intercourse; of these, 24 occurred in hotel rooms and another five outside the home. Eighty percent of such deaths occurred during extramarital affairs.[37]

Obviously, a great deal of research needs to be done in this area.

As with every other aspect of human contact, the effects of sexual activity on the heart are multifaceted and very complex; every case is clinically somewhat unique. The advice given by Dr. George Griffith [38] of the University of Southern California summarizes, as well as any, the state of knowledge about and therapeutic attitudes towards sexuality in the postcoronary patient:

> As confidence is regained by the patient and the partner, very frequently a gradual return to the pre-illness sexual routine is accomplished. Congenial partners who are accustomed to each other and whose technique is habituated can achieve sexual satisfaction without great strain on the heart. Mutual tenderness and intelligent cooperation lead to expressions of affection and post coital rest and relaxation. Sexual relationship fulfills an important role in the lives of all people—the young, the middle-aged and even those at older age levels. That fulfillment depends on the manner in which it is accepted and accomplished. . . . A loving sexual relationship brings peace and contentment which cannot be obtained at any price (p. 73).

The contentment Dr. Griffith refers to has clearly been attained by many postcoronary couples. Certainly the woman who described her struggle to help overcome sexual problems following her husband's heart attack provided the vital love and support that led to their mutual contentment and his recovery. The inability of many to achieve this type of interpersonal contentment after a heart attack is part of a human tragedy.

## SUMMARY

Individual human interactions produce cardiovascular changes that can be rather easily monitored. Such changes range from minimally significant heart reactions in healthy people to major heart reactions that can even be deadly. These clinical observations offer an important and different perspective on the relationship between companionship and health. In the macroscopic, statistical overview, the lack of human contact seemed to be the crucial force leading to premature death. But the clinical cases just reviewed indicate that *both the presence and the absence of human contact can be critical forces leading to disease and premature death.* An understanding of the relationship between health and companionship must include a recognition of the potentially devastating impact of terribly unpleasant human interactions. The mere presence of another human being is obviously not an unmitigated blessing for one's health, for unpleasant human interactions may even be physically destructive. In this regard, the heart of human companionship clearly involves something that goes far beyond the mere presence of other human beings.

What does emerge consistently from the clinical cases and mortality statistics reviewed thus far is that human contact is more than a trivial or incidental aspect of health. In many cases, it is the central issue.

Finally, the individual medical-social life histories of the patients described in this chapter force one to realize that there are limits to an objective-scientific analysis of human relationships. Clinical descriptions of individual cases ultimately move beyond the pale of science into a world in which the health implications of human relationships are far more difficult to gauge precisely.

Few experiences have made this fact more apparent to us than our attempts to assess the medical impact of human relationships on the hearts of patients in hospital intensive-care units. It is to this clinical world that we now turn our attention.

# CHAPTER 5

---

# Human Contact in
# Life-Threatening
# Environments

A man wholly solitary would be either a god or a
brute.

—Aristotle
(384–322 B.C.)

When faced with danger or the threat of danger, human beings can derive an enormous sense of comfort from their fellow man. Whether the danger is artificially contrived in a laboratory or part of the infinite variety of real life stresses, human beings instinctively seek out each other's company in adverse circumstances. The child frightened by the darkness of night reflexively cries out to its parents for reassurance and comfort. Indeed, all of us seek human reassurance. The idea of being alone, all alone, in the face of danger terrifies children and adults alike.

History is filled with examples that demonstrate how human contact acts as one of nature's most powerful antidotes to stress. There is a quality about human companionship in life-threatening situations that helps accentuate its biological and psychological power. Throughout the first nightmarish winter of the siege of Leningrad in World War II, the city's radio station remained on the air to reassure the people that they were not alone. When the radio announcers were too weak or cold to play music or recite the news, they would turn on a metronome which monotonously clicked back and forth, echoing through loudspeakers on the streets to reassure the people they were not alone.

Apart from physical torture and death, solitary confinement has long been recognized as one of the most dreaded of human experiences. And those who endure unusually harsh prison environments frequently credit their survival to the strength they were able to derive from their fellow men. Dr. Joel Dimsdale, a psychiatrist, recently described his interviews with survivors of Nazi concentration camps during World War II. Many of the survivors listed the strength they were able to derive from their fellow prisoners as the most significant factor in their will to live. On the other hand, many victims who were suddenly torn away from their loved ones succumbed to a syndrome that was labeled "musselmann" by their fellow inmates. Unable to relate to others in the camps, they often gave way to profound despair, lost hope, and perished.[1]

But while almost everyone would agree that human relationships are critical to survival, it is not at all clear just what it is about the presence of another human being that is so important, especially in life-threatening environments. It is this lack of clarity about a phenomenon universally recognized as important that has led us to reexamine two environments in which sudden death is an ever-present danger: coronary care units and a hospital shock-trauma unit. We studied the effects of human contact in an especially intimate way by monitoring the hearts of patients whose lives were in mortal peril. Unlike other life-threatening environments, these units held patients who were totally helpless; they could not seek out other human beings, but were instead forced by their physical weakness to wait until someone came to their bedside. Our interest in studying these critically ill patients was prompted by evidence suggesting that human interactions could alter heart rhythm.[2]

Since cardiac arrhythmias* in the wake of a heart attack are the primary cause of sudden death, understanding the effects of human contact in these environments seemed to us to be vitally important.

---

* See Appendix A for a description of the physiological bases of normal and abnormal heart rhythms.

## HUMAN CONTACT IN CORONARY CARE UNITS

Coronary care units are specialized hospital areas that have gradually evolved over the past two decades. These units were developed when it was recognized that many cardiac patients, who might have been saved with appropriate medical care, were needlessly dying after suffering heart attacks. Of special concern was the fact that many of these patients were already in hospitals and had appeared well on the road to recovery. Not infrequently it was noted that nurses would check on these patients, report that they looked quite healthy, and then return a few minutes later to find them dead. These sudden, unobserved hospital deaths led to the realization that these patients ought to be placed in special units and watched constantly for a few days after a heart attack. If recurrent cardiac complications did occur during this period, then the medical personnel could at least take immediate measures to aid the patient. One of the major sources of complications stemmed from the fact that there is a marked rise in the incidence of abnormal heartbeats in the first 24 to 72 hours after a heart attack. These abnormal beats have the potential for seriously disrupting the normal rhythm of the heart and can lead to ventricular fibrillation and sudden death.*

Among the major advances stimulated by the creation of these units was the development of an electronic system that could continuously monitor the heartbeats of all patients. With this device, physicians could constantly watch each patient's heartbeat and thus anticipate the development of cardiac problems, often long before such problems could become more serious. A procedure for maintaining a continuous intravenous drip in the patient's arm was also developed so that the medical staff could quickly give medications needed to help suppress the incidence of cardiac arrhythmias as

---

* It is the occurrence of these abnormal beats which makes it imperative that a person be taken to a hospital as soon as possible after a heart attack. During this crucial period, even if a patient feels better, his life can be in mortal peril.

well as promptly inject any other necessary medications. Special equipment for delivering emergency treatment should the patient's heart suddenly "arrest" (that is, stop beating) was also developed. But the single most important development was the introduction of specialized training courses—given not only to cardiologists but to all the medical staff, including resident physicians and nurses—enabling all coronary care personnel to recognize cardiac problems before they developed into major difficulties. All staff members were also trained to deliver emergency treatment in the event of cardiac arrest. This training was of special importance, since for long periods, especially at night in local hospitals, nurses are the only staff on immediate floor duty and are often the first to be confronted with sudden cardiac arrest. The medical effectiveness of these units was convincingly established when it was shown that the incidence of sudden death dropped by 35 to 40 percent in hospitals that were equipped with these facilities and had specially trained staff.

The continuous monitoring of each patient's heartbeat also enabled researchers to observe the effects of human interactions on the heart in a way that had previously been impossible. Before the development of such units, records on the effects of human companionship in times of distress depended either upon observations of how people behaved in such situations or upon their reports as to how they felt during these experiences. A person's reactions could not be directly linked to any physical changes because no means existed for continuously recording those changes.

Yet, beyond the objective benefit of viewing a person's heart in a way that was previously impossible, it is important to note that these clinical environments also generate impressions and feelings that are difficult to describe with words alone. This difficulty is felt not just by scientists conducting research in such units but by everyone involved in the drama—patients, loved ones, and medical staff. Certainly anyone who has ever visited a loved one or who has ever been a patient in such a unit will understand the problem. Such units generate powerful emotional reactions. These vary somewhat, depending on why the person is there, but in almost every case the impressions are long-lasting.

Because these units have evolved gradually over a long period of time, medical personnel have gradually been able to adapt to the new medical technology. But to heart patients, many of whom may not have been in a hospital since their birth decades earlier, such units are totally strange and overwhelming. The psychological impact of suddenly finding oneself a patient in such a unit can be devastating. Lying in bed with needles in one's arms, tubes in one's nose, sensors on one's chest recording every heartbeat on a television screen, being forced to use a bedpan, threatened with imminent death, rendered totally helpless and dependent on others—the experience is shattering.

As his heart blips ominously on a television screen next to his bed, a patient's life is reduced to a few essentials. What does it all mean? Is he going to die? Would he have done anything differently? The world of the patient's wife or children or loved ones is also reduced to a few stark essentials, for the man or woman they visit in such a unit may not be alive the next time they come back. What do you say in such circumstances—what can you say to help —what is important to communicate? For the medical staff the trauma is somewhat different, although deep down, usually buried from their own awareness, they know they are looking at their own ultimate fate. Yet they also know they must watch the television screens at the central desk, remain detached, but be kind and compassionate, competent, and prepared for emergenies. How do they communicate to a patient—what can .they say to reassure them— how do they feel when their patients die?

The very existence of units that house people faced with the imminent possibility of death helps outline in stark simplicity certain elementary facts about life. One of these is our basic need to communicate. When someone's life is in mortal peril, this need is stripped of all its usual complexity and is expressed most directly through simple acts like holding hands. Having watched many people visit their loved ones in coronary care units, I have been struck by the way that most people finally say good-bye. They will speak to each other, if the patient is physically able, usually in sub-dued tones; they will try to make every effort to appear confident, and sometimes they will even joke. But when they say good-bye, it is almost as if some deep, primitive, instinctive ritual takes over. Surprisingly, many wives do not kiss their husbands good-bye, as if they were afraid that such contact might hurt their ill mate. But just before leaving, they will stop speaking and silently hold the patient's hand or touch his body or even stand at the foot of the bed and hold the patient's foot. The contact is brief, yet deeply poignant. More often than not, the final good-bye does not involve words, almost as if words alone were insufficient to communicate their true feelings. The most simple and direct type of human com-munication does not need words.

Sitting in such units as observers, we could monitor this essential aspect of life . . . we could literally look into the very heart of human relationships. We could also monitor the physical effects of human interactions in a way that had never been possible be-fore. And yet, this remarkable technical capacity also made it clear how limited a scientific view of human relationships really was. While we could objectively and precisely quantify how a patient's heart changed when his wife consoled him, it was also obvious that a heart rate increase or decrease of 20 beats per minute or a burst of arrhythmic heartbeats could not describe the essence of the interaction. We could measure the effects of human interactions and human experiences up to a point—but there was something beyond. And while this idea may seem obvious to the readers of this book, the very real gap between objective measurement and subjective experience must be emphasized. For in the love expressed between a wife and her dying husband, it is clear that the heart of human relationships and human love ultimately moves beyond anything that can be objectively described or measured. While the objective study of the cardiac effects of human interac-tions on coronary care patients is itself an extremely complex endeavor, understanding the heart of human relationships is not ultimately a process limited by complexity alone.* There simply is a limit to science.

Nevertheless, from a scientific perspective, it was the complex nature of human interactions in coronary care units that first created serious problems for us. Before we initiated research in these hospital units, our investigations on the effects of human contact had usually been conducted within the quiet confines of research laboratories. Even when we ventured outside the laboratory, the environments in which our research was conducted were usually carefully controlled settings. The difference between these settings and work in a coronary care unit was difficult at first to reconcile. Just before beginning research in one of these units, we had been studying whether the cardiac system of horses responds to human contact. It had been a particularly beautiful spring morning, and few places could be further removed from the peaceful atmosphere of the countryside than a coronary care unit. The contrast was startling, and my initial reaction upon first entering an intensive-care environment was not unlike that reported by many patients who suddenly find themselves in similar hospital units. It was an overwhelming experience. At first I found it difficult even to glance at the patients lying quietly in their beds. Naïve though it seems in retrospect, I still remember being shocked by the realization that people really were struggling to survive even on a beautiful spring day.

For days that stretched into weeks and then into months, I watched rows of heartbeats move rhythmically across the central monitoring television screens, while the patients whose hearts were on display rested in beds 8 to 20 feet away. The patients' heartbeats usually moved across the screens in steady, trancelike rhythms, reminiscent of the monotonous clicks that measure a train's passage over a smooth but endless track. Occasionally the monotonous rhythm would suddenly change, and strange-looking beats would appear on the screen, causing a red light to flash.

Unlike a carefully controlled laboratory, this coronary care unit was a very complicated world. The patients included old and occa-

* This issue is discussed in more detail in Chapters 7 and 9.

sionally young, male and female, black and white, rich and poor, some had no formal education, while others were lawyers, physicians, or college deans. A variety of diagnostic labels such as atherosclerosis, pulmonary edema, congestive heart failure, myocardial infarction, ventricular tachycardia, and atrial fibrillation were attached to various patients' names. A barrage of different medications that had labels such as atropine, propranolol, quinidine, Valium, digoxin, Lanoxin, Coumadin, nitroglycerin, and Xylocaine were given to different patients. All of the factors which customarily appear in mortality statistics were no longer abstract numbers to me. They were, instead, individual patients struggling for their lives. The married, the single, the widowed, the divorced, the lonely, those who had been only children, those who had many siblings, those who had been orphaned or abandoned many years earlier by their parents, and those who seemed to have lives that were filled with love—over the period of the next few years, every type of patient seemed to appear in the unit.

Not only did the patients vary considerably during this period, but the atmosphere of the coronary care unit itself could change dramatically from one moment to the next. One moment the place could be very quiet and peaceful, and the next it could be filled with medical "alert teams" frantically trying to revive a patient whose heart had suddenly stopped beating. The types of human contact that could occur seemed almost limitless. Patients came in "contact" with each other by simply looking at the next bed; in a sense they were looking into a mirror, for there lay another human being also threatened with death. But one had to wonder whether the patients saw or came into "contact" with what we saw, or whether they viewed this world differently. Doctors visited patients; nurses came to and left each patient's bedside; anxious wives visited their husbands; men and women visited their critically ill parents; sometimes parents visited their stricken sons or daughters; priests, ministers, and rabbis visited their parishioners; cleaning ladies mopped beside patients' beds; prison guards occasionally sat quietly near the bed of a critically ill "patient-criminal"; dietitians discussed luncheon menus; young medical residents daily went on their ward rounds. And yet, for long periods during the day, the rhythmical flash of each patient's heartbeat was the only stimulus occurring in an otherwise tranquil environment. For some patients this constant rhythmical flash of their own heartbeats must have had the same impact that the rhythmical beat of the metronome had for the beleaguered citizens of Leningrad; it assured them that they were still alive and that they were not alone.

It was easy to see that human contact was very important to these patients. Many of them developed understandably strong attachments to the doctors and nurses in this unit, a staff that was, in many cases, the only barrier between them and death. But while the general impact of human contact was easy enough to observe, assessing its specific medical effects, especially on the heart, was a different matter.

Paradoxically, many of the coronary care medical personnel *already seemed to know the answer to our questions.* "Of course human contact affects the human cardiovascular system," a nurse commented after asking what we were trying to study. "Everyone knows that you have to measure a patient's blood pressure several times in order to get an accurate reading." "Everyone realizes that sometimes patients are frightened and anxious when a doctor first examines them," commented a medical resident, "that's why bed-side manner is so important!" The answers to the questions we were asking seemed, at first glance, to be so obviously just "common sense" that a rather bewildering state of affairs only gradually became apparent. Everyone was so certain that human inter-actions, such as pulse taking, could affect patients' hearts that no one in this unit, or indeed in any coronary care unit, had ever systematically analyzed it. There were no scientific data about a phenomenon first recognized by Celsus 2,000 years ago and which everyone had subsequently assumed was "common sense." Nor did it take us very long to realize why there had been no systematic investigations in this area. For the search for scientific answers to this commonsense question had to be conducted in the most un-common fashion.

A paramount consideration in studying human contact in coronary care units was the fact that the patients being observed were very sick human beings. Given this reality, it was clearly impossible to do anything to these patients that was not part of their routine clinical care. The experimental observations, therefore, had to be made in a social environment in which nothing was scientifically controlled. This was a dimension of human contact that scientists usually avoid—human contact that was chaotic and unpredictable, a large number of events occurring in a world where each patient could choose to attend to all or none of the social stimuli occurring around his or her bedside.

On the other hand, the heartbeat of each patient could be observed from a distance, without the patient's awareness. Physicians and nurses could also be observed interacting with patients, and usually neither the patients nor the medical personnel were consciously aware of the fact that they were being watched. Thus, at least theoretically, it was possible to determine whether these interactions affected the hearts of patients.

Several previous studies had suggested that human relationships are indeed an important part of coronary care. Dr. Klein and his colleagues at the Duke University Medical Center studied 14 patients who were transferred from their coronary care unit to an ordinary medical ward where their heart activity was no longer continuously monitored.[3] The first seven patients were moved abruptly, without advance notice and without having the coronary care nurse or personal coronary care physician visit them after their transfer. Of these seven patients, five had serious recurrent cardiovascular complications while still in the hospital. They complained of being lonely and depressed, and felt they had been abandoned by the coronary care team which had previously cared for them.* The next seven coronary care patients to be transferred out of this

---

* Almost 20 years ago, Dr. Klaus Järvinen, a physician at a medical clinic of the University of Helsinki, raised the question of whether the medical rounds themselves could not be a danger to patients who had had a heart attack. He observed that 6 out of 39 patients stricken with an acute myocardial infarction who died after seven days of hospitalization did so during or shortly after ward rounds. Two of the cases involved a medical decision as to whether the patient should be discharged from the hospital upon the finish of the ward rounds. In another two cases, the ward rounds were made by the physician-in-chief, who only visited once or twice a week.[4]

same unit were each prepared in advance for the transfer, and one of the coronary care nurses and the same physician followed them through the remainder of their stay in the hospital. While these seven patients also experienced some emotional reactions, none had any recurrent cardiovascular complications. When the relationship with the familiar medical team was not abruptly terminated, these patients experienced no cardiac difficulties upon transfer out of the unit.

In another type of intensive care unit, a metabolic ward, Dr. William Schottstaedt and his colleagues at the Oklahoma Medical School Hospital observed that various ward stresses could significantly alter certain vitally important hormones—and consequently alter the outcome of treatment. Interestingly, these investigators observed that "interpersonal difficulties were the most common source of stress to be associated with metabolic deviations. These accounted for twenty-eight of the forty-six stressful situations associated with such deviations. In general, they seemed to center on the most significant relationships. Interpersonal stresses arising between individuals without strong ties were less often associated with significant repercussions in the metabolic data." [5]

Drs. Stewart Wolf, Schottstaedt, and others then used this metabolic ward to study whether human interactions might alter levels of serum cholesterol in patients suffering from heart disease in an environment where diet and exercise could be rigidly controlled.[6] Their findings indicated that reassuring and supportive types of relationships could significantly lower the levels of serum cholesterol of patients in an intensive-care environment, while stressful human interactions could significantly elevate cholesterol levels. Within the hospital setting, the patients' serum cholesterol levels changed according to the nature of the human interactions they experienced. Perhaps one case they relate will help describe their general findings. The patient was a 49-year-old man who had had several previous heart attacks and a history of disrupted human relationships. During hospitalization, they reported,

the patient seemed happy and reasonably relaxed, although very eager to please during the first few days of the study while receiving daily visits from his new woman friend. When she left town for a few days without telling him, however, he became anxious. Serum cholesterol concentration rose somewhat until she returned, revisited, and reassured him. During this visit, however, she had met another man whom she preferred. Her daily visits to the patient fell off and on November 13, 1957, she told him that she had abandoned the plan to marry him and would not see him again. He became intensely depressed. Again the serum cholesterol rose and the following day he had a recurrent myocardial infarction. Four days later he died (p. 384).

Observations such as these made it all the more imperative that the immediate effects of human contact on the coronary care patients' hearts be carefully examined. Yet it was difficult, from a scientific viewpoint, to know precisely where to begin or even precisely what to look for. Our first study began, therefore, by our simply plugging a recorder into the heart monitor of one of the patients, picked randomly from all the patients who happened to be in the unit that day, and recording that patient's heart rate all day long on a polygraph. Eventually the heart rates of 20 additional patients were recorded in this fashion. These patients had all been admitted to the coronary care unit at least 24 hours prior to our observations, in order to allow them to adjust to the unit and to recover somewhat from the initial shock of major cardiovascular difficulties. Each patient's heart rate was continuously recorded for an eight-hour period, and only one patient was monitored at a time. All events that occurred in the unit (e.g., any alarms, noises, crises, deaths, etc.) were marked on the polygraph immediately as they happened. In addition, all personal contacts with the patient, including physician's visits, nursing interactions, and family visits, were immediately marked and coded on the patient's heart rate record. The nature of these interactions was described in a log book by nurses who had been assigned the exclusive task of observing the patients. Since nurses were routinely assigned observational functions in the coronary care unit, it was easy to mesh this type of activity into the usual unit routine without arousing the attention of the unit's patients.

The observational techniques could not have been simpler, yet our attempts to analyze patients' heart reactions to various types of human contact quickly made it apparent why cardiologists had generally avoided this type of research. In order to detect any change in the patient's beat-to-beat heart rate, we usually had to run the recording paper 25 millimeters per second. Running recording paper at that speed for eight hours produced a paper record for one patient's heart rate that stretched for about .50 mile. Then to detect subtle changes in the heart rhythm of that patient, the distance between each and every heartbeat had to be visually examined. After we measured 20 patients for eight hours each, the records of the patients' heart rates stretched for almost 10 miles!* Each patient's heart record and his or her reactions to human contact in the coronary care unit quickly became a meticulously detailed cardiac biography coded in mile upon mile of paper records. Were it not for the fact that patients' heart reactions to such routine events as pulse taking seemed at times to be so striking, these difficulties would have led us to abandon the study.

Since our chief concern was to study the heart reactions of patients in the typical coronary care setting without either the patient or the medical staff being aware of it, no attempt was made to control any of the interactions experienced by the patients. Since many of the interactions were quite complex—a nurse coming to the patient's bedside while a physician was examining a patient— attention was focused on interactions that were less complex, such as pulse taking, measurement of blood pressure, visits of relatives, and so on. When changes in heart rhythm were observed during such interactions, the entire context of these interactions had to be examined. (Part of the criteria for what was considered a less complex interaction included the stipulation that the patient rest quietly alone for a minimum of three minutes before and after any interaction, and that the environment be quiet during this period; this criterion was necessary in order to allow us to assess reactions to events such as pulse taking within the larger context of the patient's

---

* These types of analysis can now be done by computers in a few minutes. Records that took weeks to analyze just a few years ago can now be evaluated in seconds.

usual ongoing heart rate and rhythm.) Were abnormal beats occurring before the nurse came to the patient's bedside, or was the frequency of occurrence of such abnormal beats changed by the nurse's approach to the bedside? Were such cardiac changes limited to clinical interactions such as pulse taking, or were they a more general phenomenon of human contact with coronary care patients? Were such reactions regularly elicited from certain patients, or did they only occur infrequently? Were such reactions limited to coronary care patients with certain types of heart pathology, or did they occur in patients with different types of cardiovascular disorders?

These questions are especially important in view of the clinical situation faced almost daily by physicians. Cardiologists frequently observe abnormal heartbeats when they look at a patient's heart monitor or listen to the patient's heart with a stethoscope. The question at such times is whether these abnormal beats were occurring before the physician looked or listened—or are they the result of his very attempt to look at, or listen to, the patient's heart. Most clinicians have witnessed cases where significant heart reactions occurred when they or other people came to a patient's bedside. Most of these observations do not appear in textbooks but arise at social gatherings when one talks to physicians about bedside manner. Many physicians tend to shrug these observations off, because they cannot ever be certain that such heart changes would not have occurred by chance anyhow. Our studies began to indicate that there was a connection.

## A CASE STUDY

One of the very first patients monitored was a 72-year-old woman who was in the coronary care unit because she had what is known as 2:1 heart block (Figure 3); that is, the upper portion of her heart (called the atrium) would begin the beat, but only every other beat would cause the remainder of her heart (the ventricles) to beat.

The very first human interactions monitored by us in this unit are shown in the following graphs. The first event was a routine pulse taking by a nurse, before and after which the patient rested quietly in bed for three minutes. During the pulse taking, the patient's heart rate began to vary from its pattern of 2:1 block, changing back and forth from 2° to 1° block. In essence, her heart began to change from 30 up to 60 beats per minute.

During two other episodes of pulse taking and one episode of blood pressure measurement, very similar cardiac reactions occurred. While this patient was still in heart block, however, there was one other episode of pulse taking during which there were no heart rate or heart rhythm changes. For three minutes prior to a sequence in which a nurse came to this patient's bedside simply to give her a pill, the patient's heart rate had been a regular 2:1 heart block with a rate of 35 beats per minute. But during the entire one minute the nurse was at her bedside, the patient's heart rate abruptly changed to a different mode of conduction and her heart rate was 70–75 beats per minute, only to change back abruptly to a rate of 35 beats per minute and 2:1 heart block for the three minutes after the nurse left the patient's bedside. A similar reaction occurred when the nurse brought this patient lunch.

Later that same day, the medicine(atropine) the cardiologist had prescribed took effect, and the patient was no longer in continuous 2:1 block. During this period we again monitored an episode of pulse taking. This time the beat-to-beat heart rate both before and after pulse taking was approximately 70–75 beats per minute, with only periodic episodes of heart block occurring. However, when the nurse took the patient's pulse, the heart rate was slightly elevated, the beat became quite rhythmic, and the periodic pattern of heart block was completely abolished.

Note that the episode of pulse taking shown in Figure 4 is an inverted mirror image of the cardiac reaction to pulse taking this same patient had shown earlier in the day. In light of the type of

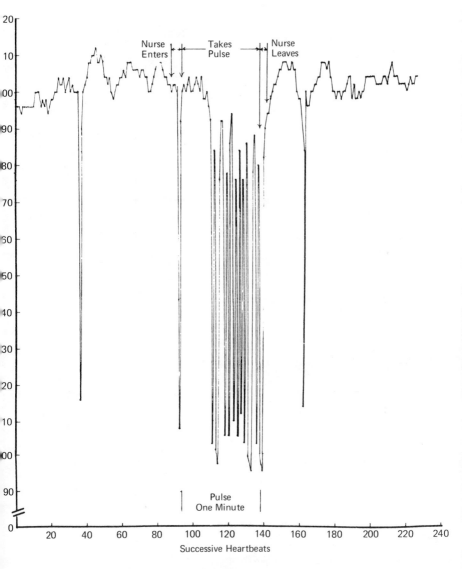

## FIGURE 3

*Effect of Pulse Taking on Heart Rate of Patient with 2:1 Block*

Beat-to-beat heart rate of patient before, during, and after pulse taking by a nurse. Heart rate data are plotted such that 2.00 equals a heart (ventricular) rate of 30, while 1.00 equals a heart (ventricular) rate of 60, and so forth. R-R intervals refer to one aspect of the heartbeat.

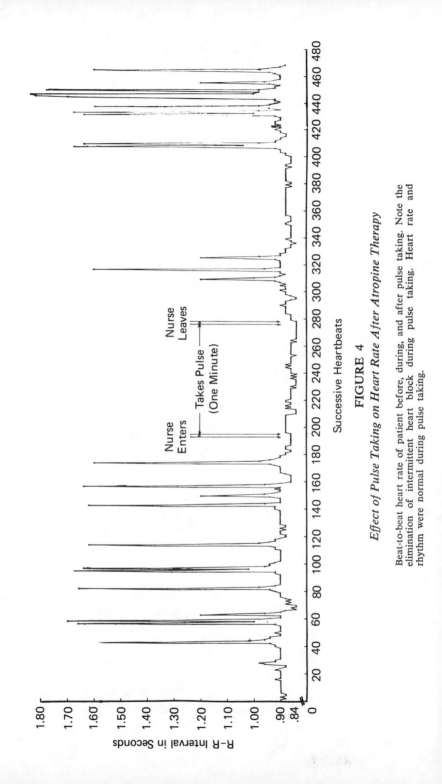

FIGURE 4

*Effect of Pulse Taking on Heart Rate After Atropine Therapy*

Beat-to-beat heart rate of patient before, during, and after pulse taking. Note the elimination of intermittent heart block during pulse taking. Heart rate and rhythm were normal during pulse taking.

cardiac problems experienced by this patient and the medication she was given, it was not difficult for us to deduce the changes in the patient's nervous system that were producing these reactions. Understanding those physiological mechanisms, however, did not help us to understand why the nurse had had these effects on the patient's heart.[7]

We began to see heart rhythm changes in other patients, and occasional changes in the frequency of abnormal heartbeats when people were at a patient's bedside. Sometimes the frequency of these abnormal beats would increase, more often they would decrease, and sometimes there were no apparent changes, leading us to wonder whether these changes in arrhythmia were spontaneous fluctuations that would have occurred whether a person came to the bedside or not. The answer to this question soon became apparent.

For example, for one elderly woman, routine nursing interactions were the only human contact that occurred during the day. The patient had been in the coronary care unit for eight days, and therefore had become quite accustomed to the nursing staff and the unit routine. While her overall frequency of abnormal beats was low during the day of our observations, twice as many abnormal heartbeats occurred when various nurses came to her bedside as when she was resting alone. To put it another way: there were twice as many abnormal beats during the 40 percent of the time that nurses were at her bedside.[8]

These observations of the effects of varying types of human contact on the frequency of cardiac arrhythmia only deepened the mystery. Why were these abnormal heartbeats occurring? Were these observations unusual? Were these patients unusual? Or were such heart reactions typical of coronary care patients?

The complex nature of these questions made it clear that to continue measuring every heartbeat in mile upon mile of records would be an overwhelming task. We were literally being buried in heart rate records and an ever-burgeoning catalogue of different types of human interactions. It also became increasingly apparent that many, many more patients would have to be monitored. Considering the numerous factors that might influence heart reactions, the many types of cardiac pathologies, the various patient personalities, and the variety of human interactions, we had no choice but to enlarge our sample of patients as quickly as possible. The only way to do that was to restrict the amount of time spent observing any one patient. What was needed was to concentrate on some type of human contact that was relatively simple yet experienced by all patients in the unit. Pulse palpation seemed to best fit this requirement. Every patient in the coronary care unit routinely had his or her pulse taken by a nurse every four hours, day or night, waking or sleeping. Furthermore, this was a human interaction which involved touch, was discrete, and of relatively short duration, required no conversation, and demanded no physical exertion on the part of the patient.

We thus began to examine the effects of pulse palpation on the heart rate and rhythm of over 300 coronary care patients, both during daylight hours and during the night when the patients were sleeping. Each pulse taking was examined only if the patient was resting alone for three minutes before and three minutes after this event. To summarize very briefly: after examining these patients it was clear that even the routine event of pulse palpation could alter the frequency of cardiac arrhythmia in coronary care patients. In some of the patients, indeed, pulse taking had the power to completely suppress arrhythmias that had been occurring.[9]

Most of the medical implications of these studies need not detain us here, except to point out that the simple act of touching can have important influences on patients' heart rate and rhythm. These observations did, however, raise many questions. Did pulse taking frighten the patients? After all, they were in coronary care units and were undoubtedly concerned with the status of their hearts. Or, conversely, did the pulse taking comfort them and reassure them that they were under continuous care? And what specifically led to the changes in the frequency of arrhythmia? Did the patients move physically in bed or change their manner of breathing in ways not noticed? Or was it an emotional response that influenced these heart rhythms? Any of these factors could have produced the heart reactions we were observing. An even larger question began to be of concern: was it only patients with cardiac pathology that reacted to human touch, or did patients without heart problems react similarly? These questions led us to shift our studies temporarily from coronary care units to one of the most acute clinical areas in any modern hospital, a shock-trauma unit.

## HUMAN CONTACT IN A HOSPITAL SHOCK-TRAUMA UNIT

A few years ago the University of Maryland Hospital developed one of the first shock-trauma units in the United States. This unit, the Maryland Center for Emergency Services, became a prototype for similar units being developed throughout the country. The highly specialized Maryland Center was developed to cope with life-threatening medical emergencies, usually involving a patient who had suddenly experienced severe trauma and often had lapsed into a state of circulatory shock and coma. About 60 percent of the 1,000 victims treated annually in this unit were flown in by a state-operated helicopter medical service. Typical patients included victims of serious automobile accidents, industrial accidents, or gunshot wounds. Most patients flown to this unit were in acute danger of death if multiple medical and surgical procedures were not immediately performed.

This shock-trauma unit itself was far more complex than a coronary care unit. The unit had 12 beds in an open rectangular area, in the center of which was a central monitoring station. Each bed unit was completely autonomous, with its own medical and patient care supplies: refrigerator, sink, running water, respirator, wall suction, wall air and oxygen, equipment for continuously monitoring the patient's electrocardiograms and blood pressure, and so forth. Each bed unit was equipped with all the facilities necessary to conduct almost every emergency medical procedure. At the central desk all patients' electrocardiograms, as well as a number of other bodily changes, were continuously monitored. A computer constantly scanned each bed, hourly printing out each patient's heart rate, blood pressure, temperature, respiration, and any other physiological data desired by the attending medical teams.

The possibility of monitoring the effects of human contact in the shock-trauma unit was of special interest because, unlike the patients in the coronary care unit, many of these patients were much younger, and most had no intrinsic heart pathology. Treatment for many of these patients involved the introduction of certain extreme medical procedures. One that was of special interest was the use of d-tubocurarine, a drug originally developed centuries ago by the Amazon Indians. The Indians placed the drug, curare, on the tips of arrowheads because it had the capacity to paralyze and kill wild animals immediately. In its modern medical use as d-tubocurarine, this drug temporarily paralyzes every muscle in the body, so that the patient cannot move, speak, open his eyes, or even breathe on his own without being artificially respirated. Yet curare still leaves a person perfectly aware of what is going on. If conscious, therefore, the patient can hear and feel what is going on in the world around him, but he cannot move any muscles. This drug was occasionally administered in the shock-trauma unit when patients had uncontrollable seizures, or when they were delirious or violently struggling against medical procedures being used to save their lives.

This clinical procedure allowed the exploration of certain questions raised by the coronary care observations. Would patients' hearts react to human contact when the patients themselves could no longer move or change their breathing pattern, or when the patients had no discernible cardiac disease? In extreme cases, would these patients react to human touch even if they were delirious or in deep comas? [10]

Two types of human interactions were studied. The first type consisted of relatively simple spontaneous clinical interactions, such as a doctor's visit, in which neither patient nor staff were aware they were being observed. The second type involved planned interactions in which nurses who were aware of the purpose of the study took the patient's pulse, held the patient's hand, or touched his arm and verbally comforted him with the following type of statement:

(First name of patient), *my name is* (first name of nurse) *and I am a nurse. I know you can't answer me when I talk to you even though you can hear me. That's because of your medication. You're receiving a drug called curare which has temporarily paralyzed you so that you are unable to respond in any way. The drug has also blocked your respiration, so there is a machine at your bedside breathing for you, which you may be able to hear. This medicine is an unpleasant but very necessary part of your therapy, so please try to relax and bear with it. As I said before, the effect will only be temporary, and once the drug is discontinued you will be able to move as before. We will try to anticipate your needs, since you are at present unable to communicate them to us. There is always a doctor or nurse at your bedside, so please try not to worry.*

This statement was not memorized or delivered verbatim; rather, the nurse reacted to each patient in an individualized manner. Whenever possible, three-minute resting periods prior to and following both types of interactions were obtained.

Although a nurse holding a patient's hand and comforting him was among the simplest human interactions that we could analyze, even this most elementary human contact proved to be quite difficult to study within the context of the shock-trauma environment. Various clinical personnel were almost always at the patient's bedside, and it was not uncommon for as many as seven or eight physicians and four or five nurses to be around the patient. Then there were the telephones at the central station, which were constantly ringing. The intercom system frequently paged various physicians, and several patient monitoring devices also emitted noises. This complex array of stimuli frequently made it necessary to watch curarized patients for as long as four to five hours before a period would occur in which the patient was left alone for as long

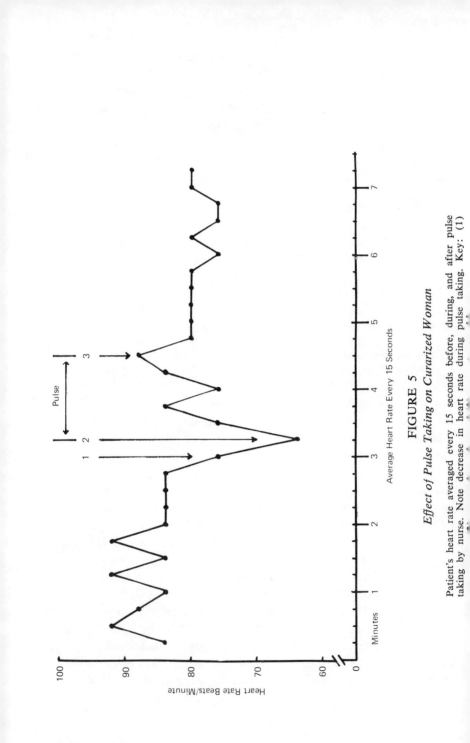

## FIGURE 5
### *Effect of Pulse Taking on Curarized Woman*

Patient's heart rate averaged every 15 seconds before, during, and after pulse taking by nurse. Note decrease in heart rate during pulse taking. Key: (1)

as seven minutes, the minimum time period necessary to evaluate patient reactions. Since patients were curarized for various periods of time, there was no precise way of determining whether the patient was conscious during the interactions. The research team relied on the attending physician's general assessment of mental status during periods when the curare effect was transiently reversed by a drug that counteracts its action. However, one of the patients was studied immediately after he was given d-tubocurarine. Since he was talking with the physician just before he was given d-tubocurarine, it is reasonable to assume that he was conscious during these observations.*

In spite of the large number of environmental stimuli bombarding each patient, the common types of human contact seemed to produce dramatic changes in the patient's heart rate. For example, Figure 5 shows the heart rate of one 31-year-old woman critically injured in an automobile accident. Her heart rate slowed almost 20 beats per minute when a nurse quietly took her pulse. When the episode was recorded, this patient had been in a coma for two days. A similar change in heart rate was observed in a 30-year-old man who had suffered severe chest injuries in an accident. The nurse in this instance held his hand and quietly comforted him (Figure 6). The power of human contact on this patient's heart rate was again seen by us later in the day, quite by chance. As is shown in Figure 7, while we were monitoring this patient seven doctors came on medical rounds to his bedside to discuss his case.

After a few minutes they left, and several minutes later another physician came in to perform a tracheal suction on the patient. This uncomfortable procedure made it necessary for the physician to periodically turn off the patient's respirator during a one-minute period—at which point the patient could no longer breathe. It is difficult to imagine a more psychologically frightening or physically distressing sensation, and we may assume that the resulting heart

---

* Our research team did not participate in any clinical decisions regarding these patients and had no prior knowledge as to when a patient might be curarized. We were able to monitor these patients only by remaining on 24-hour call.

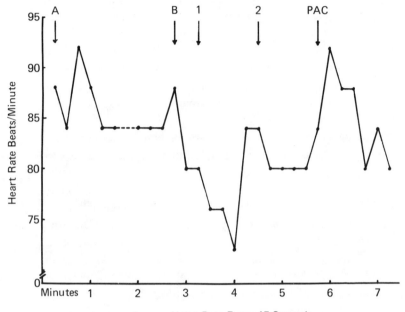

## FIGURE 6
*Effect of Comforting on Curarized Man*

Heart rate of patient before, during, and after comforting by nurse. Key: (A) nurse remaining quietly by bedside; and (B) nurse out; (1) nurse comforts patient; and (2) nurse leaves. PAC means premature atrial contraction, which was observed about one minute after second nurse comforted patient.

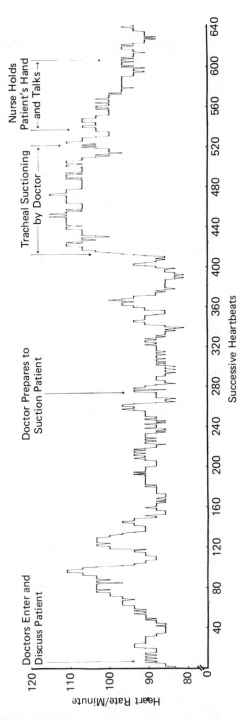

*Effects of Multiple Interactions on Curarized Man*

FIGURE 7

Beat-to-beat heart rate of patient during doctors' rounds, tracheal suctioning, and comforting by nurse.

rate increase was about as great as could be elicited under these extremely traumatic conditions. It is therefore of great interest to note that the heart rate increase was almost as great (although nowhere near as sustained) while the seven doctors chatted about this patient.

Finally, Figure 8 shows the heart rate change induced in an 11-year-old girl when a nurse quietly held her hand. This young girl had been struck by a car and had sustained a skull fracture and multiple fractures in her pelvis. She was in a coma when first brought to the shock-trauma unit and gradually recovered during the next eight days. Then she suddenly became restless, confused, and in great respiratory distress, and was curarized at this point. For the three minutes before the nurse approached her bedside, the girl's heart rate was cycling rather rhythmically from a maximum of 125 beats per minute to a low of 105 beats per minute. No unusual change in heart rate was observed during most of the period that the nurse quietly held her hand. However, just as the nurse let go of the girl's hand, her heart rate increased to a peak rate of 136 beats per minute and then fell to about 95 beats per minute before cycling back into the previous pattern. During the entire seven-minute period, the highest and lowest heart rates occurred within 30 seconds after the nurse let go of the patient's hand.

It must be recognized that observations such as these—especially those of the two patients who were in deep comas, one of whom died shortly after our observations—take us to the very limits of our knowledge. It can never be established with 100 percent certainty that these heart rate changes would not have occurred by chance, and there is no way to repeat these observations to conclusively answer that question. All of these shock-trauma observations were unique and poignant human interactions, and from a scientific point of view this uniqueness must be recognized as both a strength and an unavoidable weakness. The events monitored in this study can never be replicated within the precise context of their occurrence. They were simply unique human interactions in a terribly traumatic environment.

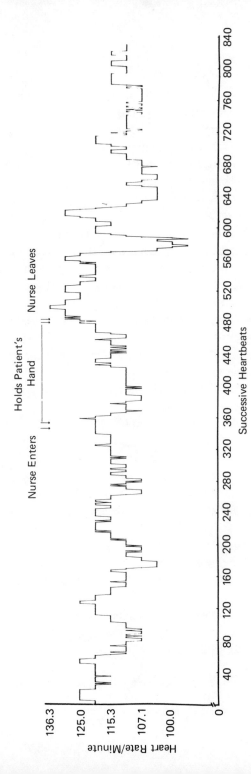

## FIGURE 8

*Effect of Comforting on Curarized Girl*

Beat-to-beat heart rate of patient before, during, and after nurse held patient's hand. Note increase and then abrupt decrease in heart rate at cessation of hand-holding.

The shock-trauma heart rate data did show that the cardiac changes seen in the coronary care unit were not unique to human beings with cardiac pathology. They also convinced us that the effects of holding a patient's hand could be seen even in the most intense of clinical environments. Human contact seemed to be all the more important to patients the more traumatic the environment became. If anything, the reaction of the heart rate to human contact seemed to increase in magnitude under these extreme conditions.

The magnitude of these reactions must also be viewed in the context of the acute clinical environment in which these measurements were taken. These patients, especially those in the shock-trauma unit, were literally bombarded by a wide array of changing environmental stimuli, any one of which could easily have had a greater impact on heart rate than the touch of one human hand. The "control periods" just before the human contact were by no means periods of quiet relaxation for the patients. It is also important to reemphasize that these patients varied from the very young to the very old and that they varied in terms of their cardiovascular pathology, physiological status, and the types of medicines they were being given. The fact that the effects of something as routine as human touch or quiet comforting could still be observed, despite all the factors that could potentially mask its influence, serves to underscore the vital importance it has for our hearts.

Like all scientific endeavors, these observations have posed far more questions than answers. Some conclusions do emerge, however. By no means should it be concluded that human contact is "dangerous" or "bad" for patients. Quite the opposite. Human contact seems to be desperately important to patients in these acute clinical settings, and the heart seems almost hyperreactive in these environments to even the most ordinary types of personal contact. It is our hope that by paying attention to the effects of various types of human contact and to the emotional context of these interactions, we may one day be able to isolate the types of patients and kinds of social interactions that produce therapeutic benefits for the heart.

From spending many hours observing doctors and nurses in

these acute clinical areas, we have also come to recognize that while these individuals spend an extraordinary amount of time with their patients, very little of it is spent simply chatting with them. Almost everything physicians and nurses do is, of necessity, concerned with the patient's illness rather than with the patient himself. So even though a great deal of human contact takes place, some patients feel socially isolated and lonely. One can only speculate, but perhaps it is this peculiar aspect of social interactions in intensive-care units that makes the hearts of so many patients so sensitive to human contact. Dr. Gunnar Bìörck, a Swedish cardiologist, recently reiterated Sir William Osler's advice on bedside manner when he wrote in the *American Heart Journal*: [11]

Physicians should be careful of their own attitudes, from the time of the first contact with the patient, in taking the history and in making the physical and other examinations, because the first contact will, to a great extent, determine the future interrelationship between the patient and his physician. An optimistic attitude is essential. . . . In dealing with cardiac patients, much may be learned by listening to their heart with the stethoscope, but it may be even more important to listen to the patient himself without a stethoscope (p. 417).

### THE WILL TO LIVE AND THE WILL TO DIE

In 1973, Stephan Lesher described in the Sunday *New York Times Magazine* the feelings of anxiety and depression that almost overwhelmed him when at the age of 38 he suffered a heart attack.[12] His feelings of bewilderment, depression, and fear during those first few days in a coronary care unit almost caused him to give up his struggle for life. Then, as he describes it, out of his despair there arose in him an intense "will to live," and with every emotional fiber at his command he began to fight to survive. Few physicians would minimize the importance of these feelings, especially in life-threatening environments. Indeed, many would contend that they can make the difference between survival and death.

Some years ago, there was a professor of surgery at The Johns Hopkins School of Medicine who felt the will to live was so important that he refused to operate on any patient who did not believe that he or she was going to survive surgery.[13]

In 1961, Drs. Avery Weisman and Thomas Hackett, physicians at the Massachusetts General Hospital, described a remarkable series of interviews with patients who had lost their will to live and had premonitions that they were going to die imminently.[14] All these patients succumbed almost precisely when they predicted they would. Although they differed widely in the seriousness of their illnesses (some were not even in critical condition) all had one thing in common: they were lonely and isolated. In the words of Weisman and Hackett:

Death held more appeal for these patients than did life because it promised either reunion with lost love, resolution of long conflict, or respite from anguish. Each patient was emotionally isolated during the final admission. Their "loneliness" was of several different kinds: one man was a semi-vagrant who had never known emotional intimacy; another man had exiled himself from his family; one woman had suffered successive deaths of her husband and members of her family; another woman had repudiated all but the most formal relationships throughout her life; a young girl had not only lost a close friend by death but was deserted by her physicians and family (p. 254).

One cannot help but be struck by the marked differences in the social support different patients receive in intensive-care units. Some patients seem to have more than ample social support; one literally has to fight off the large numbers of solicitous friends and relatives who want to visit them while they are still in the hospital. Other patients lie in their beds for weeks in the hospital, and only medical personnel visit them. We have also been trying to determine whether a patient's ability to survive a heart attack is influenced by the amount and quality of social support he receives, both in the hospital and at home.* While it will take years of continued study to arrive at a definite answer to this question, what is clear is

---

* As noted in Chapter 4, it has already been shown that people living alone are far more likely to be totally incapacitated by chronic diseases than married people afflicted with the same diseases.

that some patients' lives are very lonely. Like the patients described by Weisman and Hackett, they seem to have little reason to live; death would be a welcome relief from their loneliness.

Some of the patients we interviewed had heart attacks within six months of the deaths of their lifelong mates; they seemed totally overcome by the sudden loss and the subsequent experience of being forced to live all alone. One 50-year-old single woman who had a heart attack mentioned that she didn't know the first name of anyone in the neighborhood she had lived in for 45 years. A 44-year-old woman who had been widowed for four years wrote after being released from the intensive-care unit: "I was just filling out one of the folding envelops [our means of keeping in monthly contact with patients] 2 days before I received your letter [if a patient does not send a letter back promptly each month, we inquire about his or her health]. It makes me feel very good to know someone is concerned about me." A 50-year-old single man who survived his heart attack told us he could not recognize a single familiar person on the street. While he claimed to be only slightly lonely, he could list only a single person we would be able to contact in case he suddenly moved. He didn't seem to know anyone else who would be even slightly interested in him.

Despite recent social trends, and while it will take many more years to be certain, we suspect that Mr. Lesher was right: there *is* a will to live, and that will is fueled by human concern and human companionship. We suspect that the patient who told us that it makes her feel very good to know someone is concerned about her, expressed the source of the will to live most eloquently.

During 1975 and 1976 we were able to take detailed social histories on 154 cardiac patients in our coronary care unit.* Eighty-eight of these patients were between the ages of 45 and 65, while 17 were younger than 45. The population studied was approximately 50 percent white and 50 percent black. Among the more

---

* These data were collected by Erika Friedman as part of her doctoral dissertation on social and psychological predictors of survival from a myocardial infarction.

startling findings was the fact that only 57 percent of this group of
patients were married—43 percent were either single, widowed, or
divorced. We were at first quite surprised by this statistic, and were
initially certain that this sample was very different from the community at large. It came, therefore, as quite a shock for us to learn
that for similar age, sex, and race ranges in the Baltimore metro-
politan region, 45 percent of a similar adult population was not
married. Baltimore in 1976 clearly was very different from the
Framingham of 1948 and even different from the Reno of 1960,
which now by comparison seems like a very stable world socially.

## A POSTSCRIPT

Ideally, clinical cases ought to be juxtaposed with population mortality statistics in the depiction of any relationship as complex
as that between companionship and health. Yet sometimes the gap
between individual cases and population statistics is so great that
one is left with a sense that the health mosaic may be too complex
to put together. In the earlier chapters of this book, statistics enu-
merating the mortality ratios of single, divorced, and widowed
people suggested the possibility that what caused the sharp rise in
premature mortality was human loneliness, isolation, anxiety, or
depression. But the statistics can only hint at that possibility, and
the very objectivity of the numbers tends to make discussion of
loneliness more an exercise in intellectual curiosity than a real
attempt to come to grips with human suffering. The full impact of
the awesome destructiveness of loneliness, human isolation, and
bereavement does not strike home until you look at heartbroken
patients "being saved" by medical technology, lying all alone in
coronary care units. While there are many patients whose lives
have been filled with love, it is difficult to describe the emptiness
and pain that fill some of these patients' lives, and it is clear that no

antiarrhythmic drug by itself will prolong their lives much longer. These patients are not abstract statistics at all—they are old men and women, sometimes even young men and women, whose children have gone far away, or whose loved ones have recently died, or who don't know the names of even one person in their neighborhood, or who don't know who you should notify in case they die, and who lie in hospital beds for weeks without visitors. They are literally brokenhearted—there really is no other term to describe it —and something beyond drugs, heart transplants, coronary bypass operations, or artificial pacemakers is needed to save them.

# CHAPTER 6

---

# Bridging the Gap:
# Lessons from the Laboratory

> Although the emotion of love . . . is one of the strongest of which the mind is capable, it can hardly be said to have any proper or peculiar means of expression.
>
> —Charles Darwin,
> *The Expression of the Emotions in Man and Animals* (1872)

Between large-scale mortality statistics and individual clinical cases lies a gap that is difficult to bridge. The statistics appear to be scientific, precise, and rather easy to comprehend, while the clinical cases are very complicated, often hard to interpret, and sometimes impossible to replicate.

The clinical cases described in the last chapter drew attention to this gap. Every case was unique, very little was overtly "manipulated" or probed, nor could any of the human interactions be precisely duplicated within the context that they occurred. Nevertheless, the gap between these two extremes—the clinical and statistical—can be bridged in laboratories. But to do this, scientists are often forced to move away from humans, the ultimate objects of their investigations, and turn instead to animals.

While the entire thrust of this book so far has been on experiences that might be considered uniquely human, many of the effects of social contact on the heart can be studied in animals. Indeed, some of the more significant cardiac reactions to human contact have been observed in animals rather than in humans. Like humans, animals develop intense bonds of attachment to each other. Furthermore, humans themselves derive a great deal of companionship from animals, forming social bonds that have provided us with perhaps the best means for experimentally evaluating why and how human contact has such potent influences on our bodies.

Throughout history animals have served dual roles as servants and companions to man. As servants they have provided man with his food, done his physical work, transported him, gone to war with him, provided him with sport, play, and amusement, and given him much of his sense of beauty and grace. Animals have also been sacrificed by uncounted millions so that man could more effectively combat disease. And over and above these services, animals have always been man's constant companions. In this latter capacity, few companion animals have maintained closer ties to humans than the dog. Ample archaeological evidence from prehistoric cave paintings attests to the fact that man's relationship to the dog goes back all the way to the dawn of civilization.

Modern man maintains this extraordinary attachment with animals such as the dog. In his book *Intimate Behavior,* Desmond Morris points out that in the United States alone more than $5 billion is spent annually on household pets. He estimates that in the United States there are 90 million cats and dogs kept as household pets, and these are by no means man's only animal companions.[1]

Yet until very recently, relatively few scientists probed the nature of this relationship. Once again, the reasons for this peculiar state of affairs can best be understood by examining deeply embedded attitudes that most people, scientists included, maintain regarding the nature of companionship. Two opposing but simultaneously held attitudes pervade the history of research in this field. The first attitude is that the importance of companionship is obvious. Common sense, or common knowledge, tells us that social contact is vitally important to human beings, just as it is to animals like the dog. And being common sense, the question can be raised as to why anyone would want to study such an obvious question? The second attitude holds, paradoxically, that companionship is such a complex subject that it would be difficult, if not impossible, to analyze in a scientific laboratory. And since this is such an incredibly complicated subject, how could one ever hope to study it scientifically? The parallel between these attitudes and those of the coronary care personnel who believed that it was only "common sense" that human contact would affect patients' hearts is not accidental. These attitudes pervade the laboratory, the clinic, and society at large.

That is why, before proceeding to describe the cardiovascular reactions that an animal like the dog exhibits to human contact, it is necessary to put the evolution of research in this field in perspective. For the beliefs and attitudes about human relationships formulated in laboratories are the very same ones now commonly adopted in our society.

## EMOTIONS AND HUMAN RELATIONSHIPS—
### A LABORATORY PERSPECTIVE

The roots of many modern beliefs about human emotions, human relationships, and disease can be directly traced back to ideas formulated in animal laboratories at the beginning of the twentieth century. For example, a significant number of people now seem quite willing to accept the idea that there is a connection between stress, anxiety, and physical disease. Mass media advertising, especially those commercials marketing a wide range of anti-anxiety or analgesic agents, are but one of many sources that serve to make everyone conscious of this idea. Growing numbers of people, for example, now accept the idea that emotional stress might predispose them to develop heart problems. Yet at the same time, far fewer seem ready to accept the possibility that the lack of human companionship could do the same thing. In the context of human disease, stress and anxiety are now generally accepted as "bad" for one's health, while human companionship is still generally viewed as irrelevant. These are not distinctions that are consciously taught or even thought about a great deal; rather, they are attitudes deeply embedded in our society. As was noted at the very beginning of this book, descriptions of emotional states involving stress, pain, fear, rage, and hunger can be found in almost every modern physiology textbook while the topics of love and human companionship are notable for their total absence.

Even the growing willingness to accept a link between emotional stress and disease is itself a very recently acquired cultural attitude. One hundred years ago this idea was taken seriously by very few physicians or educated persons, and certainly the majority of people overlooked its influence. In order to understand why the idea that companionship is related to physical health was ignored in the Framingham studies only three decades ago, and is still overlooked by our society, it would be helpful to first review why the basic idea that emotions influence the way the body functions was also resisted for so long.

Attitudes and beliefs about physical health are formulated by medicine, which is itself only one of many technical branches of applied science. Modern science can roughly be dated back to about 1500, a period now widely known as the Renaissance. The prevailing viewpoint that propelled the scientific revolution between 1500 and 1850 was remarkable in its simplicity. The world was divided into two spheres: one, the physical world, was a world of things and objects which could be measured scientifically; the second, the spiritual world, a nonmaterial sphere of mind, feelings, and thoughts, was a reflection of the human soul, which could not be measured. Science turned its attention exclusively toward the world of things and objects and left the spiritual world of mind and feelings to religion and philosophy.

Given this dichotomy between mind and matter, between science and religion, it was inevitable that medicine, as a branch of applied science, would also adopt the same distinctions. In order to remain a scientific technology, medicine began to seek out the "real" organic-physical causes of human disease. For 350 years medical science ignored relationships between emotions and physical illness because science ignored the study of emotions (since emotions were a reflection of the human soul) and instead focused exclusively on the physical causes of disease.

The utility of the scientific point of view in medicine speaks for itself: many of mankind's most dreaded afflictions were successfully conquered, and a whole host of germs that caused diseases were identified and controlled. Clearly the scientific perspective that medicine accepted proved to be a smashing success. Nevertheless, this dichotomy between mind and matter did have some very unfortunate consequences for the therapeutic efficacy of modern medicine.

One of those consequences was alluded to earlier in this book. The germ theory of disease not only gave people a distorted idea about the relationship between their own behavior and their health, but it also led them to believe that human emotions had nothing to do with disease. By the beginning of the twentieth century, ideas about physical health were rigidly fixed. Germs were outside and they somehow got inside the body, leading people to believe that they were the passive victims of external forces in nature. It was widely held that human behavior did not cause disease; rather, humans were victimized by it. Once you were stricken by these foreign invaders, the only logical course of action was to go to a physician and be purged of your illness. Until the late nineteenth century, most people did not believe that they were responsible for their own physical health, a belief that has lingered on into the late twentieth century. Even today, many people resist the idea that there is a connection between *their* overeating, *their* lack of exercise, *their* smoking, or *their* loneliness and their health. They still believe that human disease is caused by germs "out there" and that nothing they do matters.

Very similar beliefs about mental disease dominated nineteenth-century thinking. Mental illness was thought to be caused by something foreign to the human body. Since it was a "mental problem," it had to involve the human soul, and so the source of these problems was attributed to an invasion of evil spirits or possession by devils. Since the mind was a reflection of the human soul, mental disturbance could only be caused by agents which disturbed the soul, namely devils. The attitude toward human emotions followed precisely the same line of thought. Emotions were viewed as a quality of the human soul; they were nonmaterial, and therefore had little to do with physical disease. Like mental disorders, emotional disorders were viewed as an indication of a disturbed soul and somehow caused by evil spirits or devils. If a person was emotionally upset, then he prayed for spiritual guidance.

For centuries these ideas remained firmly entrenched. While investigators probed deeper and deeper into the mysteries of chemistry, physics, physiology, astronomy, mathematics, and biology, most scientists continued to view human emotions, especially emotions like love, as something personal, internal, hidden, mystical, religious, and beyond scientific analysis. Such emotions could be described by mystics, poets, musicians, and artists, but clearly they were outside the scientific domain. Love and human companionship were not viewed as "things," but rather as qualities of the human soul or the human spirit. Most eighteenth- and nineteenth-century scientists would have considered the idea of studying love scientifically absurd, perhaps even humorous.

All of these ideas, however, suddenly and dramatically changed with Charles Darwin's proposal in the mid-nineteenth century that man had evolved from lower species of animals.[2] The shock waves created by his writings are still being felt today, for they profoundly influenced how twentieth-century man views himself and his internal feelings. Darwin's concept of evolution implied that the differences between man and lower animals were not nearly so marked as humans had thought. Darwin also proposed a second and related idea, that the expression of emotions in higher animals, such as dogs and monkeys, was strikingly similar to the way man expressed emotions. While Darwin's views were bitterly contested by various religious groups and outwardly rejected by many others, his views gained quick acceptance in scientific circles. By the beginning of the twentieth century, scientists began to believe that they could study emotions once thought peculiarly human by studying dogs and other animals.

The peaceful coexistence between science and religion that had held for 350 years since the Renaissance was under clear assault. It seems ironic that religious groups fought Darwin on his theory of evolution, when in fact his real encroachment on religion came from his theories on emotions. The revolutionary nature of his doctrine and the far-reaching consequences of the acceptance of his beliefs cannot be overestimated. The Western world would eventually be turned upside down.*

Darwin's writings are filled with examples of this new doctrine. In his book *The Descent of Man,* he went so far as to suggest that even the emotions involved in "religious devotion" could be seen in animals and scientifically studied.[3] In *The Expression of the Emotions in Man and Animals,* published in 1872, Darwin went beyond his initial challenge to the Biblical account of the origin of the human species and outlined a radically new idea about human feelings.[4] Not only had man evolved from lower animals, but his way of expressing emotions was very similar, if not identical, to the manner in which lower animals expressed emotions. Thus, scientists, and not theologians, writers, poets, musicians, and philosophers, should be the ones to study emotions. Darwin proposed that emotions were "serviceable habits" and were expressed in a manner designed to "effectively communicate" to others what was being felt inside. Emotional expressions served definite purposes: they mobilized the animal into some definite course of action, and/or they communicated a specific message to other animals which led them to behave in a certain fashion. Darwin observed that emotions were expressed in similar ways among all animal species, only becoming more refined and differentiated as one moved up the phylogenetic scale. Darwin also proposed one other fundamental concept about emotions that has been almost totally glossed over by the scientists who have made use of his ideas. He stated that the emotion of love was an exception to all the general rules—it was the strongest of all emotions, and yet it was the only one that had no peculiar means of expression. He struggled to

---

* As will be discussed in the final chapters, this revolution has not necessarily been an unmitigated blessing. Among other problems, Darwin's theories blurred the limits of science, leading to the widespread illusion that science was unlimited.

arrive at a means of describing the emotion of love, but in the end he concluded that it was an impossible task:

> Although the emotion of love, for instance that of a mother for her infant, is one of the strongest of which the mind is capable, it can hardly be said to have any proper or peculiar means of expression; and this is intelligible, as it has not habitually led to any special line of action. . . . A strong desire to touch the beloved person is commonly felt; . . . love is expressed by this means more plainly than by any other. . . . We probably owe this desire to inherited habit, in association with the nursing and tending of our children and with the mutual caresses of lovers. With the lower animals we see the same principle of pleasure derived from contact in association with love. Dogs and cats manifestly take pleasure in rubbing against their masters and mistresses, and in being rubbed or patted by them (p. 215).

Thus, according to Darwin, love is the most difficult of all emotions to study because it has no "peculiar means of expression." ("Pleasure derived from contact in association with love" was one expression of love that he thought might allow one to begin studying the phenomenon.) One must, however, underscore Darwin's observation that "the emotion of love . . . is one of the strongest of which the mind is capable." For no sooner had scientists accepted Darwin's point of view about emotions than they began to ignore completely the study of love. Something happened during the twentieth century that led scientists to accept Darwin's theories and yet neglect the study of the emotion he deemed the most important.

## THE SCIENTIFIC NEGLECT OF HUMAN COMPANIONSHIP AND LOVE

Darwin's writings had an immediate and major impact on two of the leading physiologists of the twentieth century: Ivan Petrovich Pavlov, a professor of physiology in Leningrad, and Walter

Cannon, a professor of physiology at Harvard University.* Both these scientists conducted significant pioneering research on the heart. Both published major textbooks demonstrating convincingly that physiological processes were influenced by emotional states, that our bodies were affected by the way we think and feel. These two scientists, whose achievements provided the framework within which twentieth-century scientists have studied the physiology of the emotions, approached the study of this topic in slightly different ways. Yet both neglected the emotion of love, which Darwin had labeled "the strongest of which the mind is capable."

In 1929, Cannon published his classic text *Bodily Changes in Pain, Hunger, Fear and Rage*, which laid the scientific groundwork for the now generally accepted position that our bodily organs, including the heart, are greatly influenced by our emotions, by the way we feel and think.[5] Cannon's book was by any standard a milestone in the history of physiology and psychosomatic medicine, for it exquisitely described the effects of various emotional states on physiological functions and disease states. Remarkably, while Darwin's classic had described the expression of five major emotions in animals—pain, hunger, fear, rage, and love—Cannon dropped one of these emotions, love, from the title of his book. Although Cannon described vividly the effects of petting and human handling on the physiological functioning of various animal organ systems, he seems to have had no context in which to place them. He labeled them "remarkable perturbations" and simply noted them in passing.

Cannon's treatise, by the force of its clarity and excellence, profoundly influenced the way modern medicine and psychology began to view human emotions. His treatise permitted both modern medicine and modern man to come to grips with the fact that human emotions could be studied and that our emotions significantly affect our physical and mental well-being. Cannon pleaded with physicians to carefully attend to human feelings, pointing out that if they

* Darwin's impact, however, ranged far beyond his influence on these two scientists. Perhaps his most important influence was on Sigmund Freud. After Darwin legitimized the scientific study of emotions, Freud was essentially free to develop his "scientific psychoanalysis" of human thought and feelings.

ignored or denied the importance of emotions, they would be unable to understand the roots of many crippling diseases:

A too common unwillingness among physicians to regard seriously the emotional elements in disease is due perhaps to the subtle influence of two extreme attitudes and disciplines. . . . So triumphantly and so generally have the structural alterations which accompany altered functions been demonstrated under the microscope, that any state which has no distinct "pathology" appears to be unreal or of minor significance. Fears, worries and states of rage and resentment leave no clear traces in the brain. What, then, have physicians to do with them? . . . If physicians show this indifference, however, is it surprising that men and women, beset by emotional stresses, turn from them and go for help to faith healers and to others who recognize the reality of these disturbing states (p. 262)?

Cannon's reasons for not studying the emotion of love did not stem from any lack of appreciation of its importance, but rather emerged from the scientific methods he employed in examining the physiology of emotions in animals. The evolution of his methods paralleled methodological developments by Pavlov at about the same time.

Pavlov was the first physiologist, as well as the first Russian scientist, ever to win the Nobel Prize. He, like Cannon, was concerned with the "unnatural" manner in which animal organ systems were studied by physiologists at the beginning of the twentieth century. He pondered the problem of how he could study physiological functions like digestion without either altering the organ or injuring the animal. Gradually he evolved a technique whereby he was able to continuously monitor organ systems such as digestion and still keep the animal healthy. He surgically constructed a fistula system in a dog's stomach, his now famous "Pavlov Pouch," which permitted him to feed the dog various foods (meat, milk, bread, etc.) and monitor how the stomach acids operated to help digest them. He emphasized that he chose the dog for his research because it was so devoted to human beings that it would tolerate almost any surgical procedure and cooperate in any experiment.[6]*

* For his part, Pavlov also deeply admired the dog. In the courtyard in his laboratory in Leningrad he erected a marble fountain with a statue of the dog placed high above the middle of the fountain on a column. That fountain and statue still survive, as does his laboratory in Leningrad.

Initially, Pavlov's surgical preparation worked well. He could feed the dog meat, wait 3–5 minutes, and then observe how the various stomach acids digested the food. Soon, however, he was confronted with a very peculiar yet consistent phenomenon. If he repeated the feeding procedures a few times, the dog's stomach would secrete acids more quickly; eventually it would secrete acids even before he gave the dog meat. He recognized that this was a strange and previously unrecognized type of digestion. How could the sight of a human cause the dog's stomach to secrete acids as if to digest food that was not yet present in the stomach? As he studied this new phenomenon in detail, Pavlov was struck by the fact that of all the stimuli that affected the dog, none was more powerful than human contact. He noted that the human so "distracted" the dog that it was extremely difficult to study these newly discovered stomach reflexes. And so he placed his dog in an isolation chamber, a "Pavlovian chamber," in which the influence of human beings and all other environmental stimuli could be controlled or eliminated.

What emerged from this research is now well known. Pavlov's observations of a new type of stomach reflex led to an entirely new method for studying emotions and learning, which in turn profoundly influenced modern education, psychology, psychiatry, and medicine. Most high school students are now familiar with the picture of Pavlov's dog salivating to a tone signaling food—the dog all alone in an isolation chamber, and the human outside recording all the physiological changes.

As research on emotions evolved in the twentieth century, similar types of chambers were generally adopted by other scientists. Today, a wide variety of controlled isolation chambers exist in psychology, physiology, and medicine to help scientists study emotions. Whether they are "Skinner boxes," Pavlovian chambers, or other types of controlled environments, all have one thing in common—human contact is scientifically controlled and excluded, while emotional states such as hunger, pain, fear, and rage are studied in great detail. The power of human contact is implicitly recognized as being so important by most modern scientists that they carefully exclude it or "control" it in their research studies.

## THE "EFFECT OF PERSON" ON THE HEART

By the first quarter of the twentieth century, Pavlov's research was beginning to have a significant impact on American psychology and physiology. One of those who helped bring this research to America was W. Horsley Gantt, an American physician who had worked with Pavlov in the Soviet Union for almost seven years. He had originally gone there in 1922 to help work in the Leningrad sector of the Russian Medical Relief Mission, organized by Herbert Hoover to help alleviate the disastrous famines that swept Russia after World War I. While in Leningrad, Gantt met Pavlov and decided to study with him. During the seven years he stayed in Leningrad, he translated Pavlov's research into English and helped bring this work to the attention of American scientists. After returning to America in 1929, Gantt continued to study conditioning at the Johns Hopkins University School of Medicine. Working on the newly discovered Pavlovian conditional reflexes, he and his research associates began to monitor the canine cardiovascular system. They observed, much like Pavlov had earlier while studying the salivary conditional reflex, that humans could influence the dog's heart. But instead of viewing this influence as a scientific nuisance, they began to use Pavolv's isolation chamber to study the very thing these chambers were originally designed to control—human contact. The results of this change in perspective were most impressive, for Gantt began to see that human contact was one of the most potent of all influences on the cardiac system. Here is an example of the type of heart reaction to human contact he began to observe [7]:

When alone [in the Pavlovian chamber] the dog's heart rate was quite rapid, varying from 120–160 beats per minute. Immediately after the person entered the room, the heart rate would decrease 20–30 beats per minute, and with the approach of the person would fall even more. During petting, the heart rate fell to the lowest value during the entire session which was, in many experiments, in the neighborhood of 40–50 beats per minute. Another procedure used at times involved the person entering the room and sitting next to the dog throughout the rest of the session. Then the person would pet the dog at 2–3 minute intervals for 60 seconds each trial, 5 to 10 trials per session. On these occasions [his] heart rate was remarkably lower and less variable while the person was in the chamber than when the dog was alone, and during petting the heart rate would go as low as 20 to 30 beats per minute. In addition, on several occasions the heart rate slowed to the extent that there was sinus arrest, that is, the heart would pause for 6–8 seconds. On several occasions, when blood pressure was measured, it fell from 140 mm HG systolic while the dog was alone, to around 75 mm HG systolic during petting (p. 55).

To my knowledge, heart rate and blood pressure changes of this magnitude are among the most marked that have ever been reported in a dog under any conditions (short of seriously injuring or killing the animal). And while this particular dog routinely showed these major cardiac changes to human contact, it nevertheless lived for 14 years in the laboratory.

The extraordinary manner in which some dogs reacted to human contact encouraged further study of this phenomenon. In a lengthy series of research investigations, Gantt and his colleagues began to observe that two of the most ordinary aspects of human contact, the simple presence of a human being and human petting, exerted the most potent effects on the dog's heart, a phenomenon that he labeled the "effect of person." The entrance of a person into the experimental room was usually followed by increases in the dog's heart rate averaging 20–60 beats per minute. Human petting, on the other hand, prompted sudden and marked decreases in heart rate from the usual resting rate (10–60 beats per minute decrease). As already noted, individual dogs varied considerably in their cardiac reactions to human contact.

It was also noted that human contact could have a striking influence on coronary blood flow in dogs. The coronary arteries, the vessels that supply blood to the heart muscles themselves, are vital to the healthy functioning of the heart. While evaluating the effects of eating and exercise on coronary blood flow, Drs. Joseph Newton and R. Walter Ehrlich at The Johns Hopkins Medical School began to notice that human contact could dramatically influence the flow of blood through the dog's coronary arteries.[8] This particular facet of the dog's cardiovascular system seemed even more reactive to human contact than heart rate or blood pressure. The investigators commented that "during experiments on the effects of eating and exercise on coronary blood flow, we were surprised to find such large coronary flow increases due to a person entering the room. Indeed, in some dogs the person was almost as potent a stimulus to coronary flow as violent exercise on the treadmill, despite the small increase in motor activity caused by the person." In light of this observation, one has to wonder whether human contact has similar effects on coronary flow in humans. Unfortunately, even today we do not have the answer to this vitally important question.

These general findings on the effects of humans, and petting by humans, on the cardiovascular system of the dog provided a simple yet powerful technique for studying some of the emotional concomitants of human contact. They also prompted a variety of questions about how these heart responses first develop and what environmental and genetic factors might modify these responses.

When I first joined Dr. Gantt's laboratory in 1962, a fascinating research project on human contact was being carried out. A dog was given a moderately painful electric shock on its forelimb without any warning signal, and the degree of heart rate increase to this unsignaled shock was carefully measured. After obtaining consistent heart reactions to this shock over a period of days, a person would go into the room and pet the dog during the electric shock. I was certain that the dog would bite the person when shocked, but much to my surprise, the petting seemed to make the pain of the shock far less severe. The heart rate increase resulting from the shock was, in fact, half as great during petting as when the dog was alone in the room.[9]

My colleague Dr. John McCarthy and I repeated this study with modifications by first pairing the painful electric shock with a tone that would warn the dog 10 seconds in advance that it was to be shocked.[10] In this situation, after a number of training trials, the dog's heart rate usually accelerated about 50–100 beats per minute when the tone was sounded. This necessarily unpleasant situation allowed us to evaluate whether human contact could alter the dog's heart rate response to intense fear and pain. What we observed was, at first, difficult to understand or believe. If the person petted the dog during both the tone and the shock, the usual marked increase in heart rate to the tone and the shock was either eliminated or changed to a decrease in heart rate! When petted, some of these dogs did not even give the usual flexion response to the shock. And this effect was just as marked on the sixth day of the experiment as it was on the first day (Figure 9).*

If Darwin was correct in believing that contact and petting in animals represent one manifestation of their expression of love, then we were witnessing a remarkable example of its power. Human contact so influenced these dogs that apparently the exact same tone-shock situation was in one case extremely upsetting to

---

* Shortly after these studies had been completed, Dr. Ruth Gattozzi examined whether analogous reactions to a similar "aversive" situation might exist in humans. She tested 13 normal and 13 hospitalized schizophrenic patients by giving them 100 trials of a ten-second tone followed by a shock, over a five-day period. She presented this tone and shock under four different conditions: when the subjects were alone in the experimental room, when a person was present in the room, when a person talked to the subject, and when a person massaged the subject's shoulders during the tone and shock. The heart rate of normal individuals reacted in a manner that was similar to the dogs' reactions; that is, their heart rates rose significantly less to the tone and shock when a person was in the room with them than when they were alone. Interestingly, however, the presence of human contact seemed to make the aversiveness of the situation far worse for schizophrenics; their heart rates increased significantly more to the tone and shock with the person present than when they were alone! Not only could human contact *not* comfort these schizophrenic patients during an aversive situation, but the presence of another human only seemed to make matters worse! The inability of human contact to comfort schizophrenics and their consequent withdrawal and social isolation has often been observed by psychiatrists and psychologists, leading to the widespread belief that human companionship not only influences our emotional and physical well-being but also our mental well-being. As was briefly noted earlier, a significant number of emotional disorders (particularly schizophrenia) seem to involve disrupted human relationships, social deprivation, and social isolation, especially during critical early developmental periods.

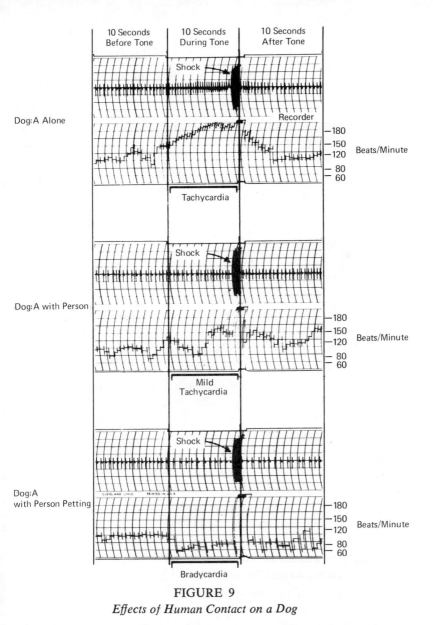

**FIGURE 9**

*Effects of Human Contact on a Dog*

The effect of three experimental conditions on a classically conditioned heart rate response to a tone followed by shock. When alone, this particular dog's heart rate increased from a rate of 100 beats per minute up to 200 during the tone and shock. However, when the person petted the dog, the heart rate decreased from 100 beats per minute to 60. Thus the same tone, signaling the same electrical shock, given at five-minute intervals, caused a heart rate difference of up to 140 beats per minute, depending on whether the dog was alone or a person petted him. Human petting had the powerful effect of eliminating the usual cardiac indicators of both fear and pain, as well as eliminating the usual behavioral reactions to a painful shock.

the dog, and in another situation not upsetting at all! Human contact had made an enormous difference.

Most people have observed the intense bond of attachment that usually develops between a mother and her child, a bond that enables a mother to pick up a hurt or frightened child and rapidly eliminate all external signs of pain and fear. Dr. Howard Liddell of Cornell University showed that similar maternal capacities exist in animals such as sheep and goats.[11] He observed that if a kid or lamb was subjected to a stressful environment (such as shock) in the presence of its mother, the kid or lamb could readily resist this stress, while if these same stresses were presented to their twin siblings without the mother's presence, the stresses would rapidly and sometimes permanently disturb these animals. How an animal tolerated these early traumatic experiences seemed to have a permanent effect on how the animal tolerated stress in later life. Similarly, Drs. Scott and Fuller and their colleagues at the Roscoe Jackson Laboratories in Bar Harbor, Maine, showed that once puppies become attached to a human, they will readily and repeatedly run across an electrified grid in order to be close to their human masters.[12] The pain the puppy had to endure in order to reach its master apparently did nothing but strengthen its attachment to humans. Our studies on the effects of human contact during aversive conditioning in dogs demonstrated that not only could the external signs of fear, worry, and pain be eliminated by human contact, but the internal indications of such fear, as manifested by the heart, could also be eliminated.

At the same time that the early developmental basis of social attachment was being examined by many investigators, animal research by Dr. Oddist Murphree and his colleagues at the Veteran's Administration Research Center in Little Rock, Arkansas, documented important genetic factors that also appear to determine the dog's emotional responsiveness to human contact.[13] For over a decade, these investigators bred and studied two groups of pointer dogs, one quite "nervous" and another very "normal," as judged by a number of behavioral tests. These two different strains of dogs were reared in similar environments, especially similar social environments. Despite their common social experiences, the neurotic dogs and normal dogs showed very different behavioral and cardiac changes to human contact. In a fashion reminiscent of the schizophrenic patients, the neurotic dogs, on being approached by humans, typically retreated to a corner of the kennel, usually crouching down as if they were terrified of human contact. When placed in experimental chambers, the neurotic dogs showed none of the usual heart rate responses to human contact, while behaviorally normal dogs showed all the typical responses. No amount of "special handling" or extra contact with humans has yet been able to make these neurotic dogs respond in the usual way to human contact.

Dr. Murphree's observations on the difficulty of modifying neurotic dogs' cardiac reactions to human contact raised many questions, but perhaps the most fundamental was *whether the behaviorally normal dog's cardiac reactions to human contact were modified by social experiences.* That is, how adaptive is the normal dog's heart to human contact? Why does the normal dog's heart rate change when a person enters an experimental chamber, and what determines the degree and pattern of the heart rate change? Many research studies had shown that the dog's heart rate responds to a variety of environmental stimuli, ranging from simple tones to shock or food, and that the pattern and degree of the cardiac response depends upon a number of environmental and physiological circumstances. For instance, it had been observed that a tone, paired just once with an electric shock, would elicit marked increases in heart rate for many trials when the tone sounded without any additional shock reinforcement. That is, the cardiac system could be readily conditioned, a fact that made that system very adaptive and reactive, but also potentially maladaptive.* The con-

---

* If, for example, a dog's heart continues to react strongly to a signal once paired with shock long after the shock has been discontinued, then such a reaction becomes maladaptive. In essence, it is a form of biological preparedness that is no longer necessary—and would eventually "wear out" the heart.

ditionability of the cardiovascular system led us to suspect that a normal dog's cardiac response to humans was, at least in part, a conditional response, dependent upon *past* experiences with people.

Viewed through the eyes of the dog, what did a person signify? To analyze this question, the same person would enter the experimental room for three successive weeks, and each time his entry would be followed by one of three different events: (1) the dog was petted, (2) the dog would receive a moderate electric shock to his paw, or (3) the person would simply exit, without petting the dog and without any shock being given to the dog. Each day the person entered the experimental chamber ten times during an hour. The same reinforcement—petting, shock, or nothing—was given consistently for one week and then switched. The same person's entry on three successive weeks thus signified three very different types of events or experiments. The largest cardiac increase occurred when a person's entry was followed by a shock, and the smallest heart rate change occurred when the person's entry was followed by petting. In addition to these different cardiac responses, the behavior of the dog indicated that his response to human contact was in part dictated by the events associated with that contact. For instance, during the person-shock sequence, after a few trials the dog would draw away from the individual and instead flex the paw through which it was being shocked when the person entered the room, keeping it flexed until the person left. In one of these dogs, the foot flexion response was so well established that even when that person would enter the animal's kennel (which was at some distance from the experimental chamber) the dog would flex his paw, although it did not flex its paw to other people who entered the kennel. The person elicited cardiac, respiratory, and motor responses from the dog which were dependent on the reinforcement associated with that individual.[14]

These experiments also help to illustrate once more a fact about human contact discussed in an earlier chapter: while a potent source of comfort, human beings can also become signals that elicit extreme anxiety and pain. To see human contact as either exclusively "good" or exclusively "bad" would fly in the face of reality. Although this book has emphasized the biological importance of human companionship, that does not mean that it cannot be modified by life experiences and become a source of lethal distress. The net effects of human contact on the heart depend on a number of factors, not the least of which is previous experience with humans.

While the effects of human contact on the dog's heart are important, the question of how these relationships—and more particularly, the cardiac indices of these relationships—first develop in the "normal" dog remains largely unresolved. Much of the pioneering behavioral research on the development of social relationships in animals was conducted by Drs. Scott and Fuller at the Roscoe Jackson Laboratories.[15] They noted that the puppy forms social attachments in a critical period between the third and twelfth week after birth, a period in which it is particularly sensitive to its immediate environment and first begins to recognize familiar aspects of its surroundings. One of the key elements involved in determining which social attachments the puppy will develop is the sensation of unpleasantness that the animal experiences when it is placed in unfamiliar surroundings. Scott concluded that the puppy learns that it is unpleasant to leave a familiar group of animals, a familiar human, or familiar objects, and hence becomes attached to these various environmental factors because they reduce the anxiety which is part of facing the unfamiliar.

In a preliminary study in which these ideas were tested, we observed that in a three-month-old puppy who had been familiarized with people, the cardiac and behavioral responses to a person's entry into the experimental chamber were quite different from those of an adult dog. The adult dog, after having been habituated to the laboratory environment, was relatively quiet in the experimental chamber and responded to a person's entry with an increase in heart rate. By contrast, this puppy struggled violently and yelped constantly when left alone in the experimental room. Social isolation in the chamber was very upsetting to it; however, when a person entered the room, the puppy immediately became quiet, and its heart rate fell as much as 20–40 percent from the pre-entry levels. Thus, while a person usually served as an excitatory stimulus to an adult dog, he was a quieting influence on the puppy. A curious aspect of this study, and something observed earlier in the laboratory, was that petting did not slow the heart rate in the puppy any more than it had already been slowed by the physical presence of the person. At what age and under what conditions the cardiovascular effects of petting first appear in the dog is still uncertain.*

While the bulk of research described in this chapter has focused on interactions between dogs and humans, cardiac changes to human contact are by no means peculiar to the canine species. This point was reinforced one evening quite by chance. While I was attending a dinner at the home of one of my colleagues, a guest asked, "Have you ever studied the reactions of cats to human contact? I've often heard that Siamese cats are so attached to their owners that if you must leave them with a veterinarian or board them when you travel, some of these cats get so upset they will refuse to eat! You know you ought to look into that phenomenon." A second guest jokingly countered with: "Cats and dogs can't even begin to compete with horses in the way they react to human contact. Why doesn't someone study how the horse's heart reacts to

---

* Developmental differences in responding to fear and pain are not restricted to animals. Dr. Aaron Katcher and his colleagues at the University of Pennsylvania have shown that about 50 percent of all children placed in the "stressful environment" of a dental chair do not exhibit overt signs of fear. That is, when they are placed in dental chairs, when they are given a topical anesthetic, or even when they are given a local anesthetic injection, they do not move around or struggle. What was of special interest, however, was that if a child showed no bodily movements, then no heart rate changes were observed. Only when they moved in the chairs or struggled with the dental assistant did these children show heart rate changes. Like the puppies in the isolation chamber, their anxiety or fear was expressed simultaneously in both their behavior and their hearts. This is in marked contrast to adults who often show striking cardiovascular changes in threatening environments without exhibiting any overt behavioral movements. There is a marked split in some adults between what they exhibit behaviorally and what is exhibited in the hearts. Dr. W. Horsley Gantt was the first to analyze this phenomenon systematically; he labeled it "schizokinesis." Gantt proposed that this splitting of heart rate reactions from overt behavioral reactions might be one of the sources of the development of heart disease.[16]

human contact?" While a number of studies had shown that the cardiac systems of many species of animals, including monkeys, guinea pigs, rats, rabbits, and cats, respond to human handling, I was unaware of any similar studies with horses.

The question seemed hard to resist. Why not pet horses? One of my colleagues quickly volunteered his horses for study. Knowing nothing about the cardiac system of the horse, or even how we would go about measuring a horse's heart rate, we were fortunate to meet Dr. Fred Fregin of the University of Pennsylvania Veterinary School, an equine cardiologist. Dr. Fregin had already developed all the techniques needed to monitor the cardiac systems of horses, even horses galloping full speed around a race track. The results were clear. Horses not only reacted to human petting in a way that was every bit as striking as in the case of dogs, but their heart rates slowed so precipitously while being petted that they began dropping heartbeats. In one of the horses we observed 29 episodes of dropped heartbeats during a one-hour period, and 23 of these episodes occurred while the horse was being petted, although this contact occupied only a small percentage of the time we recorded the horse's heart rate.[17] The precipitous heart rate slowdown in these horses was reminiscent of the heart reactions seen earlier in some dogs. As we noted earlier, on several occasions, human petting produced cardiac arrest for as long as eight seconds in a dog who was otherwise quite healthy and who lived for 14 years in the laboratory.

From all of these studies, a number of comments can be made. First of all, it is readily apparent that while behavioral observations can reveal certain features of an animal's social interactions with humans, an analysis of the cardiac responses provides an additional view of the animal's emotional response to these interactions. Second, the heart exhibits a wide range of responsiveness to human contact, dependent to some extent on the particular circumstances of the experiment. But in general, social interactions with man can have noticeable, and at times profound, effects on the cardiac systems of animals. Third, human contact can alter and even eliminate the usual cardiac responses to fear and physical pain. Fourth, it is apparent that early experience, subsequent learning, and genetic predisposition all play significant roles in determining the pattern and degree of cardiac response elicited by human contact. All these factors interact in a highly complex fashion to determine an animal's emotional responsiveness to human contact.

The animal studies described thus far all closely parallel the studies of transient types of human interaction described in Chapter 4. What is the relationship between these transient interactions and the more enduring, chronic social experiences of animals, and how do these relate to health? Among the wide variety of experimental approaches that have emerged in the past few years to examine this question, one of the more interesting has been an approach pioneered by Dr. Harry Harlow at the University of Wisconsin. His research has provided one of the more clear-cut and convincing demonstrations of the biological importance of early social contact. Dr. Harlow took infant monkeys away from their mothers at birth and placed them in environments where they were totally isolated from all other living creatures. At the same time, he carefully tended to all their other needs, even ingeniously creating a variety of lifeless surrogate mothers, akin to the mannequins seen in department store windows. These he placed in the monkeys' cages. The surrogate mothers conformed to the bodily size of the infants' biological mothers. Some were made of wire on which the infant monkey could climb up to get food; other surrogates were covered with soft terry cloth.

Dr. Harlow's research quickly revealed how important "contact comfort" was for infant animals. He observed that the isolated infant monkeys maintained continual contact with the soft terry-cloth surrogate mothers. With their biological mothers removed from their lives, the infant monkeys would cling desperately to the soft terry-cloth "surrogate mother" rather than go to "wire mothers" where they could receive food. So powerful was the need for contact comfort in infant monkeys that these animals became terrified if the terry-cloth surrogate was removed from their cages. And yet, even the continual presence of the terry-cloth surrogate mother was not sufficient for these infant monkeys. Irrespective of what type of surrogate was used, the social isolation ultimately destroyed them emotionally. When they matured, they refused to breed, and some killed their own offspring when impregnated, convincingly demonstrating the biological importance of early social contact.

The overwhelming physical and emotional destructiveness of this type of early social deprivation was clear. Psychologically the monkeys reared with surrogate mothers or in social isolation exhibited severe depression that usually remained long after they were removed from isolation. They remained emotionally scarred for the remainder of their lives.[18]

Dr. Reite and his colleagues at the University of Colorado Medical Center repeated aspects of these studies and also noted, as Harlow had earlier, that infant monkeys who were separated from their mothers for varying periods of time exhibited profound signs of emotional disturbance, including acute depression.[19] Apart from the behavioral signs of depression, they added the interesting observation that the infant monkey's heart rate at rest was significantly lower after separation from its mother than that observed in normal infants. Thus the link between the absence of maternal contact, depression, and altered cardiac status, reminiscent of that observed by Drs. Greene and Schmale in hospitalized patients in Rochester, could be reproduced in isolated monkeys also.

In addition to these studies of social deprivation, a series of experiments have demonstrated that the early social experiences of various animal species routinely used in medical research significantly influence their ability to resist experimentally induced diseases. Resistance to diseases as varied as cancer, malaria, and tuberculosis has been shown to be significantly changed by early social experience.[20] For example, the manner in which a rat or mouse is handled, the numbers placed in each cage, and other factors all significantly influence the animal's ability to resist experimentally induced infectious diseases. It is important to emphasize here that the manner in which early social experiences influence an animal's resistance to disease and death is complex. Specific types of early human handling cannot be judged as either unequivocally "good" or unequivocally "bad" in terms of subsequent health. Sometimes early human handling produces striking increases in an animal's ability to resist one type of infectious disease while lowering resistance to another. The precise nature of these relationships will require far more research before a total understanding can emerge. What is clear at present is that these early social experiences do significantly alter an animal's resistance to infectious diseases and even an animal's ability to survive.[21]

Animal research on the relationship between social contact and heart function, like the investigations on humans described earlier, is still in an embryonic stage of development. And yet, in spite of its recent birth, this research has made it clear that social interactions can profoundly alter the cardiovascular systems of animals. These parallels in findings between human and animal research have created the foundations of a structure which will eventually help scientists bridge the gap between mortality statistics and clinical observations. It seems only fitting that man's "best friend" has served in the vanguard of this research endeavor.

# CHAPTER 7

## Toward a Medicine Beyond Science

It is now biologically possible to teach people how to be happy and serene. —A. H. Maslow (1971)

Where are love hormones?
—Question raised in 1973 by a graduate student in nursing school

In the last several chapters, we have described the heart reactions of dogs, monkeys, horses; cardiac patients; neurotic and schizophrenic patients; the married, divorced, single, and widowed; children and the aged; psychotherapists; coronary care and shock-trauma patients. All this served to emphasize a point that most physicians would readily acknowledge—human interactions can produce measurable, sometimes dramatic, and occasionally even lethal effects on the heart. These illustrations were also cited to help support the central and certainly more controversial thesis of this book:

> *The lack of human companionship, the sudden loss of love, and chronic human loneliness are significant contributors to serious disease (including cardiovascular disease) and premature death.*

This central thesis was buttressed with various mortality statistics which suggested that living alone can significantly shorten life. Here we made a distinction between factors that *predispose* an individual to diseases, such as cardiovascular disease, and factors that *precipitate* immediate heart changes, some of which can lead to sudden death. The statistical data on the relationship between marital status and heart disease were cited to suggest that slowly developing degenerative diseases, such as atherosclerosis, can be influenced and accelerated by a life setting devoid of human companionship and love. A similar suggestion was made about children who suffer from parental loss or abandonment. The individual clinical cases we described also indicated that unpleasant human interactions or the recall of traumatic events could also precipitate life-threatening cardiac changes in individuals already predisposed to show such changes.

Admittedly, this central thesis and the health mosaic mirroring this thesis are still far from complete. Gaps in vital information remain; essential research data still must be collected. (Indeed, it should be emphasized that critical data supporting this thesis are lacking precisely because little prospective research has been conducted in which human relationships and health have been specifically examined.) Nevertheless, while this health mosaic has pieces still missing, the outlines of the picture are clear enough and the data consistent enough for even the most skeptical to sense that the correlation between deficient human relationships and premature death is worth exploring further.

But will it be? Will a massive, concerted research effort be made on the relationship between human contact and health? No nation spends more money on biomedical research than the United States. "Total war" has been declared on heart disease and on cancer, and billions of dollars have been spent by the U.S. government to "eradicate" these diseases. Loneliness seems to be a serious problem in our society, and for many the task of easing this affliction seems to be an overwhelming burden. Yet while the relationship between disease and loneliness seems both empirically and intuitively obvious, our government has never declared "war" on loneliness. Our nation may very well have reached a point where it is working feverishly to control diseases that we ourselves are causing.

What is it that allows us to wage "war" against heart disease while at the same time ignoring the correlation between divorce and premature coronary death? Why do we so readily tolerate social situations that seem to lead inexorably to our own physical destruction? Why do we build elaborate and expensive hospital coronary care units to save peoples' lives, only to discharge some of them back into homes of such acute social isolation that their lives will be quickly terminated?

Apart from these medical dilemmas, there is an even larger social paradox. Very few people want to be lonely. Most try to find love. Very few individuals marry with the intention of getting divorced or rejoice over the loss of their children through divorce. No one really wishes to live in constant interpersonal chaos or to be the cause of frequent disruptions of human relationships. Loneliness, the lack of love, divorce, and the loss of one's children or loved ones—these are not situations enthusiastically embraced by the vast majority of people. Why then are they such common experiences in modern society? How did we manage to create a society in which these signs of disrupted interpersonal relationships seem to be growing so quickly?

All of these complex problems ultimately lead to a key question that still must be addressed in this book: What can be done to help alleviate the spread of loneliness-induced disease in our society?

The very complexity of the issues involved in human loneliness make it clear that no simple or single approach will successfully provide all the answers. Divorce, for example, may involve questions about health, but it also involves legal, moral, financial, social, cultural, and personal questions as well. This chapter will therefore restrict itself to medical approaches that may help alleviate loneliness-induced disease. The next two chapters will describe other approaches that are more personal, individualistic, and nonmedical in character.

Loneliness is ultimately an internal, subjective human experience. Therefore, in order to effectively combat its lethal influence, medicine must adopt techniques and approaches that go beyond the current scientific-objective approach to disease. Medicine must move beyond science to deal with this problem. Indeed, later in this chapter, I shall suggest that the very use of scientific objectivity to help us understand human relationships is a philosophical attitude widely shared in our society that is causing rather than alleviating loneliness.

## THE SCIENTIFIC-LOVE-AVOIDERS

Earlier in this book, I expressed the view that deeply rooted beliefs about the causes of disease and death have tended to influence the manner in which health problems have been studied. For example, research efforts to find the causes of disease have usually not included social factors as a potential causative agent. The Framingham studies were cited as an example of how the use of static and stable populations for prospective medical research inherently prevented investigators from observing the impact of social disruption on disease. These studies were also cited as an example of the widespread and implicitly accepted belief that childhood experiences are not an important etiological factor in the appearance of disease decades later. Since these implied beliefs were deeply rooted in medical thinking, it was inevitable that similar attitudes would also be adopted by society in general.

In light of this historic neglect of social factors in disease, it would seem that the first and most important step medical science could take to alleviate loneliness-induced disease would be to recognize that its own assumptions have affected the way people now behave in our society. If medicine is to begin to cope realistically with such disease, it must first put its own house in order. In a sense, medical science must acknowledge that its implicit denial of the importance of social factors in physical disease has contributed to, and perhaps even fostered, cultural attitudes that have blinded people to such relationships. Beyond that, medical science must begin to support research that is specifically aimed at examining the connection between disease and all the varied aspects of human relationships. In short, it must begin to take human relationships every bit as seriously as it has taken such physical factors as serum cholesterol levels or blood pressure. As advisers to our society, moreover, medical practitioners must make people aware that their family and social life are every bit as important to health as dieting and exercising.

There is another attitude prevalent among scientists and physicians that needs to be reexamined, an attitude that can best be described as a covert form of therapeutic nihilism. As stated earlier, few physicians would deny the reality of a broken heart. But at the same time, most feel they can do precious little to influence psychosocial factors that cause disease, or to alleviate the physical impact of divorce or bereavement. These seem so complicated and overwhelming when compared with other, more precise aspects of modern scientific medicine—a specific antibiotic for a specific infection—that many clinicians see the whole problem as unmanageable.

This was not always the case, however. Before 1900 very few medicines were available that could be prescribed effectively to combat disease. Physicians were forced, therefore, to rely on the power of their own presence, and bedside manner was recognized as a potent source of healing. As scientific medicine began to develop drugs that were outstandingly effective as healing agents, there seemed to be less and less need for bedside manner. And so the weight of attention shifted more and more to scientific medicine, and away from the healing power of human contact. Objective knowledge and not the person dispensing such knowledge—the pill rather than the pill-giver—was seen as the key factor in healing. The role of bedside manner as a healing agent was gradually minimized, until by the mid-twentieth century it was relegated almost to the status of a historical curiosity.

Public reaction to this change was, in general, most enthusiastic. Of course, not all was well. Quite apart from the spiraling cost of medical care, there were increasing complaints that physicians no

longer seemed to care about human beings. But such complaints
were greatly overshadowed by the apparent effectiveness of the
new scientific healing, and the public generally admired the results.

Indeed, this change in the nature of medicine had a definite
influence on the way society in general began to view human relationships and disease processes. As is true with all other scientific-
medical attitudes, the downgrading of the importance of human
contact as a healing agent in medicine was accompanied by the
adoption of similar attitudes by society in general.* It became
increasingly difficult for individuals to see the importance of human
contact as a healing force in the lives of those suffering from illness.
For those suffering from physical infections, this change in attitude
proved highly therapeutic, but for those suffering from loneliness-
induced diseases, this change ultimately compounded their problems. Lonely people who began to develop physical symptoms were
sent by other human beings to drugstores to buy aspirins, tranquil-
izers, or antidepressants. They were denied the only effective healing agent—human contact—that could possibly have cured loneli-

* While the topic would require a book in itself to be thoroughly discussed, the
adoption of scientific ways of thinking had far reaching consequences for many
aspects of society. One of its more dramatic influences occurred within
formalized religions, especially Christianity. Part of the driving force behind
the growth of Christianity resided in the fact that it was a religion of healing—
it was a form of religious medicine that transcended Greek-rational medicine.
Christ was a healer; one of the transcribers of the new Gospel, Luke, was a
physician and much of the New Testament described miracles that involved the
healing of disease. Until the twentieth century, healing was one of the most
highly visible social functions of religion. Catholic churches all over the Western
world, for example, had shrines filled with crutches and other medical para-
phernalia, left as obvious evidence that cures had occurred there. The attraction
of major shrines, such as Lourdes, resided in the fact that these centers seemed
especially potent places of healing. A prerequisite for canonization as a saint
in the Roman Catholic Church involved the working of miracles—which most
often involved the restoring of health to someone deemed incurably ill.

With the growth of scientific medicine in the twentieth century, two things occurred. First of all, people saw less need for this type of "magical" religious
healing. Secondly, and perhaps of greater significance, churches themselves
adopted objectivity as a means par-excellence for examining their own beliefs.
This latter stance of objectively assessing faith systems and theology, I believe,
proved to be an especially disruptive posture for religion, and one that had
immediate consequences. These two changes brought about a dramatic decline in
the healing aspects of religion, as well as a consequent decline in interest in
religion itself. Only in the last few years has a resurgence of faith healing re-
appeared and the reasons for this resurgence will be discussed later in the text.

ness, because no one any longer believed it to be very effective. The idea that simple human compassion and comfort could heal was almost totally abandoned, swept away in a euphoric flood of "objectivity" that came in the wake of medical science's triumphs.

This scientific tide continued to rise for over 60 years, reaching its high water mark a little over a decade ago. Objective medical science crested in an especially dramatic way when in Cape Town, South Africa, a young surgeon, Dr. Christiaan Barnard, performed the first heart transplant operation. The public reaction was electric —overnight this operation became a sensation, one of the major news events of the era. American surgeons literally stumbled over each other in a headlong race to be the first in this country to duplicate the feat. The costs of a few of these operations soared into the millions of dollars, but the cost did not seem to matter. The symbolic seat of all human emotions—the very symbol of love —was being lifted from one human and put into another.

The impression was clearly left that in a few short years medical science would arrange it so that a person could do anything he wished, eat any food, behave in any way he chose, and if his heart got "smashed up" in the process, a new one could be put in. The idea was circulated that the human heart was really like an automobile tire that could be replaced every 40,000 miles. Of course, no one explicitly said that this procedure would be used to replace lonely and broken hearts—at that time that just wasn't an issue. The implicit medical belief, widely accepted, was that the heart was a pump, that surgeons were scientific plumbers, and that humans were machines.

When the first blush of this surgical triumph had paled somewhat, the heart transplant operation forced everyone to take a second look at medical beliefs, especially scientific-medical beliefs. The operation made it clear that the physician, the healer, the human element, was in danger of being totally purged from medicine and replaced by machines, techniques, pumps, valves, and drugs. And yet, when the problem was outlined in such bold relief, some physicians began to recognize that something was missing, that such an exclusively scientific approach to disease was also limited and restricted. True, such an approach might temporarily *repair* a broken heart, but it was totally ineffective in preventing the heart from breaking in the first place. It was also clear that no one could stockpile spare parts to heal a lonely heart, and the evidence was growing daily that such emotions did influence the physical functioning of the body. The central issue was one of proportions; rather than putting forth a major effort to prevent disease, medicine was in danger of becoming a repair service equipped to deal only with problems after they had occurred.

Today, for the first time since the beginning of the twentieth century, the scales have begun to right themselves. And yet it is still far from clear that these scales will inevitably swing back to a healthy balance between what was historically called the art of medicine—bedside manner—and the science of medicine. In fact, current evidence suggests that the swing will be far from balanced. The danger arises from the fact that the historical distinction between art and science in medicine has been blurred. Instead of restoring a humanistic bedside manner, medicine may substitute another approach—something that seems more analogous to a "scientific" bedside manner.

## THE SCIENTIFIC-LOVE-SEEKERS

As was discussed in Chapter 6, prior to the twentieth century problems of the human spirit, human feelings, and human relationships were not considered scientific problems at all. But Darwin's ideas on evolution and the similarity of emotional expression in man and animals challenged these traditional views and led to a significant shift in the way scientists began to think of human emotions. With the gradual acceptance of Darwin's ideas, there arose an entirely new belief, one that has been growing slowly but surely ever since, a belief in the possibility of what I have labeled scientific-love-seeking.

As the name implies, the scientific-love-seekers do not avoid objective studies of human relationships. On the contrary, they deeply believe that science offers not only the best hope for understanding such relationships, but also the best hope for improving understanding between human beings.

For the love-seekers, Darwin's writings became the foundation of an entirely new belief system about science. William James, one of America's foremost philosophers and the architect of the modern American system of education, accurately foresaw that Darwin's theories would lead to the emergence of a new faith system: a belief in the ability of scientific techniques to abolish grief, loneliness, and sadness just as they had already eliminated some of mankind's dreaded physical diseases. He called it the pursuit of the "mind cure," and he recognized that the scientific pursuit of the "mind cure" would replace the traditional religious pursuit of the "soul cure" for large numbers of people. As James wrote in *The Varieties of Religious Experience* [1]:

If we were to ask the question "What is human life's chief concern?" one of the answers we should receive would be: "It is happiness." . . . But in the theory of evolution which, gathering momentum for a century, has within the past twenty-five years swept so rapidly over Europe and America, we see the ground laid for a new sort of religion of Nature, which has entirely displaced Christianity from the thoughts of a large part of our generation. . . . We find evolutionism interpreted thus optimistically and embraced as a substitute for the religion they were born in by a multitude of our contemporaries who have either been trained scientifically or been fond of reading popular science (pp. 78–91).

James predicted where the ranks of the scientific-love-seekers would come from: "our contemporaries who have either been trained scientifically, or been fond of reading popular science."

Perhaps one way to clarify the belief system of the scientific-love-seekers would be to focus on some differences of opinion within this group. On the one hand, there is the rather optimistic

view of a minority of this group that science is now so advanced
that, in the words of Dr. Abraham Maslow (a former president of
the American Psychological Association), *"it is now biologically
possible to teach people how to be happy or serene."* [2] On the other
hand, there is the more general but ill-defined feeling among many
scientific-love-seekers that something is wrong with modern life.
Ironically, these love-seekers blame science for being too preoccupied with external objects rather than human beings, and they
actively criticize scientists for "dehumanizing" society. They are
aware of the isolation and loneliness of modern life, and they constantly talk about the human estrangement that seems to abound in
our culture. They do not, however, question scientific endeavor
itself, but only its current directions. By studying human emotions
and human relationships, they hope to put "human concerns" back
into scientific awareness, back into medicine, and consequently
back into our modern scientific culture.

Common concerns lead all scientific-love-seekers to ask the
question "What is love?" Those love-seekers who acknowledge that
love does exist point toward a wide range of scientific evidence to
prove their contention. We shall return to this group momentarily,
for their belief system has to be clarified in light of the theme of
this book.

Other scientific-love-seekers, however, have arrived at the conclusion that there is no such "thing" as love. They are profound
believers in the reality of things that can be "weighed"—that is,
objectively defined. They believe that the only reality is one that
can be measured. As one nurse in graduate school recently asked
with a kind of bemused skepticism, "Where are love hormones?"

Actually, love-seekers who use scientific logic to conclude that
love does not exist are still only a minority. Far larger numbers
seem to be using the same scientific approach to reach the opposite
conclusion . . . love does exist. As noted earlier, they point toward
a wide variety of scientific evidence to support that conclusion,
and right now tactile contact seems to be one of their favorites. As
the zoologist Desmond Morris has written in the introduction to
his recent book *Intimate Behavior* [3]: "Our intimate encounters

involve verbal, visual and even olfactory elements, but above all, loving means touching and body contact." "Getting in touch" has become one of the more commonly used phrases in modern American parlance.

But this position, too, can quickly lead to absurdity. The previous chapters of this book described in detail the powerful influence of tactile contact on the functioning of the heart in dogs, horses, and humans. It is, however, one thing to demonstrate that human touch affects the heart, and quite another to fractionate love into a variety of sensory modalities in an effort to assess which sensory modality is "most important." And yet, that is precisely what many love-seekers are trying to do.

Several years ago, while describing the effects of human contact on the heart to a group of graduate psychology students, I mentioned that human petting usually slows the heart rate of a dog. In the ensuing discussion, one of the students stressed the need to separate the effects of my petting of the dog from mere tactile stimulation. "Is it," he asked, "your petting that is causing the slowing of the dog's heart rate, or is it merely tactile contact on the dog's head?" This question was undoubtedly important, but, before the comment could be answered, the students began debating how they might be able to adequately explore this problem. One suggested that the way to test this question would be to develop a "mechanical petter." "The best experimental control would be to develop some type of artificial hand on a stick that one could insert into the experimental chamber in which the dog was housed in order to stroke the dog's head." The seriousness with which this suggestion was made, as well as the imagery it conjured up, gave me pause. One can only wonder how perplexed a dog would be if a "hand on a stick" quietly slipped into a room to stroke him on the head! In an attempt to reduce petting to its component parts, the human was immediately eliminated from the petting—a type of reductionism that, it seemed to me, eliminated the phenomenon.

Such ideas as "mechanical petters" are by no means restricted to a few graduate psychology students. Rather, they embrace what is in essence a spreading machine-oriented view of human relationships. Love and human companionship are now constantly equated with things, and an endless variety of commercial products promise relief from loneliness. For example, a recent television commercial for a particular brand of coffee depicted an attractive housewife who had recently moved into a new neighborhood and was desperately anxious to meet her new neighbors. Finally, someone rings her doorbell; it is the next door neighbor. Thank God she just happens to be brewing coffee, because if she were not, the neighbor just might go away and never come back. If coffee can help fill the void of loneliness, then why not buy it?*

The programming of "human concerns" as a legitimate scientific endeavor represents the central hope of all scientific-love-seekers. Thus we have seen the emergence of such oddities as "scientific institutes" designed to teach humans how to once again "get in touch" with one another. Rather than promising to deliver love through soaps, toothpastes, aspirins, or automobiles, or to alleviate loneliness through coffee, health tonics, or cigarettes, these institutes sell another product—"objective knowledge"—that can deliver love and cure loneliness.

The last two sentences in Desmond Morris's book *Intimate Behavior,* describe one aspect of this new development. He states:

> We laugh at educated adults who pay large sums to go and play childish games of touch and hug in scientific institutes, and we fail to see the signs. How much easier it would be if we could accept the fact that tender loving is not a weakly thing, only for infants and young lovers, if we could release our feelings, and indulge ourselves in an occasional and magical return to intimacy (pp. 243–244).

As Morris suggests, the signs are clear—loneliness is indigenous to our culture and growing numbers of people now seek out human

---

* It is interesting to note the extent to which commercial television also suggests the opposite point of view, that social interactions are usually very unpleasant experiences. Viewers are left convinced that the only thing that can protect them from other assaultive human beings is their particular product. Thus, if you invite people to your home, they will tell you your home has peculiar odors, your floor is yellow, your breath smells, your collar is dirty, or your underarms are offensive. You are left convinced that you are a living cesspool, and who needs other people to remind you of that fact! The message is clear . . . either buy the products or avoid other people!

intimacy in scientific institutes or at least turn to scientists (physicians, psychologists, psychiatrists, medical newspaper columns, etc.) for help in alleviating their loneliness. One can also readily agree with Morris that it is not at all humorous that adults play childish games of touch and hug. But it is surely an extraordinary sign of our times that adults feel the need to relieve their loneliness by going to *scientific* institutes, and that they should need scientists to legitimize human intimacy. Equally remarkable and ironic is the fact that scientific institutes feel they have the "scientific data" that legitimizes behavior like hugging.

Quite apart from this movement to get people literally to hug and touch, universities and scientific institutes all over the country are now engaged in an astounding variety of "group therapies," group encounters, nude marathons, sensitivity groups, family therapy, T groups, and so on—again, all designed to get people in touch with one another. It is almost as if we were trapped in some huge marketplace of loneliness, with a thousand hawkers selling different "scientific" remedies.

I do not mean to imply that these various psychotherapeutic techniques are no good, or that they do not help people. On the contrary, for many individuals these meetings and therapeutic encounters now provide an exclusive outlet for human relationships and emotional relief from a pervasive, overwhelming loneliness. The point is not whether these therapeutic encounters work, but rather *why* they work? Why are they needed on such a widespread scale? As implied earlier, at least part of the reason such encounters seem to provide relief is their constituents' belief that these groups are based on scientific principles. Few who attend such meetings would be willing to view them as some type of novel religious revival movement. Why they are needed on such a widespread scale also seems clear: the human spirit is in distress, and the more traditional methods for alleviating distress—including traditional medical approaches—do not seem viable for large numbers of people.

This brings us back to the distinction between the art and science of medicine, a distinction that has been largely blurred in the twentieth century. Science functions by being objective—that is, by putting physical distance between you as observer and the object you are trying to look at. For instance, in order for you to see an object in a microscope, there must be some distance between your eye and the object you are viewing, otherwise you could not see it. The object you view must be at some distance, be all alone, and be isolated. But such scientific ways of interacting with objects are diametrically opposed to the way human beings relate with each other, as Martin Buber, among many others, has pointed out.[4] Human relationships are *not* objective, and the very attempt to objectify them creates distance between you and those individuals with whom you are trying to relate. Those aspects of human relationships that can be weighed objectively are not the same as those aspects of human relationships that are experienced personally. This does not mean that one cannot *look* objectively at two people relating to one another and assess objectively various aspects of their relationship. Their hair color, dress, language, etc., etc., can all be objectively defined. What cannot be objectively defined, however, is the very process of communication, for objectively examining a conversation is diametrically opposite to engaging in one. To assess the process objectively, one must detach oneself from it.

The main dilemma confronting the scientific-love-seekers is that their belief system dictates that love either must be some *thing* or it cannot exist. This mentality leads to the belief that love can be synthesized in a test tube . . . one part handholding, two parts conversation, three parts sex, shake vigorously, and let stand for ten minutes—and presto, the distillate will be love! And if love cannot be produced with this formula, then other formulas can be tried. Perhaps love can be produced by Esalen weekends or transcendental meditation, or perhaps it exists in massage parlors, cruise ships, graduate schools, or various scientific institutes. Love must be tactile contact, or it must be some type of transactional *I'm O.K., You're O.K.* type of communication. Or it must be in group sex, or "open marriage," or in "primal screaming," or God knows where else. And all the while, the divorce rate continues to skyrocket, the number of people living alone rises rapidly, and the toll exacted in human disease and early death continues.

And yet, the growth in interpersonal chaos is having at least one beneficial effect. It is leading increasing numbers of scientists to understand why a purely objective approach toward human relationships is doomed to failure. Paradoxically, this message is coming from where you would least expect it. It is not generally coming from psychiatrists, psychologists, sociologists, anthropologists, or even theologians. Rather, it is coming from physicists, chemists, mathematicians, and molecular geneticists, for the most basic disciplines are beginning to acknowledge openly that love is neither an object nor a "thing." Indeed, variations on this theme have been expressed by many of the most eminent scientists of the twentieth century. For example, Max Born, in his autobiography *Physics in My Generation,*[5] described his youthful hope that a complete understanding of physics would help improve human relationships (the central dogma of every scientific-love-seeker), followed by his belated realization that such a belief was nothing more than self-deception:

In 1921 I believed . . . that science produced an objective knowledge of the world, which is governed by deterministic laws. The scientific method seemed to me superior to other, more subjective ways of forming a picture of the world—philosophy, poetry and religion; and I even thought the unambiguous language of science to be a step toward a better understanding between human beings.

[By the 1950s, however], I believed none of these things. The border between object and subject had been blurred, deterministic laws had been replaced by statistical ones. . . . I now regard my former beliefs in the superiority of science over other forms of human thought and behavior as a self-deception due to youthful enthusiasm (p. vii-1).

Writing on the same theme Erwin Schrödinger, the discoverer of wave mechanics, challenged the beliefs of the scientific-love-seekers in his book *Mind and Matter* [6] as follows:

Dear reader, or better still dear lady reader, recall the bright joyful eyes with which your child beams upon you when you bring him a new toy, and then let the physicist tell you that in reality nothing emerges from these eyes; in reality their only objectively detectable function is continually to be hit by and to receive light quanta. In reality! A strange reality! Something seems to be missing in it (p. 132).

It is difficult to believe that Born or Schrödinger would have taught that it is "biologically possible to teach people how to be happy and serene." And similar sentiments expressed by hundreds of eminent scientists could easily fill the remainder of this book.

This growing disparity between the beliefs of the scientific-love-seekers and the attitudes of our most eminent scientists has created a paradoxical situation: a majority of people are rushing in one direction to embrace the beliefs of early twentieth-century science, while many scientists of the late twentieth century are rushing in the opposite direction. Medicine—as an applied branch of science—is caught in the swirl. Medicine is in many ways still searching for absolute causes of physical illness. Only slowly is the idea of relativity creeping in; medicine is only just beginning to accept the idea that disease may have statistical rather than absolute causes.

And while medicine is slowly absorbing these changes, it is even more hesitatingly coming to grips with the revolutionary implications of Heisenberg's uncertainty principle,* which brought about the most dramatic shift in twentieth-century science. Heisenberg demonstrated that you could not look at any physical object without changing that object, that objects are changed by the very process of observation. He proposed that no complete description of any physical object was theoretically possible—certain aspects would always remain indeterminate, unknown, and unknowable.

Ironically, nineteenth-century physicians who relied on bed-

---

* In 1927, Heisenberg proposed a new way to describe the electron. He said that the electron was a particle, but a particle that only yields limited information. If you specify where the particle is at any given instant, you cannot determine its speed or its direction when it sets off. Or if, on the other hand, you insist on projecting the electron at a certain speed or in a certain direction, then its starting point and end point cannot be specified. The fact is that the information that the electron carries is limited in its totality—its speed and position fit together in such a fashion that they are constrained by the tolerance of the quantum. Jacob Bronowski called this profound idea "one of the great scientific ideas not only of the twentieth century, but of the history of science."

side manner to cure patients knew this principle implicitly, even though they may never have heard about electrons or atomic theory. They knew that their patients were changed—physically changed—by their bedside manner. This point has been demonstrated anew with twentieth-century technology in the heart rate responses of patients to even the simplest types of interactions. The doctor—the healer—changes his patient merely by being there.

Relationships that evolve over the years cannot suddenly be disrupted or destroyed without leaving the person physically changed. There is a gap—documented not only by the physicist, but more poignantly in the responses of terminal patients to simple human comfort—and the implications of this gap ought to be recognized. The point is that the restoration of a medicine that bridges the gap, a medicine which moves beyond science, is not an issue that finds support only among foggy-eyed romanticists but is also a proposal supported by modern physics. We do not live in a solitary or purely objective world, nor can we live in isolation . . . we must either learn to live together or increase our chances of dying prematurely.

Aristotle pointed out long ago that "a man wholly solitary would be either a God or a brute." There is a brutality in many modern human relationships that directly stems from their very objectivity and the pervasiveness of such relationships in our culture is an omnipresent testimony to our interpersonal brutality. A purely objective relationship between two human beings can be brutal precisely because it is detached from human feelings—it is a relationship that by definition creates distance, loneliness, and estrangement, and which can, at its worst, permit completely inhumane actions.

Medicine, as an adviser to our society, can help restore respect for the healing power of human companionship and can help people see that they too can prevent and cure loneliness-induced disease by simply caring for one another. But in order for medicine to accomplish this mission—to once again become an effective institution that uses both science and art to heal—the essential nonobjective nature of human relationships will have to be more openly recognized.

This is a far more difficult position to arrive at than it would at first appear. In many ways, this book embodies the dilemma. Study after study has been described in which the impact of various human interactions was objectively measured. And indeed, there is an urgent need to continue to evaluate objectively, scientifically—yes, even deterministically—the physical impact of human relationships, including the medical effects of bedside manner. But these studies must be conducted with an awareness that the phenomenon under objective scrutiny is a process that ultimately moves beyond science. Medicine—as physics learned earlier—must learn to live with such uncertainty. It must recognize that in the sphere of human relationships, healing will be brought about and health maintained in some ways that will always remain uncertain, because such healing will be accomplished by the observer's simply being there.

## CHAPTER 8

# Denying the Problem: Loneliness Traps

> And the Lord said, "It is not good that man should be alone. I will make him a helpmate for him."
> —Genesis 2:18

The return to a medicine—and a society—that once again recognizes the healing power of human contact will meet resistance from many sources in addition to those outlined in the last chapter. For the point of view about human relationships outlined in this book is, in some ways, a radical prescription for the maintenance of health. Traditional medical wisdom has viewed other humans largely as a primary source of communicable disease. Leprosy was controlled by ostracizing the afflicted from the community; the spread of smallpox and tuberculosis has been restricted through quarantine. In these and other cases, human contact has been considered a means of spreading disease and death. This ancient and time-honored attitude makes it difficult to accept the fact that human relationships also function in the opposite way to prevent disease and death.

But there is an even more basic reason why so many will find it hard to accept the prescription to nourish human relationships for the sake of one's health. The reality is that all relationships inevitably will be dissolved and broken. The ultimate price exacted for commitment to other human beings rests in the inescapable fact that loss and pain will be experienced when they are gone, even to the point of jeopardizing one's physical health. It is a toll that no one can escape, and a price that everyone will be forced to pay repeatedly. Like the rise and fall of the ocean tides, disruptions of human relationships occur at regular intervals throughout life, and include the loss of parents, death of a mate, divorce, marital separation, death of family members, children leaving home, death of close friends, change of neighborhoods, and loss of acquaintances by retirement from work. Infancy, adolescence, middle age, old age—all seasons of life involve human loss.

A prescription to nourish human companionship is, therefore, a unique type of health tonic. Part of the inescapable human dilemma is that the same companionship that keeps people healthy can also seriously threaten their health when it is taken away.

Unfortunately, in many cases, this unavoidable dissolution of all human bonds is further compounded by a new type of avoidable loneliness that dominates many people's lives. Many people unnecessarily spend their lives in social isolation or in disrupted relationships that could have been avoided. But, even here, it is obvious that marital disharmony, divorce, and social isolation existed long before our society began to accept the beliefs of the scientific-love-seekers. Cain committed fratricide long before anyone suggested that human love could be scientifically understood, and unfortunately the history of man's brutality to man has continued unabated ever since. Much social disharmony, moreover, emerges out of serious emotional upheaval that has little to do with an individual belief system. Some people simply cannot live together because they are emotionally disturbed. The schizophrenic's inability to get along with his mate, for example, is far less influenced by any subtle social philosophy than it is by the devastating effects of his own psychopathology. To suggest to people who are emotionally disturbed that they ought to get along with other human beings for the sake of their health is to offer advice that will ricochet off them more certainly than a bullet will deflect away from solid granite rock.

For many people who live alone, the sad reality is that they have already repeatedly tried to develop satisfactory human relationships without success; bland advice that they should seek to nourish companionship for the sake of their health may sound like a cruel joke. Many who experience the torment of loneliness believe that they have already done everything possible to find companionship; their past failures have bred a deeply rooted pessimism that blinds them to the reality that they are still desperately needed by others.

All of these dilemmas underline the complexity of the subject matter of this book. The causes of disease are complex; survival from disease is complex; the experience of human companionship, love, loneliness, and life and death are all complex. This complexity is further compounded by the fact that these experiences must be evaluated on both an individual and a cultural level. Everyone's early childhood experiences, his history of disease, his experiences with friendships and love, marriage, interpersonal difficulties, and losses—all are unique; and guidelines for nourishing human relationships for the sake of one's health must therefore be fashioned in terms of this unique history. And yet, at the same time, these guidelines must also be fashioned in terms of the society in which we all live.

The mortality statistics cited earlier are the sum total of a large number of individual life histories—statistics which were then grouped together under certain objective social categories. But obviously, each person's experience with a social situation like divorce is somewhat different. Some people quickly remarry, others are financially ruined, some find the separation an enormous emotional relief, while others become deeply embittered. Which of these reactions contributes most to increased mortality rates for divorcees is still far from clear. In light of this current lack of information and the diversity of reactions and adaptations to the same "objective situation"—in this case, divorce—it would be difficult to give specific advice without such counsel becoming a book in itself, and a rather tenuous one at that.

Similarly, it has been established that certain predictable psychological reactions occur after human loss—for example, depression—and that such emotional reactions are preceded and followed by well-known biochemical changes that could very well contribute to premature mortality. But in spite of the importance of this topic, this entire issue has been circumvented in this book.

The fact is that there are many books available on stress, anxiety, grief, and depression. Most of these books quickly trace these feelings back to interpersonal difficulties. Rather than repeat this clinical material, I have restricted myself to a discussion of the more general social context in which such individual emotional reactions occur. That does not mean that emotional reactions like anxiety or depression are any less important. Rather, it reflects my feeling that information and guidance are already available to individuals experiencing emotional upset because their human relationships have been disrupted.*

## THE NEW LONELINESS—A SOCIAL VACUUM

In the most general sense, neither the problem of human loneliness nor its cure is particularly new. Even Adam, wandering about as a solitary creature in the Garden of Eden, was not happy until he had "a companion in his own likeness." The Book of Life hardly begins before the Creator of Paradise states that "it is not good for man to be alone." Paradise itself was imperfect without companionship. Even God could not create a Paradise devoid of companionship.

Throughout the history of mankind, this point has been readily

---

* One other personal feeling has constrained me from giving clinical advice, and that is that our society is already saturated with such counsel. There are books on bereavement, divorce, being single, anxiety, depression, etc. Almost every major U.S. newspaper has a daily advice section for interpersonal difficulties. Sometimes, however, such advice can be used as a substitute for personal action. Many bereaved individuals or anxious divorcees do not need advice at all. What they need is human compassion, human friendship—they just need you to be there. Your counsel is often far less important than your mere presence.

acknowledged. Over the course of centuries a large number of elaborate rituals, cultural traditions, and religious ceremonies have been developed to provide generalized sources of human contact and friendship for the lonely and for those who have suffered human loss. These folk traditions have been a source of comfort for uncounted millions in the past. And yet, in spite of this long historical experience of dealing with loneliness, there are more and more people who no longer seem able to find companionship within our society.

As was mentioned in the last chapter, the toll of scientific objectivity on traditional institutions has been far greater than is at first apparent. Thus, in addition to eroding the healing role of religion, for example, the posture of pure objectivity also challenged its social role. By the mid-twentieth century, people had adopted such "purist" viewpoints toward institutions like religion that going to a church or temple for any reason other than worship was regarded as a vacuous or hypocritical gesture. "He's only going to church to fill his social needs" became a common form of condemnation. And so, the very important social function of religion—structuring a means for regular social contact—was obscured. If it did nothing else, formalized religious services did tend to get people together on a weekly basis, make them feel like they were part of a community, and reduce their loneliness.* Emerson knew this full well when he wrote in 1841, "How many we see in the street, or sit with in church, whom though silently, we warmly rejoice to be with! Read the language of these wandering eyebeams. The heart knoweth."

Religion is by no means the only institution that performs this

---

* It is of interest to note that Comstock and Patridge, in a detailed retrospective study in Maryland, found that men who were frequent attenders of religious services had a coronary mortality rate that was only 60 percent of those who rarely or never attended church.[1] In women, the rate was only 50 percent. In the same article, these authors cited the work of Shamgar and Medalie in Israel who reported similar findings. Comstock and Patridge also noted that they could find no support in their data for an alternative hypothesis that the beginnings of illness reduced the frequency of church attendance in those who died subsequently. [I should add that I am grateful to C. D. Jenkins, who called these intriguing data to my attention in his article published in the *New England Journal of Medicine* in 1976, entitled "Recent Evidence Supporting Psychologic and Social Risk Factors for Coronary Disease." [2]]

vital social function; every institution that gathers people together performs this service to some degree. This nonspecific but very real social role of many institutions ostensibly founded for other purposes should be recognized. For if social institutions are to be downgraded in importance or even eliminated, we must recognize that their disappearance will create a social vacuum that will not automatically be filled by the creation of new institutions. Social needs are diffuse and nonspecific, and can best be summarized as the desire simply to be with other people. The agenda of all groups, irrespective of their ostensible reasons for meeting together, includes the satisfaction of this need of people simply to be with one another.

Beyond its impact on traditional social institutions, the new objectivity toward emotion has led many people to adopt a peculiar attitude toward companionship and loneliness. Great value is placed on independence, individualism, and new-found freedom, and correspondingly less value is placed on dependency. To need someone else is viewed as a sign of weakness, a social sin. The "free spirit," it appears, should not relate with someone else out of necessity, but only out of choice. Those who lack companionship are inadvertently encouraged to suffer in silence or, in the most subtle manner, to give up their quest for human companionship, accept the status quo, and revel in their aloneness. To be unattached and independent of everyone else is, according to this definition, to be truly free, truly liberated. In this context, loneliness is currently being packaged in an entirely new way—as the price of freedom. A second implication also emerges quite forcefully: feelings of loneliness are a sign of weakness. If a person is truly independent, then he or she should be happy rather than suffer from loneliness. The new individualists should rejoice in the knowledge that they are unattached and "have come a long way, baby." * In many ways the situation is reminiscent of the "good thinking" of Newspeak in George Orwell's *1984*—only the lonely

* The irony of equating "progress" with cigarette smoking, as that particular slogan does, speaks for itself. It is, to use modern parlance, a complete "put-on."

are not the victims of a malevolent governmental propagandist but rather are the victims of their own penchant for self-deception.

Over the past few decades our society has refined a response to human loneliness that can be described as a "cultural pact of ignorance." This is a peculiar type of conspiracy in which some of the victims of loneliness are the perpetrators of their own suffering. The conspiracy involves a subtle denial of certain aspects of loneliness. As noted previously, many people recognize that loneliness exists in our society; certainly the scientific love-seekers sense this reality. And yet, in spite of all the talk about loneliness, the word "loneliness" often seems to be completely detached from feelings, and especially detached from the idea that it involves suffering. ("If you don't tell me you are suffering from loneliness, then I won't tell you I am suffering either.") With the meanings of words changed or impoverished, the impression is created that loneliness is no longer really an issue; no one is really suffering, everyone is liberated and free to do their own thing. Anyone who wants a "relationship" can have one, and that's cool; and anyone who wants to meditate alone can do so, and that's cool; in fact, everything is cool. Many lonely people do not appear to be lonely at all—they do not look like they are suffering—and so the truly lonely individual is forced to believe that he is the only one suffering and therefore shouldn't talk about it. We live in a society in which King Loneliness has no clothing, yet, because everyone believes he is the only one who feels lonely, we tell ourselves that loneliness must be a mirage.

Our common plight is that it is becoming increasingly difficult to share the most basic of all human truths: that people desperately need each other, that we really are dependent on one another. Instead, many people console themselves with clichés such as "I'm O.K. so you must be O.K.," while all the time they are not O.K. Feelings of isolation are massaged with slogans that only serve to make people all the more lonely. In a conspiracy of silence about their true loneliness, people deceive each other, and so make loneliness and isolation all the more prevalent. Some even go a step further and begin to kid themselves, telling themselves they are not lonely, that they are self-sufficient, that they don't need anyone. This constant indulgence in self-deception eventually makes it very difficult for them to recognize their own suffering.

Since loneliness that involves pain is denied cultural status, many people no longer feel a need to protect themselves from its ravages. Since our mass media now continually suggest that it is good to become independent of other humans, many enthusiastically try to construct a world free of the "tyranny" of human bonds. Just as the iron-lung machine was quickly discarded once polio was no longer considered a threat to health, so many people have discarded basic social supports that once provided companionship. As already stated, so many traditions, cultural practices, and beliefs that once provided relief from loneliness have been eroded in the past few decades that a person cannot assume that human companionship will be available when he needs it.

This means that the burden rests upon each individual to find the supports that will help him survive the cyclical disruptions of human bonds that are an inevitable part of life. While this advice appears to be bland enough, it is a sweeping mandate. It suggests that people consider their investments in human companionship as of even greater importance than their investments in other aspects of their lives. As this book has tried to document, human companionship is quite literally an important form of life insurance.

## LONELINESS TRAPS

What can individuals do to combat loneliness? Avoiding loneliness on an individual level within a society that fosters uprootedness, disconnectedness, alienation, and depersonalization is by no means an easy task. Decisions about moving, for example, are often brutally simple—either move or lose your job. In many facets of our lives, events seem to be out of control. Taking stock of one's current social network therefore requires some recognition of the relationship between alienation and loneliness and a rapidly changing society. Moreover, as we saw in the last chapter, certain rather abstract ideas about health and human relationships must be incorporated into medical practice before a significant shift can occur in society as a whole.

And yet there are decisions which people can make even now that are quite independent of such broadly based philosophical issues. There are steps that individuals can take to combat loneliness at the individual level.

Even in an idealized social utopia, every individual would most likely experience some type of loneliness during their lives. Thus, far more problematical than a person's initial experiences with loneliness is his response to it. Even in its milder forms, loneliness hurts. It creates an uncomfortable feeling from which people almost immediately try to escape. The problem is that loneliness can be like a spider's web; if a person struggles to escape, he may become all the more enmeshed, until he becomes so entangled that escape is impossible.

Many reactions to loneliness lead inexorably to greater isolation. As already described, one of the more pervasive loneliness traps is that woven by the scientific-love-seekers. Perhaps more than any other group, they appear to be actively battling against the lack of love in our society, and yet their struggle leads to more loneliness because they equate love with objects. They try to find love through the use of objectivity, an intellectual response that can only lead to greater isolation.

In a similar fashion, an elaborate loneliness trap has been woven by those who suggest that modern men and women should be totally self-sufficient and independent. Interpersonal freedom is the melody they play, and thousands now march in step behind them. These pipers trap people because they make them feel guilty for even admitting that they are lonely; they insinuate that it is a sign of weakness to admit publicly that a person really needs someone else.

The search for interpersonal freedom and the resultant loneliness appear in many forms. One of the more fashionable forms to emerge in the last decade is the "identity crisis," which involves "knowing who you are," "doing your own thing," and "doing it your way." The most important goal is to become a "real person," and this apparently is accomplished by becoming different from everyone else. Great fear is expressed at the thought of being only marginally different—the cleavage between the individual and everybody else must be sharp and total. The search for one's own identity cannot be found with somebody else; it is a private, solitary, and lonely struggle.

Where then can people seek their identities, if not with other people? That is the "crisis question," and many resolve it by equating their "identity" with their careers. Careers become the main objective, and everything else becomes secondary. One's spouse, family, friends, relaxation, aesthetic interests, all must play second fiddle to the pursuit of a successful career. In its most acute form, this process leads to the full-blown development of the "Type A" character described by Friedman and Rosenman. Driven and work-addicted, the Type A person often ends up in total social isolation—and dies of premature coronary disease.

There are, however, far more subtle loneliness traps in our society. Not every lonely person is trapped by interest in a career, pursuit of independence, or a love-seeking belief system. Many lonely people are not particularly "hung up" about these issues. Many readily admit that they would give anything if only they could find the "right person" with whom they could share their lives. And yet they still find themselves enmeshed in isolation.

Part of the problem is that we have very few formal institutions that deal specifically with problems of human loneliness. This is a particularly glaring weakness when one considers that there are formal institutions for practically every other human problem. Hospitals care for the sick, schools teach the uneducated, Alcoholics Anonymous treats the addicted, mastectomy and colostomy groups organize to discuss their physical problems, PTA groups meet to help the schools, and so forth. On closer examination, however, it becomes apparent that the great majority of these organizations have a major covert prerequisite. The person must either already have companionship or declare himself sick. These covert requirements make it difficult for those lacking companionship to find legitimate social outlets in existing groups.

For many lonely or isolated individuals, illness itself becomes the only legitimate method for gaining attention. Many lonely people experience very real secondary gains by getting ill: at least for a brief period during hospitalization they are flooded with the compassion provided by hospital staffs, nurses, and physicians who care for them, inadvertently providing something that is missing in their lives—human attention. The typical single, widowed, or divorced individual remains far longer in the hospital for the identical medical problems than do married people . . . and the cost for the acquisition of this secondary type of human companionship soars into uncounted billions of dollars in the United States alone. For example, when one examines data on average length of time individuals spend in short-stay hospitals* one can readily see that companionship is an important factor. The National Center for Health Statistics reported in 1972 that, when you average all persons at all ages over 17, for all types of physical illness, those that live alone spend on the average 13.5 days in a hospital, while the average married individual only spends 8.5 days in the hospital for similar illnesses.[3] In a similar fashion, the typical widowed, divorced, or separated person in the age range 45–64 visits a physician 5.9 times a year, while their married counterparts make 4.6 visits. These figures are even more surprising in light of the fact that almost 78 percent of married people have hospital insurance, while only 64 percent of single, 59 percent of divorced, 56 percent of widowed and 45 percent of separated people have such insurance.[4] It would seem that society could find less expensive ways for delivering human attention.

---

* A short-stay hospital is one in which the service provided by the hospital is general—for example, eye, ear, nose, throat, maternity. This term is used in distinction to long-term hospitals such as sanitoriums and mental hospitals, where as we have seen, the nonmarried are significantly over-represented.

Experience has shown that powerful therapeutic benefits flow from meetings in which humans band together to discuss common problems. Alcoholics Anonymous, for example, produces remarkable changes in individuals who can stand up among their fellow men and admit "I am an alcoholic." The public recognition and admission of the fact that they have a problem is one major aspect of their ability to battle that problem. So too with people suffering from obesity—again the recognition and admission of a problem to a group similarly afflicted helps reduce the feelings of guilt and shame, thereby producing secondary benefits in overcoming the problem. For decades radical breast surgery for cancer in women produced serious secondary psychological consequences. Women were ashamed of their condition, and they suffered alone, silently, often to the detriment of their physical health and the disruption and destruction of their marriages. Yet the process of banding together with others similarly afflicted has produced understanding and therapeutic gains in conquering this problem. Reach-to-Recovery is but one example of a group that helps patients recognize and publicly discuss the fact that there are serious psychological and social problems that surround cancer; with the help of these groups, many who previously would never have recovered from the effects of cancer are now able to rehabilitate their lives. All these groups work on the principle that before all else you must recognize that you have a problem, then *publicly* admit it, so that you can rid yourself of the hidden guilt and shame that often accompany such a problem.

One of the basic feelings that accompanies human loneliness is shame. Unlike some cancer patients, alcoholics, drug addicts, or obese individuals, lonely people often aggravate their condition by suffering alone. Rather than publicly meeting with others similarly afflicted, the lonely tend to shun each other. Seeing other people suffering from the same problem embarrasses the lonely all the more, making them feel all the more ashamed. These feelings lead to the most fundamental of all loneliness traps. The burden of loneliness is that feelings of shame lead the lonely not only to shun other people who are obviously lonely, but also to deny to themselves their own feelings.

This silence makes lonely individuals highly exploitable. Their sense of shame often leaves them with only two alternatives: either they must withdraw from society, or they must try to find companionship as quickly as possible. Both of these impulses can, in turn, lead to even larger traps of isolation. The loneliness trap of withdrawal is self-explanatory: it is a silent admission of total defeat and a reluctant resignation to the status quo, to a life devoid of human love.

The traps inherent in attempting to find human companionship as quickly as possible are less immediately apparent. Two traps are particularly difficult to avoid. The first is the trap of panic. Because of intense feelings of shame, anxiety, and pain, the person sets out immediately to find a mate with a single-mindedness that borders on an obsession. While such a strategy may produce a mate, all too often it also produces greater loneliness. One problem is that in the single-minded pursuit of a mate, other humans who could provide companionship and friendship are discarded.

Panic and retreat, at each end of a continuum of responses, define the extreme limits of the loneliness traps. By far the great majority of lonely people fall into a more subtle trap—they deny their own feelings of loneliness, they kid themselves. They do not permit themselves to become conscious of their own feelings, a denial for which, as we have seen, they find support in many aspects of our culture. Having denied their own loneliness, they are then driven to seek out alternatives to companionship.

The denial of dependence and of feelings of loneliness even lead some people to redefine many of the terms that describe aspects of intimate relationships. Some, for example, confuse sexual intercourse with companionship. So thoroughly confused have these notions become that the word love is now frequently used as a code word for sex. "Make love," "how's your love-life?", "do you have a lover?"—these phrases refer to activities that need not necessarily include love. While sexual pleasure can be a part of a love relationship, it is clear that sexual pleasure can be achieved without any "love," dialogue, or companionship. Prostitutes and gigolos are not the only ones who have demonstrated that fact. Drs. Masters and Johnson convincingly showed that the physiological response and subjective experience of sexual pleasure are similar in both men and women, irrespective of whether the orgasm is produced by masturbation or intercourse.[5] The investigators go even further and assert that in some cases, because of timing or emotional tension, the sexual pleasure and physiological reactions experienced through masturbation can be greater than those produced by intercourse. Clearly, human love involves much more than an orgasm. While this point may seem self-evident, one need only read any of a number of best sellers to realize that this point is not all that obvious to the culture at large.

The covert, nonspecific agenda of sexual intercourse—or for that matter, of any other human relationship—often involves more than sexual pleasure or sexual exploitation. One of the agendas is companionship—real, live, honest-to-goodness companionship. And often the agenda goes even beyond companionship to include something called love. The *Westworld* fantasy of the perfect computerized mistress ultimately leaves us cold: it is as unsatisfactory as the hand-on-a-stick petting machine for dogs. Vibrators, brothels, massage parlors, and masturbation all yield pleasure, but they do not provide love or companionship.

These loneliness traps by no means constitute an exhaustive list of all the major factors that contribute to human isolation in our society. But to list all the potential sources of loneliness is like listing all the dangers of life; it is impossible for the same reason it is impossible to predict all future dangers. But beyond that, a preoccupation with danger might prove to be the greatest danger of all, producing an individual with a warped sense of proportion, trapped in a self-fulfilling prophecy. Preoccuption with the dangers of loneliness may, in the long run, be just another loneliness trap.

Many people obviously are able to avoid loneliness traps even without realizing that such traps exist. Not everyone who lives alone hurdles inexorably into physical or emotional disaster. Not every divorcee, bereaved individual, or single person is lonely, nor do they all suffer from emotional or physical difficulties. Many lead rewarding and healthy lives, sustained and enriched by many friends and acquaintances. And, conversely, simply being married or physically living under the same roof with other human beings does not by itself guarantee human companionship or good health. Many married people are far more socially isolated and lonely than those who live alone. Physical living conditions do not seem to be the critical variables. Rather, it appears that the way a person responds and interacts with his fellow human beings is the crucial factor. Living together involves the process of dialogue.

# CHAPTER 9

# Life and the Dialogue

> However gratifying it is in later life to express thoughts and feelings to a congenial person, there remains an unsatisfied longing for an understanding without words.
>
> —Melanie Klein (1963)

It seemed all so familiar, and yet my feelings were so different. On the evening of a late winter's day in 1976, a 75-year-old man lay in bed in an intensive care unit with his wife standing quietly beside him, gently stroking his hand while the flash of each heartbeat on the nurses' central monitoring station traced out the fact that he had had a severe heart attack earlier that morning. His electrocardiogram was markedly abnormal; runs of arrhythmic heartbeats caused the warning red light to flash brightly but ominously on the monitor, while intravenous needles dripped fluid into both his arms in a frantic effort to stave off the inevitable. For several hours before his life ended my father knew he was going to die, and he had only one simple request—that his wife of almost 48 years, my mother, stay by his side.

The pain from a heart that sorely ached from lack of oxygen made it difficult for him to speak, but between them words were not necessary. She gently stroked his hand for hours as his body temperature slowly dropped, until late in the evening he died peacefully, ending a lifetime of exquisite dialogue. The grief etched in my mother's face was the price of a commitment that knew no limits.

The next time I entered a hospital room I was back at work at our University Medical School. The very first patient I saw was my coronary care nursing research assistant, who was sitting up in bed, tenderly holding her one-day-old son, her first child. She too was gently stroking a human being on the arm; he too could not speak, and between them words were equally unnecessary. The joy, pride, and peace that caused her to sparkle marked the beginning of a life of dialogue that also would know no limits.

Within a brief period I had come full circle, first witnessing the death of a person loved deeply, then witnessing life renewed. Common to both was human love, and in both cases its expression did not need spoken words. The essence of both of these encounters was dialogue, nonverbal dialogue—communication between those who are alive and in love.

Staring at the lifeless body of my father in that hospital bed, I knew what had been lost. No longer could we verbally communicate with each other; our physical dialogue had come to an end. Between the mother and child it was also clear what had been born—a dialogue of love between two living persons.

This book has ranged over a large number of social situations that influence the heart. From the quiet comforting of a dying person to the cuddling of an infant—in our earliest years, in adulthood, whether single, widowed, divorced, or married, whether neurotic, schizophrenic, or normal, whether human or animal—one factor unites all of us, and that is dialogue. Dialogue is the essential element of every social interaction, it is the elixir of life. The wasting away of children, the broken hearts of adults, the proportionately higher death rates of single, widowed, and divorced individuals—common to all these situations, I believe, is a breakdown in dialogue. The elixir of life somehow dries up, and without it people begin to wither away and die. Those who lack the dialogue early in life can perish quickly, while those who lose it as children, adolescents, or adults feel acutely what they have lost and struggle to get it back.

However, identifying dialogue as an elixir that sustains our lives creates its own special problems, not the least of which is defining just what this process is. In addition, the labeling of dialogue as the common denominator of all human interactions reminds us how many issues raised in this book still remain unsettled.

Recall the research of Dr. Harry Harlow, described in an earlier chapter. In much the same way that children were once treated in orphanages, hospitals, and foundling homes, he separated infant monkeys from their mothers at birth, raised them in social isolation, but carefully tended to every physical need except their need for other living creatures. And yet, in spite of the physical care, they became profoundly disturbed; they cried, they fought, and they eventually became severely depressed. They spent a good deal of their infancy clinging to soft terry-cloth surrogate mothers, as if they were hanging on for dear life. Witnessing the destruction of these motherless monkeys, Dr. Harlow began to speak and write about the biological need for love in infant monkeys, an idea that did not endear him to a certain U.S. congressional committee, which demanded to know what type of ridiculous nonsense was being studied at the University of Wisconsin under the aegis of federally financed research grants.*

Dr. Rene Spitz,† who had spent a lifetime trying to improve the care of children wasting away from lack of human contact in foundling homes, immediately saw the importance of this work and how it related to his own clinical observations. He suggested that what had disturbed these infant monkeys was not specifically the lack of love, as Dr. Harlow had suggested, but rather the lack of something he called "dialogue." Surrogate mothers, whether wire or terry cloth, could not react or respond to the infant monkeys. When the infant cried there was no response from the surrogate; when the infant clung, the surrogate did not cling back; the black, lifeless, buttonhole eyes of the surrogate mother never changed, never responded, and so the infant monkeys were trapped in an overwhelming isolation that ultimately destroyed them.[1]

---

* Darwin notwithstanding, a great deal of residual resistance still obviously existed in the halls of Congress toward the idea that animals have emotions similar to humans.

† The title of this chapter was first used by Dr. Spitz in an article published in 1963 in which he examined the implications of Dr. Harlow's research and his own clinical observations.

The distinction between love and dialogue that emerged from these studies is one that is crucial to this book. For it was clear to Spitz that what destroyed the health of Harlow's infant monkeys was not solely the lack of love, but rather the total lack of *any* response, not just from mothers but from *any* living creature. While one type of response from a living monkey mother might have been love, other types of responses would also have occurred. Joy, pleasure, displeasure, irritation, fatigue, anger—live mothers (animal or human) have a wide range, perhaps even an infinite variety of responses, and these are all part of the dialogue.

The title of this chapter was meant to emphasize the belief that our health and our lives depend on dialogue in general and not exclusively on a dialogue of love. An individual may lack a dialogue of love and still remain relatively healthy as long as other forms of human dialogue are maintained and the individual does not become socially isolated.* What emerges from all the clinical cases and statistics described in this book is a picture of dialogue as a continuum that stretches from total social isolation at one extreme to a life totally saturated with love at the other. In between are an infinite variety of dialogues that vary in quantity, quality, intensity, and duration, all linked to our physical health in a fashion that ranges from the least to the most conducive.

In its most general meaning, dialogue consists of reciprocal communication between two or more living creatures. It involves the sharing of thoughts, physical sensations, ideas, ideals, hopes, and feelings. In sum, dialogue involves the reciprocal sharing of any and all life experiences.

As a definition, the idea of reciprocal sharing, responding to or communicating with other living creatures, sounds innocent enough. But as already suggested in Chapter 7, the process ultimately goes beyond anything that can be measured with scientific

---

* In what would perhaps be an extreme extension of this position, I would go so far as to suggest that married couples who live together in "bonds of hatred" may be physically healthier than those who live together like surrogate monkeys, without any dialogue. The total lack of dialogue between a couple "living together" may be the ultimate form of hatred.

instruments. In fact, descriptions of this process can be traced all the way back to ancient Greek philosophy.

The notion that loneliness involves the lack of dialogue did not originate in the work of Rene Spitz or Harry Harlow. The very word was first used by Plato in the *Dialogues*, written records of the conversations of his teacher Socrates. Nor was the word *dialogos* chosen by Plato at random; instead, it was the core idea of a philosophy that helped shape Western civilization. Bertrand Russell noted that from the very beginning the Greeks' *logos* was a bridge linking philosophic discourse (the word) and scientific inquiry (the measure). Plato's *logos* was a given, a necessary prerequisite for orderly philosophic and scientific discourse.[2]

It is important to add that while Plato recognized that loneliness was the end result of the lack of dialogue, he added an important dimension to the concept. He proposed that real dialogue was a *process* and not a *thing*. In a sense the same point was exacted in a painful way from Harlow's motherless monkeys—a material mother substitute destroyed their health. The profoundly depressed children that Spitz watched withering away and dying were also tragic examples of the same principle: physical care, material care, was not sufficient to keep them alive. The broken hearts of the bereaved and the terrible agony of loneliness, as well as the mortality data that fill this book, give ample testimony to this same point. No material substitute—no simple *thing*—can fill the human need for dialogue.

Other characteristics of the process of dialogue are that it is reciprocal, spontaneous, often nonverbal, *and* alive. These characteristics explain why dialogue cannot be packaged, codified, or described by a neat set of rules, laws, or classifications. If, for example, you accept the proposition that dialogue is a spontaneous process, something that is continually changing so that it cannot be fixed in time or predicted, then it becomes apparent that dialogue could never be "captured" in a microscope or quantified on a scale, for that would destroy its spontaneity. Trying to objectify dialogue in order to examine it would destroy the process.

These characteristics of dialogue also explain why we cannot raise children with surrogate (lifeless) parents, or satisfy each other as adults with material substitutes for dialogue. Toys and teddy bears, blue blankets and rotary wheels, television and tape recorders, these can never be adequate substitutes for the dialogue that we need. When a child "goos" or smiles, it is vitally important that someone else—someone alive—say "ga" or smile back. *Someone must respond.* These responses cannot be programmed. Since no one can predict when a child will "goo" or smile, someone simply has to be there, ready to respond appropriately. Someone has to care.

The Bell System notwithstanding, even devices such as the telephone will never quite be "the next best thing to being there," because most of the dialogue of life is nonverbal. Since the process is not exclusively in you or in the other person, but rather between people as a reciprocal, spontaneous, and mutually flowing process, deviousness, fraud, or artificiality will only cause static that will disrupt dialogue. While we are alive, therefore, what we have to give to each other is at one and the same time the simplest yet most sublime gift—ourselves. Material substitutes like cars and diamonds are in the end only surrogates that cannot sustain us. Even objective knowledge by itself is a lifeless surrogate that only has meaning in human dialogue.

As already emphasized there are no specific potions or magical formulas that can help an individual achieve dialogue with other people, any more than there are serums that will create love. Dialogues such as love are processes that move beyond and outside the realm of science. Knowledge about dialogue is, by itself, no guarantee that a person will be able to communicate with others or help them out of their loneliness. Indeed, knowledge about dialogue may even keep people at a distance. What often are sold in our society as guidelines for communication—rules on how you should engage your friends, how you should act toward your lover, or how you should speak to your child—seem to be the very way to disrupt dialogue. Many of the cookbook-objective rules instructing people on how to communicate with one another only seem to serve to keep people all the more isolated and lonely. The child at the mother's breast contains all the elements of perfect dialogue, and neither the mother nor the child have to work to achieve this reciprocal relationship.

This does not mean that dialogue always flows naturally. One cannot be oblivious to the fact that there are children who are battered and abandoned, and clearly many human relationships are far from perfect. Mortality statistics also bear mute testimony to the fact that dialogue is a process that can be lost. What it does mean, however, is that knowledge about dialogue can only be usefully employed when the inherent limitations of objective solutions are recognized and other, frankly nonscientific approaches are appreciated.

The scientific approach to disease specifies that if certain life situations such as divorce increase one's chances of developing coronary heart disease, then aspects of these situations which contribute to the problem ought to be identified and individuals "immunized" or prepared to take some sort of remedial action to protect their health. On the surface, this is an eminently reasonable (rational) approach that offers great hope. But what if some of the aspects of divorce or social isolation that lead to increased coronary heart disease cannot be measured? What if one of the problems is ultimately lack of love, lack of dialogue?

To assert that there are unmeasurable aspects of human relationships which affect our health is a very uncomfortable position for any scientist to assume; it suggests an endorsement of irrationalism, mysticism, or, even worse, of witchcraft and voodoo. And yet, the issue itself needs to be faced. Dialogue does involve a process that cannot be totally measured with scientific instruments. Such an acknowledgement need not be particularly startling or controversial. The fact is that many, if not most, scientists could readily agree with it. This was, after all, Schrödinger's point when he said that the gleam in a young child's eyes involved more than light quanta. Schrödinger clearly was not suggesting that physics be abandoned, any more than Charles Darwin or Walter Cannon proposed abandoning the study of emotions because the topic was hopelessly bogged down in phenomena that could not be measured.

On the contrary, their attempts to define the limits of their sciences served to guide the way in which they conducted their research and applied it to everyday life situations. Similarly, admitting that human relationships may involve nonmeasurable processes does not mean that one should abandon further scientific study. Nor does it mean that advice cannot be given or that people cannot be helped. It is, instead, a call for a return to a more balanced view that recognizes both what can be and what cannot be known scientifically about human relationships.

The need for such a balanced view seems self-evident. When we look into the eyes of another human being we are not just looking at the flashing lights of another fancy computer; people are not programmed robots. Discussing this problem in *Man on His Nature*,[3] Sir Charles Sherrington, one of the brilliant neurophysiologists of the twentieth century, commented that "a purely reflex pet would please little even the fondest of us; indeed the fondest least" (p. 199). Human relationships are no different. No one wants another human being to be totally predictable, totally programmed, any more than we would buy a dog or cat that was totally programmed. The joy, beauty, and power of human relationships reside precisely in the fact that the process is unique. And dialogue is the process that differentiates us from robots and programmed machines.

## INTERRUPTIONS IN THE DIALOGUE

But the dialogue is also fragile. As we saw earlier, interruptions in human dialogue can range all the way from very brief absences from loved ones to the permanent loss of dialogue through death. Holmes and Rahe's Life Change Index, for example, provided one yardstick for measuring the relative impact of interruptions and disruptions in human dialogue. By monitoring the occurrence of disease and even the occurrence of death, these investigators were able to weigh numerically the effects of the death of a spouse, separation, divorce, death of a close family member, children leaving home, and death of a close friend. All of these disruptions were followed by significant increases in disease and death. These statistical relationships between human loss, disease, and death suggest that those who experience interruptions and disruptions in the dialogue of life need help and support. While it is true that only individuals can love and participate in dialogue, such interactions, like chemical reactions, need the proper social milieu in order to flourish.

Thus, an individual's grief, insecure ego, inability to love, shattered dialogue, or entanglement in loneliness traps is also a collective problem for society. If children lose their parents or are abused, neglected, or abandoned by their parents, it seems obvious that someone else must help them. It is generally recognized that children need love, and if they do not receive it from their biological parents, society has an obligation to help them. The debate here centers on how such love can be effectively provided. Similarly, when adults suffer from interruptions in the dialogue of life—when they are bereaved, experiencing divorce or separation, living alone or lonely—they too need help, and it is in society's collective interest to provide it. The problem, then, is how?

First, though the emphasis in these final chapters has been on the limits of science, objective data about human dialogue are obviously useful. Psychiatrists, psychologists, social workers, and other health professionals *do* know a great deal about bereavement and loss, and they are on the whole quite cognizant of the physical and emotional impact of disruptions in dialogue. An entire new discipline called *crisis intervention* has developed within the past decade specifically designed to begin immediately helping those experiencing interruptions in the dialogue.

These professional groups are performing a vital, and in many cases, absolutely essential, service. What is at issue here is the usefulness of an *exclusively* objective approach to aiding people in trouble. Ironically, the most problematic aspect of these professional efforts is that they now seem to be so necessary. They seem to be filling a void that is constantly growing. One is left to conclude that either people who suffered interruptions of dialogue a few decades ago were not cared for properly, or that the sources of support that once existed have now been eroded and are no longer viewed by society as particularly helpful.

It is my opinion that in much same way that medicine slowly abandoned its appreciation for the healing role of bedside manner, society has abandoned its appreciation for the healing capacity of human contact. Emotional support that once came from families, neighbors, friends, ministers, rabbis, and priests is now purchased from psychiatrists, psychologists, and various social service agencies. While delivering needed support to people, these professional helping groups have also tended to usurp our functions and relieve us of our sense of personal responsibility.

Understanding the nature of human dialogue and the degree to which an individual's very existence is sustained by other human beings helps explain why the loss of a loved one or the lack of love can be so devastating. It also suggests why those who are suffering interruptions in the dialogue are often avoided. To engage a bereaved person in dialogue means sharing his or her pain. What emerges from the eyes of a bereaved individual is grief, what emerges from the eyes of those recently divorced is anxiety; what emerges from the eyes of those who live alone is loneliness; what emerges from the eyes of the unloved adolescent is frightened anger. These people all need to share these painful aspects of their lives through dialogue. The dialogue of pain, anxiety, anger, and loneliness is also part of life, but it is a dialogue that can be both frightening and painful. How convenient to label these as scientific-medical problems and therefore have others look into their eyes.

## DETERIORATION OF DIALOGUE

Although interruptions in human dialogue may be very painful, at least they are clear-cut. Individuals may suffer acutely when they lose a loved one, but they usually realize they are suffering, and they know why. The vital force missing in their lives is recognized and acknowledged. There is, however, another dimension to human dialogue that is far more subtle and often quite difficult to recognize. For if dialogue can grow, it can also deteriorate, slowly and subtly, to the point where an individual can be trapped in a totally impoverished relationship without even being able to recognize what happened or why. The process is very similar to the way the body grows and ages, on a day-to-day basis, without any visible change. The very fact that a person can tolerate deteriorated dialogue and sometimes even encourage it is something that we would often prefer to deny, for reflecting on the implications is not pleasant. Since dialogue involves reciprocal sharing with other human beings, its deterioration must also be reciprocal, and each person must share part of the responsibility. An individual can only receive to the extent that he gives, and, in that sense, dialogue is a mirror of his personality.

This idea is neither particularly new nor radical. Psychoanalysts spend years in personal analysis trying to understand their own personalities, because they recognize that if they are not aware of their own anxieties, then their own insecurities will block them from listening to their patients. In the dialogue of psychotherapy the patient can only communicate those thoughts and feelings that the therapist is willing to share, and this reciprocity can be burdensome, anxiety provoking, depressing, or exhilarating. The psychoanalyst tries not to indulge in the delusion that all the difficulties in psychotherapy arise from the fact that the patient has problems. If the patient flees from the therapy or terminates the therapeutic dialogue prematurely, psychotherapists reflexively begin to search for their own unconscious contributions to this disruption.

A similar situation exists in all human relationships. Take, for example, the erosion and dissolution that occurs in so many marriages. Problems seldom emerge unilaterally from the behavior of only one of the partners; usually both contribute to the deterioration. This is not a particularly easy idea to accept, especially for those who have gone through the trauma of divorce, for it is always easier psychologically to blame the other person for problems than to search for one's own contributions.

Understanding the life-threatening nature of the lack of dialogue makes it easier to comprehend the radical, often violent manner in which many people flee from situations of deteriorated dialogue. Sometimes individuals who have been married for years suddenly up and leave without warning, to live with another person. Frequently they leave at great personal cost. They may be drained financially; often they are cut off from their own children and their social circle; their careers are placed in jeopardy and sometimes ruined; material possessions that they slaved for years to acquire are quickly cast aside. At the same time, the person left behind is often totally shocked, left with a profound sense of rejection, resentment, or even hatred. Crushed beyond the point of recovery, the abandoned mate may even die. We have encountered such people in earlier chapters.

In the most ironic fashion, marital separation and divorce stand as mute testimonials to the Platonic idea of the nonmaterial nature of human dialogue. Few individuals who leave their mates ever gain materially from the separation. Why then do they leave? What are they escaping from? What are they searching for? What do they hope to get in return? Why do people who have comfortable material existences and physically stable environments suddenly abandon it all? It seems that what they sense is that they are being slowly choked to death in their current environment, that their very existence is being threatened. Dialogue has deteriorated below a certain critical threshold, until one of the partners can no longer tolerate the isolation.

If only he left because of money, sex, or emotional disturbance, then the one mate's flight might not be so crushing to the one left behind. If it were only some-*thing* that caused him to leave, then it all would be easier to accept emotionally. But usually it isn't some-*thing* that causes the disruption—it is some-*one*. Both individuals contribute to the breakdown in dialogue, and no idea can be more painful than that, no idea can be more threatening. Divorce is a

major life-threatening event not just because a couple's children
may be emotionally and possibly physically harmed, their financial
position eroded, their house jeopardized, their social circle shattered. No, the central threat is to the individual's very existence, his
humanity. In divorce the individual is rejected and left to feel like a
profound failure. Life is dialogue, and in divorce that idea crashes
over the individual like a tidal wave. It is a major threat to life, as
is readily verified in health statistics.

Although the vast majority of divorces occur within the first five
years of marriage, very few occur immediately. More typically the
relationship erodes slowly over a period of time, an insidious process that only gradually leads to the termination of all dialogue.
While the deterioration can be precipitated by any of a large
number of factors, usually the psychological state of anxiety pervades the entire period of erosion. The dialogue becomes a mutual
struggle, not unlike the struggle between a psychotherapist and
patient, in which a significant degree of growth occurs only when
both individuals become aware of their anxieties.

There is a widespread illusion that "good" dialogue must always
be pleasant, that you must make the other person feel good. In its
most innocent form, this attitude is reflected in the behavior of adolescents, who always try to "look good" and "act well" around
their boyfriends or girlfriends. The "ugly side" that the adolescent
may recognize as part of his personality is revealed only to his parents, mainly because he feels secure that his parents will still love
him despite these problems. The "uglier" or "bad" sides are aspects
of the adolescent's personality that he himself does not particularly
like, and he fears that if he publicly revealed these negative aspects
of his personality to others, he would be rejected. Consciously putting your best foot forward, always looking good, is an essentially
adolescent attitude, yet many adults enter marriage with these adolescent notions about dialogue.

This human tendency has led many people to believe that trial
periods of living together before marriage would be preferable to a
lifelong commitment to another individual about whom so little is
known. In a sense, this situation seems to support the position of

the scientific-love-seekers, who argue that test periods or experiments in living together would help prevent many of the marriages that end so disastrously for the couples and children involved.

Considering the enormous pain and trauma of divorce and situations of deteriorated dialogue, any proposal that offers the hope of reducing their prevalence holds great appeal, especially for people who "want to avoid the mistakes their parents made in getting married." Unfortunately, this problem cannot be solved merely by living under the same roof or in the same bed with someone else for a trial period. A total commitment with no preconditions cannot be simulated by a test period with such preconditions. This does not mean that marriage relationships are always necessarily "better" in terms of human dialogue than those of couples who just live together without any formalized commitments. Clearly, many informal relationships develop spectacularly, while over 1 million formalized marriages in the United States ended in divorce in 1975 alone. What is medically important is the *way* we live together—the dialogue. The very idea that there are no cookbook rules for human dialogue precludes the establishment of an "ideal" objective condition in which human dialogue can flourish. The issue boils down to one of premises about human relationships and what it is about their context that allows dialogue to develop.

The only major precondition for dialogue is trust. If trust exists between two people, then dialogue will naturally develop. Melanie Klein emphasized the fundamental nature of trust when she stated that the need to establish nonverbal dialogue, the need to pursue understanding without words, exists in all of us. This pursuit she traces back to the relationship a child establishes with its mother.[4] She points out that it is one of absolute trust, unimpeded by language. As we mature, language becomes part of our repertoire, but the essential core of all dialogue—as was poignantly observed in the coronary care unit—remains nonverbal in character.

Trust between two people is a gradually emerging process that involves ever greater degrees of commitment. All dialogue involves commitment to a contract that is both implicitly understood and explicitly documented. Regardless of whether the contract is "until death do us part" or for a two-year trial period—"let's live together and see what happens" or "let's be friends"—both the explicit and implicit aspects of the contract modulate the level of trust and consequently the nature of the dialogue. A lifelong commitment to another person, while no guarantee that dialogue will flourish, at least provides the framework in which trust can grow. Since the commitment is more total than that of a mere trial period, each individual is psychologically free to make mistakes and still feel assured that the dialogue will not be lost.

In addition to degree of commitment, predictability is one of the core aspects of the growth in trust. If either person becomes unpredictable in areas of behavior crucial to the other person, then trust is placed in jeopardy. This can happen if both components of the contract, the implicit commitments and the explicit commitments, are not adhered to. Generally in human relationships it is the violation of implicit commitments that leads to a deterioration of dialogue.

It is often mistakenly assumed in human relationships that the contracts made with other people are completely explicit. This is perhaps the central error of the scientific-love-seekers, who assume that in trial periods of living together all the commitments that people make to each other can be spelled out in a totally rational manner. But as any lawyer, physician, psychiatrist, or psychologist realizes, even in the most clear-cut types of human interactions, there are implicit commitments struck between the consenting parties which the parties themselves may not even be aware of. The fact is that even in the most explicit dialogue there are still many hidden assumptions.

Marriage is without doubt the single most important contract involving the greatest number of implicit commitments. In marriage the commitment to dialogue is generally regarded as total—for better or for worse—and for life. While the explicit commitment is indeed total, there are also a host of implicit assumptions that give marriage its special meaning. These commitments are modulated by trust, which grows as the dialogue grows. Trust sets the tone for all marital dialogue—trust in yourself as well as trust in the other person. The question is frequently raised about extramarital sexual affairs: What is wrong with "open sex in marriage," what is wrong with one simple interlude, one little affair of intercourse with someone other than a marital partner? Setting aside any discussion of morality here, if the implicit and explicit commitments to marital dialogue involve the promise to be sexually faithful to one another, then intercourse with another person is a breach of those commitments. After the breach a person is left with several choices. One strategy is to cover up the violation. This strategy may even be buttressed by the unfaithful partner's feeling that the mate would not understand, or better yet, that the mate would be hurt if he or she found out. The only problem with this strategy is that the commitment to total trust and complete predictability is shattered, and from then on the individual is forced to live with a secret that must be kept from the other person. With remarkable frequency, this strategy does not work, in spite of all the best efforts to conceal the episode, for the entire matter is communicated nonverbally. Not infrequently the act of infidelity is quickly found out by the mate, who, rather than challenge the integrity of their marriage, keeps all suspicions inside. This becomes a kind of tragic game—"If you won't tell me, then I won't ask"—and the victim is the dialogue. Given these new commitments to mutual deception, a kind of pact of ignorance, the dialogue deteriorates.

An alternative strategy is to "confess" and own up to the act of infidelity. This strategy is also fraught with emotional difficulties that are hard to predict. The person may be seriously wounded; even if he or she quickly forgives the act, rejecting the other person might be the subconscious response. The injured partner might consciously or, even worse, unconsciously recognize that the other person's total commitments are not in fact total, an idea that will prompt a reciprocal withdrawal from total commitment. An insidious and vague type of distrust begins to grow between the couple. Once again, the victim is the dialogue.

A third option is to use the episode constructively, perhaps to help put each other in touch with needs that they did not realize existed, perhaps to know themselves better and move on to more intimate levels of dialogue. This *is* an option, but it is the one least likely to happen, since it demands the greatest degree of emotional stability and maturity from both partners.

Extramarital sexual affairs involve issues that go to the very heart of human dialogue. The casual manner in which such issues are discussed in the press and popular books suggests that the nature of human dialogue is not particularly well understood. Extramarital affairs involve highly volatile emotional issues that cannot be brushed aside lightly or dismissed by logical arguments. Rational agreements between couples that marital swinging, group sex, or an orgiastic rumpus are all O.K. and quite independent of their total commitment to dialogue, or that these activities may even lead to greater openness of marital dialogue ignore the fact that more than rational activities are involved. While both partners may agree rationally, one has to wonder what happens to the irrational-emotional commitments implicitly assumed by both?

Dialogue is the elixir of life; without it we cannot survive. And yet, we still seem to know so little about it, and so little about the relationship between the dialogue, love, human companionship, and health. What about divorced individuals who remarry? Is their health affected by the first divorce, or is it improved by the second marriage? What about people who live together but who do not marry? Are their health and longevity affected by this particular choice of life-style? What about the future health of children whose parents divorce and then remarry? What will be the future health of children raised in single-parent households? Are children more vulnerable to the lack of dialogue at certain critical periods in their lives? What about people who live alone—people who never marry but lead full and active lives—or people who adjust to the loss of their mates and lead healthy and full lives? How do they manage to survive life stresses that seem to overwhelm so many other people?

Questions like these come in a flood. They fill this book, and they cry out for answers we do not have. We have spent most of the twentieth century searching for the causes of disease and death everywhere but we have not explored the question of the way we live together. I hope this book will help stimulate a scientific examination of the health implications of human companionship. Perhaps we shall be able to learn why people die so readily when they are lonely and isolated, and then find means to prevent such losses. Beyond that, this book would have no better fate than to help at least a few additional people to live together in love.

Examining the nature of living together, understanding the nature of human dialogue, and blending a scientific understanding of human companionship within a philosophical framework that will allow us to appreciate its complexity will not be an easy matter. Dialogue is a dynamic, ever-changing force. To repeat a point made earlier, like the billions of snowflakes that fall in a winter storm, no two human dialogues are the same. No two marriages are exactly alike; nor can divorce, widowhood, and being single be considered precisely quantifiable conditions . . . they vary as much as marriages do. Many married people live in a state of complete psychological and physical divorce, while the lives of some divorcees, widows, and single people are filled with satisfying, loving human relationships. Some children whose early lives are devoid of love are nevertheless able to establish loving relationships as adults, while others whose early lives were saturated with love lead isolated and lonely adult lives.

On the surface, the incredibly varied ways people can live together might seem to make the task of understanding the precise connections between living together and health totally hopeless. And yet, this flux of human dialogue is the very reason why the mortality statistics presented in this book are so impressive. Given the multifaceted character of dialogue, it would have been easy to obscure the obvious. And yet, in spite of all the potential factors that could have hidden the connection between living together and health, the data presented here stand as a mute testimonial to its power. The facts emerge, indeed they leap out, in spite of the variance.

Once again, the choice is ours to make. We must either live together or face the possibility of prematurely dying alone. Life and dialogue are one and the same.

# The Heart:
# Its Function
# and Malfunction

While a great deal of controversy still surrounds the question of what causes heart disease, there is general agreement on how the healthy heart functions. In order to understand the suggestion that human companionship can alter the course of heart disease, some knowledge of the heart and its circulation is necessary. The heart is a highly specialized muscle that functions to pump blood constantly to the body. In the adult, the heart is slightly larger than a clenched fist. It is located in the center of the chest, angled slightly from right to left, with the lower margin pointing to the left. The heart is encased in a membrane called the pericardium, which allows the heart to move freely while maintaining the same relative position in the chest.

The walls of the heart are made up of a muscle, the myocardium, that varies in thickness in different regions of the heart. The heart contains four chambers, two on the right and two on the left. The two top chambers are called the right and left atria (receiving chambers), while the two bottom chambers are called the right and left ventricles (pumping chambers). The right and left sides of the heart are separated by a partition called the septum, effectively creating two separate pumps within the heart. The atria are separated from the ventricles by one-way valves which effectively keep blood flowing in one direction.

On each side of the heart, the blood flows from the upper chamber (the atria) to the lower chambers (the ventricles). The valves open when the blood is flowing from the atria to the ventricles, and then these valves close again. Blood continuously fills both sides of the heart. The blood that fills the right atrium is returning from various parts of the body. It is dark and bluish in color because it has exchanged its oxygen for carbon dioxide with all the cells in the body. From the right atrium the blood then flows to the right ventricle, which in turn pumps the blood to the lungs through the pulmonary artery in order to get a fresh supply of oxygen. The oxygenated blood (now brightly red in color) then returns from the lungs to the left atrium through the pulmonary vein. It then goes to the left ventricle, where it is pumped to the entire body. The blood returns through the veins to the right atrium, to repeat the entire trip again. The normal adult heart pumps approximately five quarts of blood in a single minute, 75 gallons in one hour. During the average day, the heart pumps approximately 70 barrels of blood; and during the average normal human life span, about 70 years, the heart will pump 1.8 million barrels of blood throughout the body.

Since the right ventricle is pumping blood to the lungs while the left ventricle pumps blood out to the body, it is easy to see why the health of the lungs and the health of the entire body figure prominently in the health of the heart. If the lungs are damaged, then the heart must begin to work increasingly harder to push the blood through the respiratory system, an effort that gradually takes its toll on the efficiency of the heart as a whole. Since the left ventricle pumps blood to the entire body, it is, of necessity, the strongest part of the heart, and indeed the myocardium (heart muscle) of the left ventricle is the thickest portion of the heart. If an individual is overweight, then the heart must begin working harder to push the blood through the added tissues, an effort that can again take its toll on the efficiency of the cardiac system.

The blood flows through literally mile upon mile of blood vessels in an unending system called circulation. Blood vessels are hollow tubes that are normally both soft and elastic. They can stretch, contract, expand, and adjust in a number of ways to allow more or less blood to flow through them. There are three main types of blood vessels: arteries, veins, and capillaries. Blood flows away from the heart in very large arteries, which then branch into ever smaller arteries. From the smallest arteries the blood then flows into tiny capillaries which connect the smallest arteries to the smallest veins. The veins then bring the blood back to the heart for additional oxygen. The capillary walls are so thin that food and oxygen pass through them to all the surrounding cells, in effect allowing these cells to perform work. At the same time, the various waste products of the cells, as well as carbon dioxide, move into the capillaries, mix with the blood, and are carried away in the veins. The arteries, therefore, function to take food and oxygen to all the cells, while the veins take carbon dioxide and waste products away.

Being an extremely active and vital muscle, the myocardium itself needs a great deal of oxygen-rich blood to do its work, a task assigned to the coronary arteries. The coronary arteries supplying blood to the heart are quite large at the top of the heart, and then gradually become smaller as they course down the external surface of the heart. A process known as atherosclerosis is a gradual narrowing of the inner walls of these arteries. The arteries become narrowed when the inner layer of the artery is thickened by soft, fatty deposits called atheromas or atheromatous plaques. When the coronary arteries become rigid and narrow, the likelihood increases that the blood supply to various portions of the heart muscle could be temporarily or permanently cut off. A serious blockage of one of these arteries can cause a heart attack. Atherosclerosis can also occur in other parts of the body, and blockage in these various regions can lead to kidney problems, stroke, or blood clots. It is important to emphasize that atherosclerosis is usually a slow, progressive disease, which can begin in childhood. During its development it may produce no symptoms for 20 to 40 years, and often is discovered only on postmortem examination. Knowledge about the cause of atherosclerosis is still very limited, but it appears to be influenced by heredity, a fatty diet (high in cholesterol), obesity, lack of exercise, and the general life-style of the individual.

Two major symptoms can emerge from the gradual narrowing of the coronary arteries. The first, known as angina pectoris, is a pain in the chest (heart) caused by the lack of oxygen to the heart muscle due to a diminished blood supply. The pain occurs intermittently, often in association with physical exericse, eating, or emotional stress. These activities all increase the needs of the myocardium for blood beyond the amount that can "get through" the clogged arteries. This results in myocardial ischemia, (diminished oxygen in the portion of the myocardial tissue affected) and consequent pain. Many individuals suffer from brief, tolerable attacks of angina for many years. A heart attack occurs when the artery becomes blocked. This can be brought about by a slow, gradual narrowing, vascular spasm, or through a sudden occlusion by a clot. This blocked artery can no longer deliver the life-sustaining blood to the heart muscle, resulting in the destruction of some of the heart's tissue.

A number of warning signs often precede the actual occurrence of a heart attack. These include pain or pressure in the chest, which may occur for hours or even days before the actual attack. During a heart attack the individual can experience a variety of symptoms. Most patients experience moderate to severe tightness or crushing pain in the front of the chest; the pain may spread to the neck, jaw, shoulders, arms, or back. Sometimes the person feels nauseated and vomits, misleading him into believing that he has only a severely upset stomach. Sometimes the patient experiences shortness of breath, dizziness, or even total loss of consciousness. Sixty percent of all coronary deaths occur before the patient reaches the hospital.

Hospital coronary care units, or CCUs, evolved gradually during the last two decades after cardiologists began to realize that many individuals who died following a myocardial infarction had hearts that still appeared quite healthy upon postmortem examination. Cardiologists began to recognize that many victims of lethal heart attacks had "hearts that were too good to die." It was recognized that it wasn't the myocardial infarction itself that led to the death of the individual, but rather the electrical instability of the heart following the infarction. It was further recognized that if physicians could suppress the electrical instability that occurred during the first few days after a heart attack, then the heart had the capacity to repair itself. The coronary arteries, if given a chance, often could build and send a new supply of arteries to the injured heart tissue, a "collateral circulation" to repair its injured muscle tissue.

The healthy, adult heart beats rhythmically at a pace intrinsically determined by the heart itself. Usually this pace is set in one region of the heart, the sinoatrial node in the right atrium, which generates its own electrical impulse. The pace of this impulse is in turn influenced by two major nerves, the vagus and the sympathetic nerves. These nerves arise in the brain and are one means by which emotions are reflected in changes in cardiovascular functioning.

When the pacemaker generates an electrical impulse, this impulse soon spreads to the entire myocardium, causing the heart muscle to contract and the heart to eject the blood that is inside its chambers. The heart muscle has other "pacemakers" in other parts of the heart; these also have the capacity to generate an electrical impulse if they are disturbed. When these areas, or "foci," fire independently of the main pacemaker, the entire heart will also beat. Such pacemakers exist in many parts of the atria and ventricles. If an unusual or "ectopic" area of the atria or ventricles generates an electrical impulse, then the ongoing heart rhythm will change for the next beat, or however long this new focus continues to initiate electrical impulses. Such beats are unusual (dysrhythmic) and are called atrial or ventricular premature beats. The unusual electrical discharges disrupt the ordinary rhythm of the heart and cause the heart to beat irregularly. As noted, the incidence of these premature beats is especially high during the first few hours after a heart attack. If such abnormal beats are not controlled, the heart may completely lose control of its own natural beat, at which point it will begin beating wildly, with many areas all trying to beat at once. In this condition the heart will fibrillate, without actually contracting, somewhat like a bag of writhing worms, a process that will lead to death in seconds or a few minutes unless reversed. Fortunately, cardiologists have learned not only how to stop cardiac fibrillation but also how to prevent it. With modern drugs, most types of irregular heartbeats can be controlled. A heart which has actually stopped beating can be revived with cardiopulmonary resuscitation techniques. In order to detect and control the incidence of abnormal beats after a heart attack, most hospitals are now equipped with a special area where the heart activities of patients can be monitored continuously for one to four days after a heart attack, when the danger of cardiac arrhythmia and cardiac death through electrical accidents is highest. The development of these specialized units has led to an estimated 30–40 percent reduction in the incidence of fatal heart attacks during hospital recuperation. Each patient's heartbeat in the coronary care unit is constantly monitored on oscilloscopes, at the patient's bedside and at a central monitoring desk. These monitors allow cardiologists and specially trained nurses to recognize immediately any abnormal heart activity and take immediate steps to restore the heart to its normal rhythm.

# Statistics on Living Together and Health

Tables B1–2. Average annual U.S. death rates according to marital status per 100,000 population, between the ages of 15–64, during the period 1959–1961. In almost every case, for both males and females, widowed, divorced, and single people have significantly higher death rates than married people.

Table B3. Death rate (ratios of nonmarried to married) from all types of cancer for ages 15 and older. As can be seen in this table, death rates for almost all types of cancer are significantly higher in nonmarried individuals. These data are based on 1960 U.S. population data. There are intriguing differences in death rates that clearly need additional investigation. For example, the doubling of cancer of the respiratory system in divorced males compared to single males needs to be explored further. Whether such a large difference is due to differential patterns of cigarette smoking in these two groups is not at all clear.

Table B4. High death rates for nonmarried individuals are not peculiar to the United States but can be observed in every industrialized nation that maintains reliable health statistics. There are, however, important cultural differences, as can be seen in the extraordinarily high increase in death rates for Japanese widowed individuals between the ages of 20 and 35. This specific table shows the ratio of death rates per 1,000 population for single, widowed, and divorced individuals, compared to death rates for married Japanese based on 1970 census data. Again, to repeat a point

## TABLE B1
### Marital Status and Mortality: Males

| Cause of Death | Death Rates for White Men | | | | Death Rates for Nonwhite Men | | | |
|---|---|---|---|---|---|---|---|---|
| | Married | Single | Widowed | Divorced | Married | Single | Widowed | Divorced |
| Coronary disease and other myocardial (heart) degeneration | 176 | 237 | 275 | 362 | 142 | 231 | 328 | 298 |
| Motor vehicle accidents | 35 | 54 | 142 | 128 | 43 | 62 | 103 | 81 |
| Cancer of respiratory system | 28 | 32 | 43 | 65 | 29 | 44 | 56 | 75 |
| Cancer of digestive organs | 27 | 38 | 39 | 48 | 42 | 62 | 90 | 88 |
| Vascular lesions (stroke) | 24 | 42 | 46 | 58 | 73 | 105 | 176 | 132 |
| Suicide | 17 | 32 | 92 | 73 | 10 | 16 | 41 | 21 |
| Cancer of lymph glands and of blood-making tissues | 12 | 13 | 11 | 16 | 11 | 13 | 15 | 18 |
| Cirrhosis of liver | 11 | 31 | 48 | 79 | 12 | 40 | 39 | 53 |
| Rheumatic fever (heart) | 10 | 14 | 21 | 19 | 8 | 14 | 16 | 19 |
| Hypertensive heart disease | 8 | 16 | 16 | 20 | 49 | 68 | 106 | 90 |
| Pneumonia | 6 | 31 | 25 | 44 | 22 | 68 | 78 | 69 |
| Diabetes mellitus | 6 | 13 | 12 | 17 | 11 | 18 | 22 | 22 |
| Homicide | 4 | 7 | 16 | 30 | 51 | 79 | 152 | 129 |
| Chronic nephritis (kidney) | 4 | 7 | 7 | 7 | 11 | 18 | 26 | 21 |
| Accidental falls | 4 | 12 | 11 | 23 | 7 | 19 | 23 | 19 |
| Tuberculosis, all forms | 3 | 17 | 18 | 30 | 15 | 50 | 62 | 54 |
| Cancer of prostate gland | 3 | 3 | 3 | 4 | 8 | 7 | 15 | 12 |
| Accidental fire or explosion | 2 | 6 | 18 | 16 | 5 | 15 | 24 | 16 |
| Syphilis | 1 | 2 | 2 | 4 | 6 | 10 | 14 | 15 |

SOURCE: Hugh Carter and Paul C. Glick, *Marriage and Divorce: A Social and Economic Study*, American Public Health Association, Vital and Health Statistics Monograph (Cambridge: Harvard University Press, 1970), p. 345.

## TABLE B2
### Marital Status and Mortality: Females

| Cause of Death | Death Rates for White Women | | | | Death Rates for Nonwhite Women | | | |
|---|---|---|---|---|---|---|---|---|
| | Married | Single | Widowed | Divorced | Married | Single | Widowed | Divorced |
| Coronary disease and other myocardial (heart) degeneration | 44 | 51 | 67 | 62 | 83 | 112 | 165 | 113 |
| Cancer of breast | 21 | 29 | 21 | 23 | 19 | 26 | 28 | 27 |
| Cancer of digestive organs | 20 | 24 | 24 | 23 | 25 | 33 | 41 | 35 |
| Vascular lesions (stroke) | 19 | 23 | 31 | 28 | 72 | 89 | 147 | 82 |
| Motor vehicle accidents | 11 | 11 | 47 | 35 | 10 | 13 | 25 | 20 |
| Rheumatic fever (heart) | 10 | 14 | 15 | 13 | 8 | 14 | 12 | 13 |
| Cancer of lymph glands and of blood-making tissues | 8 | 9 | 9 | 8 | 7 | 7 | 9 | 13 |
| Hypertensive heart disease | 7 | 8 | 10 | 9 | 50 | 63 | 97 | 56 |
| Cancer of cervix | 7 | 4 | 13 | 18 | 17 | 22 | 34 | 27 |
| Diabetes mellitus | 7 | 7 | 11 | 8 | 20 | 24 | 36 | 22 |
| Cirrhosis of liver | 7 | 6 | 15 | 20 | 9 | 20 | 23 | 20 |
| Cancer of ovary | 7 | 12 | 8 | 8 | 6 | 8 | 9 | 8 |
| Suicide | 6 | 8 | 12 | 21 | 3 | 3 | 6 | 5 |
| Cancer of respiratory system | 5 | 5 | 6 | 7 | 5 | 6 | 9 | 10 |
| Pneumonia | 4 | 15 | 7 | 10 | 12 | 31 | 33 | 22 |
| Chronic nephritis (kidney) | 3 | 4 | 5 | 4 | 11 | 14 | 16 | 11 |
| Homicide | 2 | 1 | 7 | 9 | 14 | 17 | 33 | 25 |
| Tuberculosis, all forms | 2 | 5 | 4 | 5 | 8 | 24 | 19 | 16 |
| Accidental fire or explosion | 1 | 2 | 6 | 4 | 4 | 6 | 11 | 5 |

SOURCE: Ibid.

## TABLE B3
### Marital Status and Cancer Death Ratios, 1960

| Color and Primary Sites | Male Death Ratios | | | Female Death Ratios | | |
|---|---|---|---|---|---|---|
| | Single to Married | Widowed to Married | Divorced to Married | Single to Married | Widowed to Married | Divorced to Married |
| WHITE | | | | | | |
| Buccal cavity and pharynx | 2.16* | 2.12 | 4.10 | 0.87 | 1.47 | 1.67 |
| Digestive organs and peritoneum | 1.26 | 1.31 | 1.53 | 1.14 | 1.18 | 1.15 |
| Respiratory system | 1.16 | 1.45 | 2.11 | 1.04 | 1.23 | 1.49 |
| Breast | 2.50 | 2.50 | 2.50 | 1.41 | 1.02 | 1.13 |
| Cervix uteri | – | – | – | 0.60 | 1.66 | 2.38 |
| Female genital organs excluding cervix | – | – | – | 1.47 | 1.22 | 1.24 |
| Prostate | 0.90 | 1.13 | 1.30 | – | – | – |
| Male genital organs except prostate | 1.50 | 0.64 | 1.79 | – | – | – |
| All urinary organs | 1.10 | 1.28 | 1.52 | 1.08 | 1.25 | 1.40 |
| Other and unspecified sites | 1.26 | 1.33 | 1.70 | 1.17 | 1.29 | 1.22 |
| Lymphatic and hematopoietic tissues | 0.98 | 0.96 | 1.21 | 1.08 | 1.10 | 1.05 |
| NONWHITE | | | | | | |
| Buccal cavity and pharynx | 2.08 | 2.64 | 3.14 | 1.50 | 1.94 | 1.44 |
| Digestive organs and peritoneum | 1.35 | 1.76 | 1.78 | 1.21 | 1.57 | 1.42 |
| Respiratory system | 1.51 | 1.74 | 2.46 | 1.23 | 1.63 | 1.89 |
| Breast | 1.67 | 3.33 | 2.00 | 1.31 | 1.41 | 1.42 |
| Cervix uteri | – | – | – | 1.17 | 1.84 | 1.60 |
| Female genital organs excluding cervix | – | – | – | 1.44 | 1.54 | 1.45 |
| Prostate | 0.88 | 1.52 | 1.45 | – | – | – |
| Male genital organs except prostate | 1.77 | 1.54 | 2.69 | – | – | – |
| All urinary organs | 1.17 | 2.16 | 1.83 | 1.13 | 1.68 | 1.70 |
| Other and unspecified sites | 1.34 | 1.87 | 1.95 | 1.31 | 1.49 | 1.37 |
| Lymphatic and hematopoietic tissues | 1.06 | 1.34 | 1.65 | 1.12 | 1.32 | 1.71 |

* 2.16 means that the death rate for single white males for buccal cavity and pharynx cancer was 2.16 times higher than for married individuals.

TABLE B4

*Marital Status and Death Ratios in Japan, 1970*

| Age | MALES | | | FEMALES | | |
|---|---|---|---|---|---|---|
| | Single | Widowed | Divorced | Single | Widowed | Divorced |
| 20–24 | 1.83 | 31.23* | 4.56 | 1.54 | 13.46* | 4.46 |
| 25–29 | 2.07 | 25.42* | 4.50 | 2.66 | 10.82* | 2.90 |
| 30–34 | 3.39 | 7.37 | 5.61 | 4.24 | 3.14 | 3.06 |
| 35–39 | 4.80 | 4.70 | 5.45 | 3.59 | 1.62 | 2.49 |
| 40–44 | 4.45 | 3.38 | 4.96 | 3.22 | 1.39 | 1.71 |
| 45–49 | 4.23 | 3.01 | 5.07 | 3.31 | 1.39 | 1.51 |
| 50–54 | 3.76 | 2.35 | 3.07 | 3.21 | 1.23 | 1.31 |
| 55–59 | 3.40 | 2.03 | 2.48 | 3.25 | 1.19 | 1.12 |
| 60–69 | 2.81 | 1.76 | 1.65 | 2.84 | 1.29 | 1.08 |
| 70–79 | 2.30 | 1.46 | 1.18 | 2.40 | 1.33 | 1.05 |
| 80+ | 1.40 | 1.41 | 0.97 | 2.45 | 1.57 | 1.05 |

* The high proportionate death rates for younger male Japanese widows is most likely influenced by suicide, which is high in Japan for this category.

noted earlier, the 31.23 for male, widowed Japanese between the ages of 20 and 24 means that their death rate was 31.23 times higher than married Japanese males of similar age. I am deeply grateful to Satoshi Dohno, an associate professor at the Hiroshima Bunkyo University, and to his colleagues Hideko Ito and Keiko Kawashima for providing the pertinent Japanese mortality tables from which these figures were calculated.

Table B5. This table shows the marked increase in rates of residence for the nonmarried in all types of residential institutions. These data are based on rates per 10,000 population for ages 45–64. In all institutions, the nonmarried are markedly overrepresented. The tables are based on 1960 census data.

Tables B6–10. Cardiovascular death rates vary according to marital status, sex, age, and race. As can be deduced from these tables, the incidences of coronary heart disease, cerebrovascular disease, and hypertensive heart disease are all significantly lower in married individuals than in the nonmarried. Since the death ratios for *coronary heart disease* were presented in the text, that specific table will

not be presented here. All tables were excerpted from Iwao Mori-
yama, Dean E. Kreuger, and Jeremiah Stamler, *Cardiovascular
Diseases in the United States* (Cambridge: Harvard University
Press, 1971).

TABLE B5 *
*Marital Status and Rates of Institutionalization, 1960*

| Type of Institution | Married | Widowed | Divorced | Separated | Single |
|---|---|---|---|---|---|
| **MEN** In all institutions | 45 | 340 | 676 | 589 | 935 |
| Mental hospitals | 22 | 97 | 237 | 215 | 550 |
| State and local | 18 | 76 | 183 | 189 | 472 |
| Federal | 3 | 16 | 48 | 23 | 72 |
| Private | 1 | 5 | 6 | 3 | 7 |
| Correctional institutions | 12 | 84 | 215 | 186 | 103 |
| Homes for aged and needy: | | | | | |
| Known to have nursing care | 1 | 38 | 29 | 30 | 40 |
| Not known to have such care | 3 | 68 | 103 | 64 | 91 |
| Tuberculosis hospitals | 6 | 35 | 62 | 63 | 36 |
| Chronic hospitals (except tuberculosis and mental) | 1 | 16 | 26 | 27 | 24 |
| Institutions (mostly) for juveniles | 0 | 2 | 4 | 4 | 89 |
| **WOMEN** In all institutions | 37 | 99 | 193 | 247 | 475 |
| Mental hospitals | 31 | 51 | 150 | 193 | 297 |
| State and local | 30 | 48 | 144 | 187 | 286 |
| Federal | 1 | 1 | 3 | 5 | 4 |
| Private | 1 | 2 | 3 | 2 | 7 |
| Correctional institutions | 1 | 2 | 5 | 9 | 2 |
| Homes for aged and needy: | | | | | |
| Known to have nursing care | 1 | 16 | 10 | 10 | 26 |
| Not known to have such care | 1 | 21 | 17 | 12 | 38 |
| Tuberculosis hospitals | 2 | 4 | 5 | 10 | 6 |
| Chronic hospitals (except tuberculosis and mental) | 1 | 4 | 4 | 9 | 8 |
| Institutions (mostly) for juveniles | 0 | 1 | 2 | 4 | 97 |

SOURCE: Carter and Glick, *Marriage and Divorce*, p. 334.
* Slight mathematical descrepancies were unexplained in original source.

## TABLE B6
*Hypertensive Heart Disease Death Ratios, 1959–1961 ***

| Color and Age | Male | | | Female | | |
|---|---|---|---|---|---|---|
| | Single | Widowed | Divorced | Single | Widowed | Divorced |
| **White** | | | | | | |
| 25–34 | 2.50 | 2.13 | 3.25 | 2.50 | 3.00 | 2.83 |
| 35–44 | 2.81 | 2.03 | 3.67 | 1.86 | 1.82 | 1.79 |
| 45–54 | 2.18 | 2.25 | 2.99 | 1.22 | 1.61 | 1.40 |
| 55–64 | 1.64 | 1.88 | 2.01 | 1.00 | 1.49 | 1.19 |
| 65–74 | 1.50 | 1.65 | 1.71 | 0.97 | 1.35 | 1.07 |
| 75–84 | 1.20 | 1.40 | 1.43 | 1.07 | 1.28 | 1.15 |
| 85+ | 1.01 | 1.26 | 1.18 | 1.32 | 1.47 | 1.32 |
| 15 and over, age-adjusted | 1.46 | 1.63 | 1.76 | 1.09 | 1.40 | 1.18 |
| **Nonwhite** | | | | | | |
| 25–34 | 1.58 | 2.36 | 1.77 | 1.48 | 3.68 | 1.15 |
| 35–44 | 1.75 | 2.77 | 2.32 | 1.58 | 1.90 | 1.09 |
| 45–54 | 1.45 | 2.18 | 1.90 | 1.35 | 1.97 | 1.14 |
| 55–64 | 1.10 | 2.05 | 1.54 | 0.99 | 1.93 | 1.07 |
| 65–74 | 1.14 | 1.74 | 1.66 | 1.21 | 1.69 | 1.24 |
| 75–84 | 0.95 | 1.53 | 1.42 | 1.27 | 1.47 | 0.98 |
| 85+ | 0.87 | 1.30 | 0.87 | 1.07 | 1.42 | 0.82 |
| 15 and over, age-adjusted | 1.21 | 1.94 | 1.66 | 1.22 | 1.84 | 1.11 |

* It is of great interest to note that in the critical ages of 25 to 55, the death rate for non-married nonwhite males is almost always double that of married nonwhite males.

### TABLE B7
*Cardiovascular Renal Disease Death Ratios, 1959–1961*

| Color and Age | Male | | | Female | | |
|---|---|---|---|---|---|---|
| | Single | Widowed | Divorced | Single | Widowed | Divorced |
| **White** | | | | | | |
| 25–34 | 1.82 | 2.25 | 2.61 | 2.09 | 2.32 | 1.92 |
| 35–44 | 1.73 | 2.05 | 2.70 | 1.97 | 1.83 | 1.82 |
| 45–54 | 1.53 | 1.77 | 2.33 | 1.35 | 1.58 | 1.52 |
| 55–64 | 1.36 | 1.62 | 2.01 | 1.07 | 1.43 | 1.31 |
| 65–74 | 1.41 | 1.49 | 1.74 | 1.07 | 1.33 | 1.21 |
| 75–84 | 1.33 | 1.39 | 1.55 | 1.23 | 1.33 | 1.30 |
| 85+ | 1.19 | 1.30 | 1.33 | 1.55 | 1.54 | 1.43 |
| 15 and over, age adjusted | 1.39 | 1.55 | 1.82 | 1.23 | 1.43 | 1.33 |
| **Nonwhite** | | | | | | |
| 25–34 | 2.03 | 3.52 | 2.54 | 1.66 | 2.62 | 1.17 |
| 35–44 | 2.06 | 2.86 | 2.41 | 1.59 | 2.15 | 1.36 |
| 45–54 | 1.67 | 2.60 | 2.16 | 1.40 | 2.05 | 1.22 |
| 55–64 | 1.21 | 2.23 | 1.81 | 1.07 | 2.05 | 1.23 |
| 65–74 | 1.29 | 1.81 | 1.74 | 1.31 | 1.80 | 1.33 |
| 75–84 | 1.28 | 1.56 | 1.41 | 1.28 | 1.50 | 1.19 |
| 85+ | 1.22 | 1.48 | 1.41 | 1.48 | 1.64 | 1.08 |
| 15 and over, age-adjusted | 1.39 | 2.09 | 1.81 | 1.30 | 1.89 | 1.24 |

## TABLE B8
*Coronary Heart Disease Death Rates per 100,000 Population, 1959–1961* *

| Color, sex, and marital status | 25–34 | 35–44 | 45–54 | 55–64 | 65–74 | 75–84 | 85+ |
|---|---|---|---|---|---|---|---|
| **White Males** | | | | | | | |
| Married | 9.6 | 81.1 | 329.6 | 849.3 | 1,836.2 | 3,735.6 | 7,798.7 |
| Single | 14.6 | 119.0 | 458.4 | 1,086.7 | 2,512.8 | 5,053.7 | 9,913.3 |
| Widowed | 19.0 | 149.0 | 548.3 | 1,314.2 | 2,662.6 | 5,184.5 | 10,504.1 |
| Divorced | 27.2 | 200.0 | 713.3 | 1,634.3 | 3,070.8 | 5,815.5 | 10,719.6 |
| **White Females** | | | | | | | |
| Married | 1.8 | 11.8 | 60.1 | 254.4 | 864.2 | 2,401.0 | 5,374.4 |
| Single | 5.7 | 24.6 | 80.2 | 262.6 | 906.2 | 3,022.3 | 8,749.8 |
| Widowed | 9.3 | 27.6 | 101.7 | 376.1 | 1,162.9 | 3,243.8 | 8,398.7 |
| Divorced | 4.1 | 25.3 | 95.9 | 331.1 | 1,038.2 | 3,177.1 | 7,522.3 |
| **Nonwhite Males** | | | | | | | |
| Married | 14.7 | 77.7 | 257.2 | 643.1 | 1,246.1 | 1,999.8 | 3,698.9 |
| Single | 33.0 | 158.5 | 456.4 | 857.8 | 1,822.9 | 3,096.2 | 5,259.1 |
| Widowed | 62.3 | 202.6 | 682.6 | 1,442.6 | 2,285.6 | 3,175.0 | 5,850.4 |
| Divorced | 38.8 | 188.3 | 595.5 | 1,226.2 | 2,229.7 | 2,977.7 | 6,386.7 |
| **Nonwhite Females** | | | | | | | |
| Married | 9.7 | 41.4 | 147.8 | 371.3 | 677.5 | 1,337.1 | 2,312.2 |
| Single | 15.6 | 75.8 | 205.3 | 426.0 | 951.8 | 1,856.4 | 4,417.4 |
| Widowed | 23.0 | 100.2 | 318.4 | 772.8 | 1,264.8 | 2,083.7 | 4,420.7 |
| Divorced | 12.2 | 55.8 | 207.6 | 517.7 | 943.4 | 1,783.8 | 2,990.3 |

* Note that these are death *rates,* not comparable ratios of nonmarried to married people. In every case, the death rates for married people are lower.

## TABLE B9
*Hypertensive Disease Death Rates per 100,000 Population, 1959–1961 **

| Color, sex, and marital status | 25–34 | 35–44 | 45–54 | 55–64 | 65–74 | 75–84 | 85+ |
|---|---|---|---|---|---|---|---|
| **White Males** | | | | | | | |
| Married | 0.8 | 3.6 | 16.1 | 54.5 | 153.4 | 426.4 | 1,036.4 |
| Single | 2.0 | 10.1 | 35.1 | 89.6 | 230.1 | 509.8 | 1,048.0 |
| Widowed | 1.7 | 7.3 | 36.2 | 102.5 | 253.5 | 598.3 | 1,301.3 |
| Divorced | 2.6 | 13.2 | 48.2 | 109.7 | 261.7 | 609.1 | 1,221.5 |
| **White Females** | | | | | | | |
| Married | 0.6 | 2.8 | 12.6 | 43.0 | 150.6 | 468.9 | 976.1 |
| Single | 1.5 | 5.2 | 15.4 | 42.9 | 145.4 | 501.4 | 1,286.0 |
| Widowed | 1.8 | 5.1 | 20.3 | 63.9 | 203.0 | 600.3 | 1,433.1 |
| Divorced | 1.7 | 5.0 | 17.6 | 51.0 | 161.8 | 536.9 | 1,291.0 |
| **Nonwhite Males** | | | | | | | |
| Married | 11.3 | 48.4 | 116.9 | 241.2 | 436.4 | 673.0 | 1,211.4 |
| Single | 17.9 | 84.8 | 169.1 | 265.1 | 498.0 | 636.3 | 1,051.8 |
| Widowed | 26.7 | 134.0 | 255.2 | 495.5 | 758.7 | 1,030.3 | 1,575.6 |
| Divorced | 20.0 | 112.3 | 222.1 | 371.5 | 725.0 | 953.3 | 1,049.9 |
| **Nonwhite Females** | | | | | | | |
| Married | 11.0 | 49.8 | 116.6 | 224.5 | 362.9 | 601.9 | 1,075.9 |
| Single | 16.3 | 78.6 | 156.9 | 221.8 | 438.8 | 766.0 | 1,155.0 |
| Widowed | 40.5 | 94.7 | 229.4 | 433.4 | 614.8 | 885.9 | 1,528.4 |
| Divorced | 12.7 | 54.4 | 132.4 | 239.6 | 448.2 | 589.6 | 879.5 |

* As can be seen, death rates for this disease are significantly higher for nonwhites until age 75. In all cases again, for both sexes, all races, and at all ages until 85, the death rates are significantly higher for the nonmarried.

## TABLE B10
*Cerebrovascular Disease Death Rates per 100,000 Population, 1959–1961* *

| Color, sex, and marital status | 25–34 | 35–44 | 45–54 | 55–64 | 65–74 | 75–84 | 85+ |
|---|---|---|---|---|---|---|---|
| **White Males** | | | | | | | |
| Married | 3.2 | 9.4 | 35.0 | 121.4 | 443.3 | 1,434.7 | 3,651.7 |
| Single | 6.1 | 21.6 | 70.2 | 194.4 | 642.9 | 1,750.2 | 3,599.4 |
| Widowed | 8.6 | 29.1 | 78.5 | 224.5 | 698.9 | 1,904.1 | 4,348.8 |
| Divorced | 7.2 | 29.8 | 96.0 | 274.2 | 798.6 | 2,102.3 | 4,431.9 |
| **White Females** | | | | | | | |
| Married | 3.2 | 9.2 | 30.4 | 92.0 | 336.6 | 1,230.8 | 2,821.5 |
| Single | 5.4 | 15.5 | 38.8 | 95.0 | 371.5 | 1,426.7 | 4,046.5 |
| Widowed | 7.1 | 16.6 | 45.5 | 126.9 | 444.2 | 1,570.1 | 4,188.2 |
| Divorced | 5.8 | 17.2 | 47.4 | 120.5 | 413.3 | 1,578.5 | 4,038.4 |
| **Nonwhite Males** | | | | | | | |
| Married | 9.6 | 38.9 | 126.2 | 333.3 | 715.2 | 1,196.0 | 2,314.9 |
| Single | 15.7 | 79.3 | 207.5 | 370.1 | 783.1 | 1,287.3 | 2,237.5 |
| Widowed | 26.7 | 126.2 | 360.3 | 753.0 | 1,248.4 | 1,789.1 | 3,214.2 |
| Divorced | 17.6 | 92.2 | 249.5 | 541.1 | 1,201.3 | 1,435.3 | 3,062.1 |
| **Nonwhite Females** | | | | | | | |
| Married | 13.1 | 46.9 | 131.0 | 291.4 | 542.3 | 1,056.8 | 1,878.1 |
| Single | 19.1 | 59.3 | 187.0 | 299.8 | 663.2 | 1,189.5 | 2,330.3 |
| Widowed | 40.5 | 107.5 | 266.6 | 619.8 | 988.4 | 1,486.0 | 2,779.9 |
| Divorced | 13.8 | 66.4 | 137.1 | 329.6 | 708.4 | 1,269.8 | 1,934.9 |

* As was true of hypertensive heart disease, the death rates for cerebrovascular disease before age 75 are higher for the nonwhite U.S. population. In every case, the death rates for the nonmarried are significantly higher than those observed for married individuals.

# NOTES

## INTRODUCTION

1. *A National Program to Conquer Heart Disease, Cancer and Stroke,* 2 vols. (Washington, D.C.: U.S. Government Printing Office, 1965), 2:18.
2. Hugh Carter and Paul C. Glick, *Marriage and Divorce: A Social and Economic Study,* American Public Health Association, Vital and Health Statistics Monograph (Cambridge: Harvard University Press, 1970).
3. Evelyn M. Kitagawa and Philip M. Hauser, *Differential Mortality in the United States: A Study in Socioeconomic Epidemiology,* American Public Health Association, Vital and Health Statistics Monographs (Cambridge: Harvard University Press, 1973).
4. Victor R. Fuchs, *Who Shall Live? Health, Economics and Social Choice* (New York: Basic Books, 1974).
5. Alvin Toffler, *Future Shock* (New York: Random House, 1970).
6. *Essentials of Life and Health* (New York: Random House, 1972), pp. 199–204.
7. Philip Slater, *The Pursuit of Loneliness* (Boston: Beacon Press, 1970).
8. Meyer Friedman and Ray H. Rosenman, *Type A Behavior and Your Heart* (New York: Alfred A. Knopf, 1974).
9. James J. Lynch et al., "Psychological Aspects of Cardiac Arrhythmia," *American Heart Journal* (1977), in press.

## CHAPTER 1

1. *A National Program to Conquer Heart Disease, Cancer and Stroke,* 2 vols. (Washington, D.C.: U.S. Government Printing Office, 1965).
2. Victor R. Fuchs, *Who Shall Live? Health, Economics and Social Choice* (New York: Basic Books, 1974).
3. Tavia Gorden and William B. Kannel, "Section 1: Introduction and General Background," in *The Framingham Study: An Epidemiological Investigation of Cardiovascular Disease,* Department of Health, Education and Welfare, National Institute of Health (Washington, D.C.: U.S. Government Printing Office, 1968); see also William B. Kannel and Thomas R. Dawber, "Framingham Study—Follow-up Reports. Contributors to Coronary Rise: Implications for Prevention and Public Health: The Framingham Study," *Heart and Lung* 1 (1972): 797–809; William B. Kannel and Manning Feinleib, Natural History of Angina Pectoris in the Framingham Study," *American Journal of Cardiology,* 29 (1972): 154–163; William B.

Kannel and William P. Castelli "The Framingham Study of Coronary Disease in Women," *Medical Times* 10 (1972): 73–184.

4. *The Framingham Heart Study: Habits and Coronary Heart Disease,* Public Health Service Publication no. 1515 (Washington, D.C.: U.S. Government Printing Office, 1966), pp. 227–243.

5. C. B. Thomas and E. A. Murphy, "Further Studies on Cholesterol Levels in the Johns Hopkins Medical Students: Effect of Stress at Examinations," *Journal of Chronic Diseases* 8 (1958): 661; S. M. Grundy and A. C. Griffin, "Effects of Periodic Mental Stress on Serum Cholesterol Levels," *Circulation* 19 (1959): 496; P. T. Wertlake et al., "Relationship of Mental and Emotional Stress to Serum Cholesterol Levels," *Proceedings of the Society for Experimental Biology and Medicine* 97 (1958): 163; M. Friedman and R. Rosenman, "Association of Specific Overt Behavior Pattern with Blood and Cardiovascular Findings," *Journal of the American Medical Association* 169 (1959): 1286; S. V. Kasl, S. Cobb, and C. W. Brooks, "Changes in Serum Uric Acid and Cholesterol Levels in Men Undergoing Job Loss," *Journal of the American Medical Association* 206 (1968): 150; J. F. Hammarstein et al., "Serum Cholesterol, Diet and Stress in Patients with Coronary Artery Disease," *Journal of Clinical Investigation* 36 (1957): 897; W. Raab, "Emotional and Sensory Stress Factors in Myocardial Pathology," *American Heart Journal* 72 (1966): 538; W. Raab, J. P. Chaplan, and E. Bajusz, "Myocardial Necroses Produced in Domesticated Rats and in Wild Rats by Sensory and Emotional Stress," *Proceedings of the Society for Experimental Biology and Medicine* 97 (1958): 163.

6. James P. Henry, John P. Meehan, and Patricia M. Stephens, "The Use of Psychosocial Stimuli to Induce Prolonged Systolic Hypertension in Mice," *Psychosomatic Medicine* 29 (1967): 408.

7. Albert J. Stunkard, *The Pain of Obesity* (Palo Alto, Calif.: Bull Publishing, 1976).

8. Stewart Wolf and Helen Goodell, *Behavioral Science in Clinical Medicine* (Springfield, Ill.: Charles C. Thomas, 1976).

## CHAPTER 2

1. *Arteriosclerosis: A Report by the National Heart and Lung Institute Task Force on Arteriosclerosis,* DHEW Publication no. (NIH) 72–219, vol. 2 (Washington, D.C.: U.S. Government Printing Office, 1971).

2. Iwao Moriyama, Dean E. Krueger, and Jeremiah Stamler, *Cardiovascular Diseases in the United States,* American Public Health Association, Vital and Health Statistics Monograph (Cambridge: Harvard University Press, 1971), p. 2.

3. "World Health Organization Warns Heart Diseases are Becoming Mankind's Greatest Epidemic," *News Bulletin, International Society of Cardiologists,* May 1969.

4. J. Brown et al. "Nutritional and Epidemiologic Factors Related to Heart Disease," in *World Review of Nutrition and Dietetics,* vol. 12, ed. Geoffrey H. Bourne (New York: Karger, 1970), pp. 1–42.

5. C. David Jenkins, "Psychologic and Social Precursors of Coronary Disease [first of two parts]," *New England Journal of Medicine* 282 (1971): 244–254.

6. Evelyn M. Kitagawa and Philip M. Hauser, *Differential Mortality in the United States: A Study in Socioeconomic Epidemiology,* American Public Health Association, Vital and Health Statistics Monograph (Cambridge: Harvard University Press, 1973).

7. Stewart Wolf and Helen Goodell, *Behavioral Science in Clinical Medicine* (Springfield, Ill.: Charles C. Thomas, 1976), p. 18.

8. Arthur S. Kraus and Abraham M. Lillienfeld, "Some Epidemiologic Aspects of the High Mortality Rate in the Young Widowed Group," *Journal of Chronic Diseases* 10 (1959): 207–217.

9. Hugh Carter and Paul C. Glick, *Marriage and Divorce: A Social and Economic Study,* American Public Health Association, Vital and Health Statistics Monograph (Cambridge: Harvard University Press, 1970), p. 345.

10. Abraham M. Lillienfeld, Morton L. Levin, and Irving I. Kessler, *Cancer in the United States* (Cambridge: Harvard University Press, 1972), pp. 126–149; see also David L. Levin et al., *Cancer Rates and Risks,* 2nd ed, U.S. Department of Health, Education and Welfare (Washington, D.C.: U.S. Government Printing Office, 1974), p. 55.

11. Harold J. Morowitz, "Hiding in the Hammond Report," *Hospital Practice,* August 1975, pp. 35–39.

12. Cedric R. Bainton and Donald R. Peterson, "Deaths from Coronary Heart Disease in Persons Fifty Years of Age and Younger," *New England Journal of Medicine* 268 (1963): 569–575.

13. Colin Parkes, *Bereavement: Studies of Grief in Adult Life* (New York: International Universities Press, 1972).

14. Michael Young, B. Benjamin and C. Wallis, "Mortality of Widowers," *Lancet* 2 (1963): 454.

15. W. D. Rees and S. G. Lutkins, "Mortality of Bereavement," *British Medical Journal* 4 (1967): 13.

16. Brian MacMahon and Thomas F. Pugh, "Suicide in the Widowed," *American Journal of Epidemiology* 81 (1965): 23.

17. Ian C. Wilson and John C. Reece, "Simultaneous Death in Schizophrenic Twins," *Archives of General Psychiatry* 11 (1964): 377–384.

18. Walter Cannon, "Voodoo Death," *Psychosomatic Medicine* 19 (1957): 182.

19. George L. Engel, "Sudden and Rapid Death During Psychological Stress: Folklore or Folk Wisdom?" *Annals of Internal Medicine* 74 (1971): 771–782.

20. William A. Greene, Sidney Goldstein, and Arthur J. Moss, "Psychosocial Aspects of Sudden Death: A Preliminary Report," *Archives of Internal Medicine* 129 (1972): 725–731.

21. Stewart Wolf, "Psychosocial Forces in Myocardial Infarction and Sudden Death," *Circulation* (supp. IV) vols. 4–40 (1969): 74–81.

22. Arthur H. Schmale, Jr., "Relationship of Separation and Depression to Disease. I: A Report on a Hospitalized Medical Population," *Psychosomatic Medicine* 20 (1958): 259–277.

23. T. H. Holmes and R. H. Rahe, "The Social Readjustment Rating Scale," *Journal of Psychosomatic Research* 11 (1968): 213; Richard H. Rahe, "Life Change and Subsequent Illness Reports," in *Life Stress and Illness,* ed. E. K. Gunderson and Richard H. Rahe (Springfield, Ill.: Charles C. Thomas, 1974), pp. 60–61.

24. E. K. Gunderson and Richard H. Rahe, eds., *Life Stress and Illness* (Springfield, Ill.: Charles C. Thomas, 1974).

25. Richard H. Rahe and Matti Romo, "Recent Life Changes and the Onset of Myocardial Infarction and Coronary Death in Helsinki," *Life Stress and Illness,* pp. 105–120.

26. Tores Theorell and Richard H. Rahe, "Psychosocial Characteristics of Subjects with Myocardial Infarction in Stockholm," in *Life Stress and Illness,* pp. 90–104.

27. E. A. Liljefors and R. H. Rahe, "An Identical Twin Study of Psychosocial Factors in Coronary Heart Disease in Sweden," *Psychosomatic Medicine* 32 (1972): 523.

28. Meyer Friedman and Ray H. Rosenman, *Type A Behavior and Your Heart* (New York: Alfred A. Knopf, 1974).

29. J. H. Medalie, *Factors Associated with the First Myocardial Infarction: 5 Years Observation of 10,000 Adult Males, Presented at the Symposium on Epidemiology and Prevention of Coronary Heart Disease, Helsinki, 1972,* cited in *Life Stress and Illness,* p. 91.

30. I. G. Bruhn et al., "Social Aspects of Coronary Heart Disease in a Pennsylvania German Community," *Social Science in Medicine* 2 (1968): 201.

31. J. J. Groen, "Influence of Social and Cultural Patterns on Psychosomatic Diseases," *Psychother. Psychosom.* 18 (1970): 189–213.

## CHAPTER 3

1. W. F. Enos, R. H. Holmes, and J. C. Beyer, "Pathology of Coronary Arteriosclerosis," *American Journal of Cardiology* 9 (1962): 343–354; A. R. Moritz and N. Zamcheck, "Sudden and Unexpected Deaths of Young Soldiers: Diseases Responsible for Such Deaths during World War II," *Archives of Pathology* 42 (1946): 459–494; W. M. Yater et al., "Coronary Artery Disease in Men 18 to 39 Years of Age: Report on 869, 450 with Necropsy Examinations," *American Heart Journal* 36 (1948): 334–372, 481–526, 683–722; M. Newman, "Coronary Occlusion in Young Adults: Review of 50 Cases in the Services," *Lancet* 2 (1946): 409–411.

2. Lytt I. Gardner, "Deprivation Dwarfism," *Scientific American* 227 (1972): 76–82.

3. Sigmund Freud, *Mourning and Melancholia* (1917) in *Complete Psychological Works Standard Edition* vol. 14, J. Strachey, ed. and trans. (London: Hogarth Press, 1957), pp. 237–260.

4. John Bowlby, "Maternal Care and Mental Health," *World Health Organization Monograph* 2 (1951); "Some Pathological Processes Set in Train by Early Mother-Child Separation," *Journal of Mental Science* 99 (1953): 265; "Pathological Mourning and Childhood Mourning," *Journal of the American Psychoanalytic Association* 11 (1963): 500; *Attachment and Loss,* vol. 1, *Attachment* (New York: Basic Books, 1969).

5. Rene A. Spitz, "Anxiety in Infancy: A Study of its Manifestations in the First Year of Life," *International Journal of Psychoanalysis* 31 (1950): 138.

6. Nelson K. Ordway, M. F. Leonard, and T. Ingles, "Interpersonal Factors in Failure to Thrive," *Southern Medical Bulletin* 57 (1969): 23–28.

7. C. W. Wahl, "Some Antecedent Factors in the Family Histories of 392 Schizophrenics," *American Journal of Psychiatry* 110 (1954): 668.

8. Roslyn Seligman et al., "The Effect of Earlier Parental Loss in Adolescence," *Archives of General Psychiatry* 31 (1974): 475–479.

9. S. Glueck and E. Glueck, *Unraveling Juvenile Delinquency* (Cambridge: Harvard University Press, 1950).

10. S. Greer, "Study of Parental Loss in Neurotics and Sociopaths," *Archives of General Psychiatry* 112 (1964): 177.

11. I. Gregory, "Anterospective Data Following Childhood Loss of a Parent," *Archives of General Psychiatry* 13 (1965): 99–120.

12. Jay H. Nolan, "Culture and Psychosis Among the Loma Tribe of Liberia, West Africa," *Transcultural Psychiatric Research Review,* 13 (1976); 71–74.

13. Arthur H. Schmale, Jr. "Relationship of Separation and Depression to Disease. I: A Report on a Hospitalized Medical Population," *Psychosomatic Medicine* 20 (1958): 259–277.

14. Claus B. Bahnson, "Emotional and Personality Characteristics of Cancer Patients," in *Recent Developments in Medical Onccology,* Alton Sutnick, ed., (Baltimore, Md.: University Park Press, 1975).

15. Claus B. Bahnson and W. J. Wadell, "Personality Factors Predisposing to Myocardial Infarction," *Psychosomatic Medicine,* Proceedings of the First International Conference in the Academy of Psychosomatic Medicine (1966), pp. 249–257.

16. Caroline B. Thomas and Karen R. Duszynski, "Closeness to Parents and the Family Constellation in a Prospective Study of Five Disease States: Suicide, Mental Illness, Malignant Tumor, Hypertension and Coronary Heart Disease," *Johns Hopkins Medical Journal* 134 (1974): 251.

17. Ralph S. Paffenbarger et al., "Chronic Disease in Former College Students: I: Early Precursors of Fatal Coronary Heart Disease," *American Journal of Epidemiology* 83 (1966): 328; see also, R. S. Paffenbarger et al., "Chronic Disease in Former College Students. II: Methods of Study and Oberservations on Mortality from Coronary Heart Disease," *American Journal of Public Health* 56 (1966): 97; R. S. Paffenbarger, M. C. Thome, and A. L. Wing, "Chronic Disease in Former College Students. IX: Characterisistics in Youth Predisposing to Hypertension in Later Years," *American Journal of Epidemiology* 88 (1968): 25; R. S. Paffenbarger, S. H. King, and A. L. Wing, "Chronic Disease in Former College Students. IV: Characteristics in Youth that Predispose to Suicide and Accidental Death in Later Life," *American Journal of Public Health* 59 (1969): 900.

18. R. S. Paffenbarger and D. P. Asnes, "Chronic Disease in Former College Students. III: Precursors of Suicide in Early and Middle Life," *American Journal of Public Health* 56 (1966): 1036.

19. Gilbert Kliman, *Psychological Emergencies of Childhood* (New York: Grune and Stratton, 1968), pp. 1–148.

20. Quoted in "As Parents' Influence Fades—Who's Raising the Children," *U.S. News and World Report,* October 27, 1975, p. 43.

21. Quoted in "How Children Fare in Black Households," *U.S. News and World Report,* October 27, 1975, p. 43.

22. Rachel Carson, *Silent Spring* (Boston: Houghton Mifflin, 1962).

## CHAPTER 4

1. James J. Lynch et al., "Effects of Human Contact on the Heart Activity of Curarized Patients in a Shock-Trauma Unit," *American Heart Journal* 88 (1974): 169.

2. C. T. East, *The Story of Heart Disease: The Fitzpatrick Lectures for 1956 and 1957, Given Before the Royal College of Physicians of London* (London: Dawson and Sons, 1957).

3. A. C. Celsus, *De Medicina,* Liber III, 6 (Circa A.D. 30); quoted in ibid.

4. Arthur J. Moss and Bruce Wynar, "Tachycardia in House Officers Presenting Cases at Grand Rounds," *Annals of Internal Medicine* 72 (1970): 255.

5. Alberto DiMascio, Richard W. Boyd, and Milton Greenblatt, "Physiological Correlates of Tension and Antagonism During Psychotherapy: A Study of Interpersonal Physiology," *Psychosomatic Medicine* 19 (1957): 104; Alberto DiMascio et al., "The Psychiatric Interview (A Sociophysiologic Study)," *Diseases of the Nervous System* 16 (1955): 4; Roy Coleman, Milton Greenblatt, and Harry C. Solomon, "Physiological Evidence of Rapport During Psychotherapeutic Interviews," *Diseases of the Nervous System* 17 (1956): 71, 77.

6. Brigitte Stanek, P. Hahn, and H. Mayer, "Biometric Findings on Cardiac Neurosis. III: Changes in ECG and Heart Rate in Cardiophobic Patients and Their Doctor During Psychoanalytical Initial Interviews. Topics of Psychosomatic Research, 9th European Conference on Psychosomatic Research, Vienna, 1972," *Psychother. Psychosom.* 22 (1973): 289; H. Mayer, Brigitte Stanek, and P. Hahn, "Biometric Findings of Cardiac Neurosis. II: ECG and Circulation Findings of Cardiophobic Patients During Standardized Examination of the Circulatory System. Topics of Psychosomatic Research, 9th European Conference on Psychosomatic Research, Vienna, 1972," *Psychother. Psychosom.* 22 (1973): 299.

7. Robert B. Malmo, Thomas J. Boag, and A. Arthur Smith, "Physiological Study of Personal Interaction," *Psychosomatic Medicine* 19 (1957): 119.

8. Howard B. Kaplan et al., "Affective Orientation and Physiological Activity (GSR) in Small Peer Groups," *Psychosomatic Medicine* 25 (1963): 245.

9. Morton F. Reiser, R. B. Reeves, and J. Armington, "Effects of Variations in Laboratory Procedure and Experiments Upon the Ballistocardiogram, Blood Pressure, and Heart Rate in Healthy Young Men," *Psychosomatic Medicine* 17 (1955): 185.

10. W. Raab, "Correlated Cardiovascular Adrenergic and Adrenocortical Responses to Sensory and Mental Annoyances in Man: A Potential Accessory Cardiac Risk Factor," *Psychosomatic Medicine* 30 (1968): 818; T. Thorell et al., "A Longitudinal Study of 21 Subjects with Coronary Heart Disease: Life Changes, Catecholamine Excretion and Related Biochemical Reactions," *Psychosomatic Medicine* 34 (1972): 505; William W. Schottstaedt, William J. Grace, Harold G. Wolff, "Life Situation, Behavior Patterns and Renal Excretion of Fluid and Electrolytes," *Journal of the American Medical Association* 157 (1955): 1485; J. Mason and J. Brady, "The Sensitivity of Psychoendocrine Systems to Social and Physical Environment," *Psychobiological Approaches to Social Behavior,* ed. P. Herbert Leiderman and David Shapiro (Stanford, Calif.: Stanford University Press, 1964); Stewart Kiritz and Rudolf H. Moos, "Physiological Effects of Social Environments," *Psychosomatic Medicine* 36 (1974): 96; Margaret T. Singer, "Presidential Address: Engagement–Involvement–A Central Phenomenon in Psychophysiological Research," *Psychosomatic Medicine* 36 (1974): 1; John I. Lacey, "Psychophysiological Approaches to the Evaluation of Psychotherapeutic

Process and Outcome," *Research in Psychotherapy Proceedings of a Conference, Washington, D.C., April 9-12, 1958,* eds. Eli A. Rubinstein and Morris Parloff (Washington, D.C.: National Publishing, 1959), pp. 106–208.

11. M. McClintock, "Menstrual Synchrony and Suppression," *Nature* 229 (1971): 229–244.

12. John Mason, "Psychological Influences on the Pituitary Adrenal-Cortical System," *Recent Progress in Hormone Research* 15 (1959): 345.

13. Stewart Wolf and Helen Goodell, *Behavioral Science in Clinical Medicine* (Springfield, Ill.: Charles C. Thomas, 1976).

14. Medical Department, United States Army, *Neuropsychiatry in World War II, Vol. 2: Overseas Theaters* (Washington, D.C.: U.S. Government Printing Office, 1973), p. 995.

15. Irving L. Janis, *Air War and Emotional Stress: Psychological Studies of Bombing and Civilian Defense* (New York: McGraw Hill, 1951).

16. Stanley Schachter, *The Psychology of Affiliation* (Stanford, Calif.: Stanford University Press, 1959).

17. K. W. Back and M. Bogdonoff, "Plasma Lipid Responses to Leadership, Conformity and Deviation," *Psychobiological Approaches to Social Behavior,* ed. P. H. Leiderman and D. Shapiro (Stanford, Calif.: Stanford University Press, 1964).

18. E. Home, "A Short Account of the Author's Life," *A Treatise on the Blood, Inflamation and Gunshot Wounds,* by J. Hunter (Philadelphia: T. Bradford, 1796).

19. William Osler, "The Lumleian Lectures on Angina Pectoris: Delivered Before the Royal College of Physicians of London," *Lancet* 1 (1910): 839–844.

20. L. N. Katz, S. S. Winston, and R. S. Megibow, "Psychosomatic Aspects of Cardiac Arrhythmias: A Physiological Dynamic Approach," *Annals of Internal Medicine* 27 (1947): 274; W. Proctor Harvey and Samuel A. Levine, "Paroxysmal Ventricular Tachycardia Due to Emotion: Possible Mechanism of Death from Fright," *Journal of the American Medical Association* 150 (1952): 479; Samuel J. Kowal, "Emotions and Angina Pectoris: An Historical Review," *American Journal of Cardiology* 5 (1960): 427; Samuel A. Levine, "Benign Atrial Fibrillation of Forty Years' Duration with Sudden Death from Emotion," *Annals of Internal Medicine* 58 (1963): 684; Paul Dudley White, "The Historical Background of Angina Pectoris," *Modern Concepts of Cardiovascular Disease* 43 (1974): 112.

21. Ian P. Stevenson et al., "Life Situations, Emotions and Extrasystoles," *Psychosomatic Medicine* 11 (1949): 257.

22. Louis H. Sigler, "Emotion and Atherosclerotic Heart Disease. I: Electrocardiographic Changes Observed on the Recall of Past Emotional Disturbances," *British Journal of Medical Psychology* 40 (1967): 55.

23. Stewart Wolf, "The End of the Rope: The Role of the Brain in Cardiac Death," *Canadian Medical Association Journal* 97 (1967): 1022.

24. Herbert Weiner, Margaret T. Singer, and Morton F. Reiser, "Cardiovascular Responses and Their Psychological Correlates. I: A Study in Healthy Young Adults and Patients with Peptic Ulcer and Hypertension," *Psychosomatic Medicine* 24 (1962): 498.

25. William N. Chambers and Morton F. Reiser, "Emotional Stress in the Precipitation of Congestive Heart Failure," *Psychosomatic Medicine* 15 (1953): 38–60; see also, Charles R. Vernon, Dan A. Martin, and Kerr L.

White, "Psychophysiological Approach to Management of Patients wtih Congestive Heart Failure," *Journal of the American Medical Association* 171 (1959): 1947–1954; Kerr L. White, Dan A. Martin, and Charles R. Vernon, "Venous Pressure, Emotions and Congestive Heart Failure," *Journal of Chronic Disease* 10 (1959): 163–182.

26. Julius Bauer, "Sudden, Unexpected Death," *Postgraduate Medicine,* 22 (1957): A34–45.

27. James L. Mathis, "A Sophisticated Version of Voodoo Death: Report of a Case," *Psychosomatic Medicine,* 26 (1964): 104–107; Denis Leigh, "Sudden Deaths from Asthma: Physiopathological Mechanisms—Report of a Case," *Psychosomatic Medicine* 17 (1955): 232–239.

28. John C. Coolidge, "Unexpected Death in a Patient Who Wished to Die," *Journal of the American Psychoanalytic Association* 17 (1969): 413–419.

29. Gunnar Biörck, "Social and Psychological Problems in Patients with Chronic Cardiac Illness," *American Heart Journal,* 58 (1959): 414–417.

30. Z. J. Lipowski, "Psychophysiological Cardiovascular Disorders," *Comprehensive Textbook of Psychiatry,* 2nd ed., eds. A. M. Freedman, H. I. Kaplan, and B. J. Sadock (Baltimore, Md.: Williams and Wilkins, 1974).

31. R. Berg-Larsen, "A Psychodynamic Evaluation of Patients with Myocardial Infarction with Regard to Their Future Occupational and Social Adjustment. Recent Research in Psychosomatics, 8th European Conference, Knokke, 1970," *Psychother. Psychosom.* 18 (1970): 294.

32. E. Weiss and O. S. English, *Psychosomatic Medicine,* 3rd ed. (Philadelphia: W. B. Saunders Co., 1957), p. 216.

33. W. B. Tuttle, W. L. Cook, and E. Fitch, "Sexual Behavior in Post-Myocardial Infarction Patients," *American Journal of Cardiology* 13 (1964): 140.

34. Herman K. Hellerstein and Ernest H. Friedman, "Sexual Activity and the Postcoronary Patient," *Archives of Internal Medicine* 125 (1970): 997–987.

35. W. H. Masters and V. E. Johnson, *Human Sexual Response* (Boston: Little, Brown, 1966).

36. R. G. Bartlett, "Physiologic Responses During Coitus," *Journal of Applied Physiology* 9 (1956): 469.

37. M. Ueno, "The So-Called Coition Death," *Japanese Journal of Legal Medicine* 17 (1963): 330.

38. George C. Griffith, "Sexuality and the Cardiac Patient," *Heart and Lung,* 2 (1970): 70–73.

# CHAPTER 5

1. Joel E. Dimsdale, "The Coping Behavior of Nazi Concentration Camp Survivors," *American Journal of Psychiatry* 131 (1974): 792–797.

2. James J. Lynch et al., "Psychological Aspects of Cardiac Arrhythmia," *American Heart Journal* (1977). In press.

3. Robert F. Klein et al., "Transfer from a Coronary Care Unit: Some Adverse Responses," *Archives of Internal Medicine* 122 (1968): 104–108; see also W. Doyle Gentry, Gerard J. Musante, and Thomas Haney, "Anxiety

and Urinary Sodium/Potassium as Stress Indicators on Admission to a Coronary Care Unit," *Heart and Lung* 2 (1973): 875–877.

4. Klaus A. Järvinen, "Can Ward Rounds Be a Danger to Patients with Myocardial Infarction?" *British Medical Journal* 1 (1955): 318–320.

5. William W. Schottstaedt et al., "Sociologic and Metabolic Observations on Patients in the Community of a Metabolic Ward," *American Journal of Medicine* 25 (1958): 248–257.

6. Stewart Wolf et al., "Changes in Serum Lipids in Relation to Emotional Stress during Rigid Control of Diet and Exercise," *Circulation* 26 (1962): 379–387.

7. James J. Lynch et al., "The Effects of Human Contact on Cardiac Arrhythmia in Coronary Care Patients," *Journal of Nervous and Mental Disease* 158 (1974): 88–91.

8. Sue A. Thomas, James J. Lynch, and Mary E. Mills, "Psychosocial Influences on Heart Rhythm in the Coronary Care Unit," *Heart and Lung* 4, No. 5 (1975): 746–750.

9. James J. Lynch et al., "Human Contact and Cardiac Arrhythmia in a Coronary Care Unit," *Psychosomatic Medicine* (1977). In press; see also, M. E. Mills et al., "The Effects of Pulse Palpitation on Cardiac Arrhythmia in Coronary Care Patients," *Nursing Research* 25 (1976): 378–382.

10. James J. Lynch et al., "Effects of Human Contact on the Heart Activity of Curarized Patients in a Shock-Trauma Unit," *American Heart Journal* 88 (1974): 160–169.

11. Gunnar Bìörck, "Social and Psychological Problems in Patients with Chronic Cardiac Illness," *American Heart Journal* 58 (1959): 414–417.

12. Stephan Lesher, "After a Heart Attack: There Comes a Will to Live —Well," *New York Times Magazine,* January 27, 1974, pp. 9–12.

13. J. M. T. Finney, "Discussion of Papers on Shock," 100 (1934): 746.

14. Avery D. Weisman and Thomas P. Hackett, "Predilection to Death: Death and Dying as a Psychiatric Problem," *Psychosomatic Medicine* 23 (1961): 232–256.

## CHAPTER 6

1. Desmond Morris, *Intimate Behavior* (New York: Random House, 1971).

2. Charles Darwin, *Origin of the Species* (New York: E. P. Dutton, 1934).

3. Charles Darwin, *The Descent of Man, and Selection in Relation to Sex* (London, 1871).

4. Charles Darwin, *The Expression of the Emotions in Man and Animals* (New York: Philosophical Library, 1955).

5. Walter B. Cannon, *Bodily Changes in Pain, Hunger, Fear and Rage,* 2nd ed. (New York: Appleton, 1929).

6. Ivan P. Pavlov, *Lectures on Conditioned Reflexes,* trans. W. H. Gantt (New York: International Publishers, 1928).

7. J. E. O. Newton and Walter W. Ehrlich, "The History of a Catatonic Dog," *Conditional Reflex* 3 (1968): 45–61; see also W. Horsley Gantt et al., "Effect of Person," *Conditional Reflex* 4 (1966): 18–35.

8. Joseph E. Newton and Walter W. Ehrlich, "Coronary Blood Flow in Dogs: Effect of Person," *Conditional Reflex* 1 (1966): 81.

9. Sandra Anderson and W. Horsley Gantt, "The Effect of Person on Cardiac and Motor Responsivity to Shock in Dogs," *Conditional Reflex* 1 (1966): 181–189.

10. James J. Lynch and J. F. McCarthy, "The Effect of Petting on a Classically Conditioned Emotional Response," *Behavioral Research and Therapy* 5 (1967): 55–62.

11. Howard S. Liddell, "Conditioning and Emotions," *Scientific American* 190 (1954): 48.

12. John P. Scott, "The Development of Social Motivation," Nebraska Symposium on Motivation, ed. David Levine (Lincoln, Neb.: University of Nebraska Press, 1967), pp. 111–132.

13. Oddist D. Murphee, J. E. Peters, and R. A. Dykman, "Effect of Person on Nervous, Stable and Crossbred Pointer Dogs," *Conditional Reflex* 2 (1967): 273.

14. James J. Lynch and J. F. McCarthy, "Social Responding in Dogs: Heart Rate Changes to a Person," *Psychophysiology* 5 (1969): 389–393.

15. John P. Scott and J. L. Fuller, *Genetics and the Social Behavior of the Dog* (Chicago: University of Chicago Press, 1965).

16. W. Horsley Gantt, "The Cardiovascular Component of the Conditional Reflex to Pain, Food and Other Stimuli," *Physiological Review* 40 (1960): 266–291.

17. James J. Lynch et al., "Heart Rate Changes in the Horse to Human Contact," *Psychophysiology* 11 (1974): 472–478.

18. H. F. Harlow, "The Nature of Love," *American Psychologist* 13 (1958): 673; "The Development of Affectional Patterns in Infant Monkeys," in *Determinants of Infant Behavior,* ed. B. M. Foss (New York: Wiley, 1961), pp. 75–97; "Love in Infant Monkeys," *Scientific American* 200 (1959): 68; Wm. T. McKinney, "Primate Social Isolation: Psychiatric Implications," *Archives of General Psychiatry* 31 (1974): 422–426.

19. Martin Reite et al., "Depression in Infant Monkeys: Physiological Correlates," *Psychosomatic Medicine* 36 (1974): 363–367.

20. R. Ader and S. B. Friedman, "Differential Early Experiences and Susceptibility to Transplanted Tumor in the Rat," *Journal of Comparative and Physiological Psychology* 59 (1965): 361–364; Stanford B. Friedman, Lowell A. Glasgow, and Robert Ader, "Psychological Factors Modifying Host Resistance to Experimental Infections," *Annals of the New York Academy of Sciences* 164 (1969): 381–393; R. Ader and S. B. Friedman, "Some Social Factors Affecting Emotionality and Resistance to Disease in Animals. V: Early Separation from the Mother and Response to a Transplanted Tumor in the Rat," *Psychosomatic Medicine* 27 (1965): 119–122.

21. James J. Lynch and A. H. Katcher, "Human Handling and Sudden Death in Laboratory Rats," *Journal of Nervous and Mental Diseases* 159 (1974): 362–365.

## CHAPTER 7

1. William James, *The Varieties of Religious Experience: A Study in Human Nature* (New York: Longman, Green, 1908).

2. Abraham Maslow, "Toward a Humanistic Biology," *American Psychologist* 24 (1969): 724.

3. Desmond Morris, *Intimate Behavior* (New York: Random House, 1971).

4. Martin Buber, *I and Thou,* 2nd ed., trans. Roger Gregor Smith (New York: Scribner's, 1958).

5. Max Born, *Physics in My Generation,* 2nd ed. (New York: Springer-Verlag, 1969).

6. Erwin Schrödinger, *What is Life? Mind and Matter* (London: Cambridge University Press, 1967).


## CHAPTER 8

1. G. W. Comstock and K. B. Patridge, "Church Attendance and Health," Journal of Chronic Diseases 25 (1972): 665–672.

2. C. David Jenkins, "Recent Evidence Supporting Psychologic and Social Risk Factors for Coronary Disease (Two Parts)," *New England Journal of Medicine* 294 (1976): 987–994 and 1033–1038.

3. *Age Patterns in Medical Care, Illness and Disability—United States 1968–1969.* National Health Survey, Series 10, Number 70, DHEW Publication No. (HSM) 72–1026, (Washington, D.C.: U.S. Department of Health, Education and Welfare, 1972).

4. Hugh Carter and Paul C. Glick, *Marriage and Divorce: A Social and Economic Study* (Cambridge: Harvard University Press, 1970).

5. W. H. Masters and V. E. Johnson, *Human Sexual Response* (Boston: Little, Brown, 1966).


## CHAPTER 9

1. Rene Spitz, "Life and Dialogue," in *Counterpoint: Libidinal Object and Subject,* ed. Herbet S. Gaskill (New York: International Universities Press, 1963): 154–176.

2. Bertrand Russell, *Wisdom of the West* (London: Crescent Books, 1967).

3. Charles Sherrington, *Man on His Nature* (New York: Macmillan, 1941).

4. Melanie Klein, *Our Adult World and Other Essays* (London: Heinemann, 1963).

# INDEX